W9-BOA-540

Carbonica
Gladys Hariuchi
Edwin C. Heuer
Robin Kelley O'Connor
Alistair Robertson
(Louis) LATOUR
Marion R. Shanken
L.F. Bouchard
Rodney D. Strong
Rio Roffen
Stéfan M
James Trezise
David S. Hare
Louis P. Martini
E. D. Wente
Alin Lewis
Mike Stephens
Tor de Medici
Ed Sbragia
John L. Mira

Claude Taittinger
Jean Hugel
Patrick Campbell
Philip di Belardino
Robert de Goulaine
Jack Cakebread
Francisco Valle
Zelma Long
Georges Duboeuf
Hubert Trimbach
Myron S. Nightingale

WINDOWS ON THE WORLD

Complete Wine Course

WINDOWS ON THE WORLD

Complete Wine Course

Kevin Zraly

Sterling Publishing Co., Inc.
New York

ACKNOWLEDGMENTS

I am indebted to the winemakers, grape growers, and wine friends throughout the world who, over the last twenty years, have contributed their expertise and enthusiasm for this book. The signatures on the endpapers represent some of the people whose help was invaluable to me.

A special thank you to my family and friends, who have been there for me since September 11th. I can't express enough how much your support has meant to me.

I welcome your questions and comments. Please visit my Web site, *windowswineschool.com,* for updates and wine news.

PROJECT MANAGER: Laurie Kahn
PROJECT EDITOR: Stephen Topping
DESIGN: Kevin Hanek
MAPS: Jeffrey L. Ward

Original Edition and Millennium Edition edited by Felicia Sherbert
LIBRARY OF CONGRESS CATALOGING-IN-PUBLICATION DATA AVAILABLE
10 9 8 7 6 5 4 3 2

Published by Sterling Publishing Co., Inc.,
387 Park Avenue South, New York, NY 10016

© 2005 by Kevin Zraly

Distributed in Canada by Sterling Publishing, c/o Canadian Manda Group, 165 Dufferin Street, Toronto, Ontario, Canada M6K 3H6
Distributed in Great Britain by Chrysalis Books Group PLC,
The Chrysalis Building, Bramley Road, London W10 6SP, England
Distributed in Australia by Capricorn Link (Australia) Pty. Ltd.,
P.O. Box 704, Windsor, NSW 2756, Australia

Printed in China. All rights reserved.

ISBN 1-4027-2639-2

For information about custom editions, special sales, premium and corporate purchases, please contact Sterling Special Sales Department at 800-805-5489 or specialsales@sterlingpub.com.

PREVIOUS PAGE: *A vineyard near Beaune, in the Burgundy region of France, late autumn (Charles O'Rear/Corbis);*
INSETS, LEFT TO RIGHT: *Row of glasses at a wine tasting (Owen Franken/Corbis); Vineyard near Savigny-les-Beaune, in the Burgundy region of France (Georgina Bowater/Corbis); Bunches of ripe grapes from a Château Beychevelle vineyard in the Bordeaux region of France (Adam Woolfitt/ Corbis)*
NEXT PAGE: *Grapes ready for harvest in the Avignonesi Winery, Tuscany (Bob Krist/Corbis)*

It was the best of times; it was the worst of times.

Windows on the World Complete Wine Course was first published in 1985, a time when the world—and my life—was very different. I had been working at Windows on the World, the restaurant at the top of the World Trade Center, for five years when I started writing this book.

I began as cellar master in 1976 and a short time later founded the Windows on the World Wine School. As the World Trade Center evolved, my role expanded to wine director for all restaurants operating within the complex.

Windows on the World occupied the entire 106th and 107th floors of One World Trade Center. From 1976 to 1993 it ranked number one in dollar volume in the United States, generated more wine sales than any other restaurant in the world, and was arguably the most famous dining establishment on earth. What an exciting time it was, for the restaurant and for me.

Those good times came to a halt on February 26, 1993, when a van full of explosives detonated in an underground garage of the World Trade Center. Windows on the World was closed for three years while repairs were made to the building, but we were able to keep the wine school going using borrowed spaces nearby. Meanwhile, The Port Authority began a search to find an operator for the restaurant, and I had no idea if I would be invited to work with whatever new managment team they chose. It was a period of loneliness and uncertainty for me.

But when Joe Baum, the man who'd first hired me in 1976, was once again awarded the contract to open Windows on the World, I believed the old excitement would return. Soon, thanks to a daring plan to feature American cuisine, the restaurant was restored to glory, reopening almost 20 years to the date that it had in 1976.

All that vanished on September 11th, 2001. More than three thousand people lost their lives that day, including 72 of my coworkers and friends. I continue the Windows on the World Wine School and updating this book on a yearly basis; keeping both alive is my way of honoring the Windows legacy.

This book is dedicated to everyone who has a passion for wine,
from the grape growers to the winemakers, from the buyers and the sellers to,
most important, the wine consumers.

May your glass always be more full than empty.

Contents

Introduction

This book grew out of my involvement with the wine school.

WHEN I FIRST started the wine school, I searched everywhere for a simple, straightforward wine guide to use as a textbook. I would pick the few that seemed to come closest but by the end of each semester I would be looking again. Every book was either too encyclopedic or too scientific. And I wasn't the only one who was frustrated: My students were, too. Teaching and learning had stopped being fun; my students were finding the texts too complicated and I found myself referring to them less and less. So I began developing my own course material, which I kept simple, giving my students only the basic information they needed for understanding and enjoying wine.

I taught from a handwritten outline and photocopied labels, lists, and other information for each class, handing out copies to students for home study and future reference. This proved so popular that many of my students asked me to write a wine book around the materials. In 1981, five years after I started working at Windows on the World and ten years after teaching my first wine class, I set out to write this book.

Full of naïve enthusiasm, I started researching publishers, looking for the best and reading as much as I could about the business of publishing. I soon learned that, although *I* thought my idea for an easy-to-understand wine book was brilliant, finding a publisher who agreed was an entirely different matter. At least five of the largest publishers in the industry turned down my book, telling me it would never sell. "Rejection" was becoming an all-too-familiar word.

Eventually I was introduced to Sterling Publishing, a company I like to call the "little engine that could." Back then it was a small, family-owned "niche-marketing" publisher, known for its beautiful craft books. (Or, more accurately, *unknown*: Sterling was probably the most successful small publisher you'd never heard of!) Two years ago, this "little" company was purchased by Barnes & Noble, and I am proud and honored to say that *Windows on the World Complete Wine Course*, with more than 2 million copies sold to date, is the largest selling wine book in the United States!

The success of this book is due, in part, to timing: By 1985, many Americans were becoming interested in wine. They were "thirsty" to learn about all the aspects of tasting and buying wine—and they wanted it in an informative and entertaining way.

So what has happened in the wine world over the last twenty years?

I've given a great deal of thought to the changes the wine world has undergone over the past two decades as I tackled the revisions for this twentieth-anniversary edition. As I reread the first edition, I was struck by the enormous growth in the quality and selection of American wines. In 1985 there were 712 wineries in the United States; today there are more than 4,000—with wineries and vineyards in all 50 states.

I've also made many changes to the order of the book over the years. For example, On Tasting Wine has been moved up front: With wine's increased acceptance and popularity, I think understanding wine production and history are far less important than understanding how to appreciate wine. Another change is the inclusion of a 60-Second Wine Expert section, which I hope readers will find of value; it's been my most effective classroom teaching tool.

I've learned over the past twenty years that familiarity with the world's major grape varieties is essential to an in-depth understanding of wine. I've added two summaries, "White Grapes of the World" on page 15 and "Red Grapes of the World" on page 87. These will give you a quick snapshot and easy reference of the most important grape varieties.

Americans' wine-drinking habits and interests changed as we began consuming more of it. The first edition of this book emphasized French wines, with California wines a close second—although even in 1985 many "wine experts" were unconvinced of their quality. Also, the first edition did not discuss wines from Australia, Chile, or Argentina; there was no mention of Washington State or Oregon wines. All are now included.

There is an old adage that goes, "If it ain't broke, don't fix it!" The basics of winemaking haven't much changed, so the "Prelude" chapter is nearly the same as it was twenty years ago, as are the chapters on French and German wines (although the lists of vintages and better producers have been updated).

The biggest news in winemaking has come from the United States, Italy, Australia, Chile, Argentina, New Zealand, South Africa, and Spain. While I've learned a lot in the past two decades, my philosophy follows another old saying: "If I had more time, I would have written a shorter book." Despite its title,

this book was never meant to be a "complete" wine course, and in fact the hardest part of writing it has been maintaining its brevity. There are many comprehensive wine books out there and I do not hesitate to recommend them. However, my job is to cut to the chase: not presenting everything there is to know about wine—just what you need to know to be a better buyer of wine.

HERE ARE SOME OF THE MAJOR EVENTS IN THE WINE INDUSTRY OVER THE LAST TWENTY YEARS:

- Americans are drinking more and better wine than ever before; by the end of this decade the United States will be the world's biggest wine consumer. Wine is becoming more appealing to Americans than either beer or distilled spirits. The increase of wine schools around the United States is just one example of this exciting trend.

- There has been a proliferation of wine events across the United States, almost all of which donate some of the proceeds to charities. In 2004 alone, two auctions, the Napa Valley Wine Auction and the Naples, Florida, Wine Festival, raised $5.2 million and $6.6 million respectively.

- In 2004, U.S. commercial wine auctions generated more than $100 million.

- French consumption of wine has dropped more than 40 percent since the 1970s and today the French wine industry is in crisis.

- The quality of restaurant wine lists in the United States has never been better—although some restaurants have created "monster" lists for promotional purposes, creating more intimidation for "new" wine drinkers.

- Such major newspapers as *The Wall Street Journal* and *USA Today* have added full-time wine writers to their staffs. (Although *The New York Times* has had the column "Wine Talk" since the early 1970s, most other wine writing was done on a freelance basis.)

- Among all the great wine-producing countries, the biggest change has been in Italy. The quality of Italian wines has improved dramatically—not just in the historically important regions of Piedmont, Tuscany, and Veneto but also in the country's southern regions.

- Australia now produces the top-selling imported wine in the United States (Yellow Tail) and continues to make more and better wines every year.

- Chile has become the source of some of the finest Cabernet Sauvignons available and Argentina has perfected the Malbec grape, using it to make one of the best wines in the world.

- The amount of corked wines, or TCA (see page 229), has disappointed many wine drinkers. The best estimates indicate that 3 to 5 percent of all corked wines have been spoiled by this compound.

- High-quality wines worldwide are increasingly being bottled with screw caps. Expect this trend to continue.

- Gallo now produces wine in France.

- Costco is the largest retailer of wine in the United States.

- A line of inexpensive wines produced by Charles Shaw (aka Two Buck Chuck) sold more than 10 million cases in 2004.

- Through consolidation, the number of wine wholesalers in the United States has declined by 50 percent.

- The U.S. Supreme Court rules on the legality of interstate shipping of wine directly to consumers.

- You can now find more books on wine than ever before.

- After 38 years of operation as the premier winery of Napa Valley, the Robert Mondavi winery was sold in 2004.

- *Sideways,* a movie in which wine plays a central role, won the 2005 Golden Globe Award for Best Comedy and was nominated for a Best Picture Oscar.

After thirty-five years of wine study, I am still excited every time a cork is popped. Wine was, and is, my passion—a romance I hope will continue for the rest of my life.

Prelude
to Wine

❧

Grapes on the vine in Napa, California
(Morton Beebe/Corbis)

The Basics

THE FIVE major wine importers into the United States:

1. Italy
2. Australia
3. France
4. Chile
5. Spain

ITALY, AUSTRALIA, and France account for 73% of all imports into the United States.

IT IS ESTIMATED that 6,500 different wines are available to the consumer in the United States. Twenty-two brand names equal 50% of the total wine market.

Source: Impact Databank

THE TOP 10 producers of wine in the world:

1. France
2. Italy
3. United States
4. Spain
5. Argentina
6. Germany
7. South Africa
8. Australia
9. Chile
10. Portugal

ALCOHOL WHEN consumed in moderation will increase HDL (good) and decrease LDL (bad) cholesterol.

A BOTTLE of wine is 86% water.

MORE ACRES of grapes are planted than any other fruit crop in the world!

YOU'RE IN A WINE SHOP looking for that "special" wine to serve at a dinner party. Before you walked in, you had at least an idea of what you wanted, but now, as you scan the shelves, you're overwhelmed. "There are so many wines," you think, "and so many prices." You take a deep breath, boldly pick up a bottle that looks impressive, and buy it. Then you hope your guests will like your selection.

Does this sound a little farfetched? For some of you, yes. Yet the truth is, this is a very common occurrence for the wine beginner, and even someone with intermediate wine knowledge, but it doesn't have to be that way. Wine should be an enjoyable experience. By the time you finish this book, you'll be able to buy with confidence from a retailer or even look in the eyes of a wine steward and ask with no hesitation for the selection of your choice. But first let's start with the basics—the foundation of your wine knowledge. Read carefully, because you'll find this section invaluable as you relate it to the chapters that follow. You may even want to refer back to it occasionally to reinforce what you learn.

For the purpose of this book, wine is the fermented juice of grapes.

What's fermentation?

Fermentation is the process by which the grape juice turns into wine. The simple formula for fermentation is:

$$\text{Sugar} + \text{Yeast} = \text{Alcohol} + \text{Carbon Dioxide (CO}_2\text{)}$$

The fermentation process begins when the grapes are crushed and ends when all of the sugar has been converted to alcohol or the alcohol level has reached around 15 percent, which kills off the yeast. Sugar is naturally present in the ripe grape. Yeast also occurs naturally, as the white bloom on the grape skin. However, this natural yeast is not always used in today's winemaking. Laboratory strains of pure yeast have been isolated and may be used in many situations, each strain contributing something unique to the style of wine. The carbon dioxide dissipates into the air, except in Champagne and other sparkling wines, in which this gas is retained through a special process.

What are the three major types of wine?

Table wine: approximately 8 to 15 percent alcohol

Sparkling wine: approximately 8 to 12 percent alcohol + CO_2

Fortified wine: 17 to 22 percent alcohol

All wine fits into at least one of these categories.

Why do the world's fine wines come only from certain areas?

A combination of factors is at work. The areas with a reputation for fine wines have the right soil and favorable weather conditions, of course. In addition, these areas look at winemaking as an important part of their history and culture.

Is all wine made from the same kind of grape?

No. The major wine grapes come from the species *Vitis vinifera*. In fact, both European and American winemakers use the *Vitis vinifera*, which includes many different varieties of grapes—both red and white. However, there are other grapes used for winemaking. The most important native grape species in America is *Vitis labrusca*, which is grown widely in New York State as well as other East Coast and Midwest states. Hybrids are a cross between *Vitis vinifera* and *Vitis labrusca*.

Where are the best locations to plant grapes?

Grapes are agricultural products that require specific growing conditions. Just as you wouldn't try to grow oranges in Maine, you wouldn't try to grow grapes at the North Pole. There are limitations on where vines can be grown. Some of these limitations are: the growing season, the number of days of sunlight, the angle of the sun, average temperature, and rainfall. Soil is of primary concern, and adequate drainage is a requisite. The right amount of sun ripens the grapes properly to give them the sugar/acid balance that makes the difference between fair, good, and great wine.

KEVIN ZRALY'S FAVORITE WINE REGIONS

Napa
Sonoma
Bordeaux
Burgundy
Champagne
Rhône Valley
Tuscany
Piedmont
Mosel
Rhine
Rioja
Douro (Port)
Mendoza
Maipo Valley
South Australia

PLANTING OF vineyards for winemaking began more than 8,000 years ago.

A SAMPLING OF THE MAJOR GRAPES

Vitis vinifera
Chardonnay
Cabernet Sauvignon

Vitis labrusca
Concord
Catawba

Hybrids
Seyval Blanc
Baco Noir

VITIS is Latin for vine.
VINUM is Latin for wine.

THE TOP five countries in wine grape acreage worldwide:
1. Spain
2. France
3. Italy
4. Turkey
5. United States

WINEMAKERS SAY that winemaking begins in the vineyard with the growing of the grapes.

THE MOST important factors in winemaking:
1. Geographic location
2. Soil
3. Weather
4. Grapes
5. Vinification (the actual winemaking process)

VINES ARE planted during their dormant periods, usually in the months of April or May. Most vines will continue to produce good-quality grapes for 40 years or more.

DON'T FORGET that the seasons in the Southern Hemisphere—which includes Australia, New Zealand, Chile, Argentina, and South Africa—are reversed.

A VINE doesn't usually produce grapes suitable for winemaking until the third year.

"BRIX" IS the winemaker's measure of sugar in grapes.

AS SUGAR levels increase, acidity decreases.

IT TAKES an average of 100 days between a vine's flowering and the harvest.

AN APRIL frost in Bordeaux destroyed more than 50% of 1991's grape harvest.

IN 2002, THE Piedmont region of Italy (Barolo, Barbaresco) was hit with a September hailstorm that destroyed some of the best vineyards in the region.

A RAINY September made the 2001 Champagne harvest the wettest since 1873.

Does it matter which types of grapes are planted?

Yes, it does. Traditionally, many grape varieties produce better wines when planted in certain locations. For example, most red grapes need a longer growing season than do white grapes, and red grapes are usually planted in warmer locations. In colder northern regions—in Germany and northern France, for instance—most vineyards are planted with white grapes. In the warmer regions of Italy, Spain, and Portugal, and in California's Napa Valley, the red grape thrives.

When is the harvest?

Grapes are picked when they reach the proper sugar/acid ratio for the style of wine the vintner wants to produce. Go to a vineyard in June and taste one of the small green grapes. Your mouth will pucker because the grape is so tart and acidic. Return to the same vineyard—even to that same vine—in September or October, and the grapes will taste sweet. All those months of sun have given sugar to the grape as a result of photosynthesis.

June
3% acid
0 Brix

July
2.3% acid
10 Brix

August
1.7% acid
15 Brix

Harvest
September
0.9% acid
22 Brix

What effect does weather have on the grapes?

Weather can interfere with the quality of the harvest, as well as its quantity. In the spring, as vines emerge from dormancy, a sudden frost may stop the flowering, thereby reducing the yields. Even a strong windstorm can affect the grapes adversely at this crucial time. Not enough rain, too much rain, or rain at the wrong time can also wreak havoc.

Rain just before the harvest will swell the grapes with water, diluting the juice and making thin, watery wines. Lack of rain will affect the wines' balance by creating a more powerful and concentrated wine, but a smaller crop. A severe drop in temperature may affect the vines even outside the growing season. Case in point: In New York State the winter of 2003–04 was one of the coldest in fifty years. The result was a major decrease in wine production, with some vineyards losing more than 50 percent of their crop for the 2004 vintage.

What can the vineyard owner do in the case of adverse weather?

A number of countermeasures are available to the grower. Some of these measures are used while the grapes are on the vine; others are part of the winemaking process.

PROBLEM	RESULTS IN	SOLUTION
Frost	Reduced yield	Various frost protection methods: wind machines, sprinkler systems, and flaming heaters
Not enough sun	Unripe grapes	Chaptalization (the addition of sugar to the must—fresh grape juice—during fermentation)
Too much rain	Thin, watery wines	Move vineyard to a drier climate
Mildew	Rot	Spray with copper sulfate
Drought	Scorched grapes	Irrigate or pray for rain
Phylloxera	Dead vines	Graft vines onto resistant rootstock
High alcohol	High acidity	Dealcoholize

What is phylloxera?

Phylloxera, a grape louse, is one of the grapevine's worst enemies, because it eventually kills the entire plant. An epidemic infestation in the 1870s came close to destroying all the vineyards of Europe. Luckily, the roots of native American vines were immune to this louse. After this was discovered, all the European vines were pulled up and grafted onto phylloxera-resistant American rootstocks.

IN APRIL 2001, vineyards from Central California to Mendocino experienced the worst spring frost in thirty years, causing millions of dollars in damage.

THE HISTORIC 2003 heat wave in Europe changed the balance of the traditional style of wines produced in most regions on the Continent.

POOR WEATHER conditions for the 2002 vintage in Tuscany resulted in no production of Chianti Classico Reserva.

A SPRING frost damaged 80% of the 2002 vintage Champagne grapes.

FROM 1989 TO 1999 in Bordeaux, France, it rained during the harvest of eight out of ten vintages, which affected picking dates, yields, and the quality of the wine.

ONE OF THE few countries to escape phylloxera is Chile. Chilean wine producers imported their vines from France in the 1860s, before phylloxera attacked the French vineyards.

IN THE early 1980s, phylloxera became a problem in the vineyards of California. Vineyard owners were forced to replant their vines at a cost of $15,000 to $25,000 per acre, costing the California wine industry billions of dollars.

Can white wine be made from red grapes?

Yes. The color of wine comes entirely from the grape skins. By removing the skins immediately after picking, no color is imparted to the wine, and it will be white. In the Champagne region of France, a large percentage of the grapes grown are red, yet most of the resulting wine is white. California's White Zinfandel is made from red Zinfandel grapes.

What is tannin, and is it desirable in wine?

Tannin is a natural substance that comes from the skins, stems, and pips of the grapes, and even from the wooden barrels in which many are aged. It acts as a preservative; without it, certain wines wouldn't continue to improve in the bottle. In young wines, tannin can be very astringent and make the wine taste bitter. Generally, red wines have a higher level of tannin than do whites, because red grapes are usually left to ferment with their skins.

Is acidity desirable in wine?

All wine will have a certain amount of acidity. Generally, white wines have more acidity than do reds, though winemakers try to have a balance of fruit and acid. An overly acidic wine is also described as tart or sour. Acidity is a very important component in the aging of wines.

What is meant by "vintage"? Why is one year considered better than another?

A vintage indicates the year the grapes were harvested, so every year is a vintage year. A vintage chart reflects the weather conditions for various years. Better weather usually results in a better rating for the vintage, and therefore a higher likelihood that the wine will age well.

Are all wines meant to be aged?

No. It's a common misconception that all wines improve with age. In fact, more than 90 percent of all the wines made in the world are meant to be consumed within one year, and less than 1 percent of the world's wines are meant to be aged for more than five years. Wines change with age. Some get better, but most do not.

WALNUTS AND tea also contain tannin.

BESIDES TANNIN, red wine contains resveratrol, which in medical studies has been associated with anti-cancer properties.

"And Noah began to be a husbandman and he planted a vineyard, and he drank of the vine."
GENESIS 9:20–21

KING TUTANKHAMEN, who died in 1327 B.C., apparently preferred the taste of red wine, according to scientists who found residues of red wine compounds in ancient Egyptian jars found in his tomb.

THE FIRST known reference to a specific vintage was made by Roman scientist Pliny the Elder, who rated the wines of 121 B.C. "of the highest excellence."

THREE MAJOR wine collectibles that will age more than ten years:
1. Great châteaus of Bordeaux
2. Best producers of California Cabernet Sauvignon
3. Finest producers of vintage Port

What makes a wine last more than five years?

The color and the grape: Red wines, because of their tannin content, will generally age longer than whites. And certain red grapes, such as Cabernet Sauvignon, tend to have more tannin than, say, Pinot Noir.

The vintage: The better the weather conditions in one year, the more likely the wines from that vintage will have better balance of fruits, acids, and tannins, and therefore have the potential to age longer.

Where the wine comes from: Certain vineyards have optimum conditions for growing grapes, including such factors as soil, weather, drainage, and slope of the land. All of this contributes to producing a great wine that will need time to age.

How the wine was made (vinification): The longer the wine remains in contact with its skins during fermentation (maceration), and if it is fermented and/or aged in oak, the more it will have of the natural preservative tannin, which will help it age longer. These are just two examples of how winemaking can affect the aging of wine.

Wine storage conditions: Even the best-made wines in the world will not age well if they are improperly stored.

How is wine production regulated worldwide?

Each major wine-producing country has government-sponsored control agencies and laws that regulate all aspects of wine production and set certain minimum standards that must be observed. Here are some examples:

France: Appellation d'Origine Contrôlée (AOC)

Italy: Denominazione di Origine Controllata (DOC)

United States: Alcohol and Tobacco Tax and Trade Bureau

Germany: Ministry of Agriculture

Spain: Denominación de Origen (DO)

"The truth of wine aging is that it is unknown, unstudied, poorly understood, and poorly predicted!"
—ZELMA LONG, California winemaker

A WINE barrel, sometimes called a barrique, equals 300 bottles of wine.

THERE ARE more than 60 wine-producing countries in the world, producing upwards of 35 billion bottles a year.

"There are no standards of taste in wine, cigars, poetry, prose, etc. Each man's own taste is the standard, and a majority vote cannot decide for him or in any slightest degree affect the supremacy of his own standard."

—MARK TWAIN, 1895

IF YOU can see through a red wine, it's generally ready to drink!

AS WHITE wines age, they gain color. Red wines, on the other hand, lose color as they age.

ON TASTING WINE

YOU CAN READ ALL THE BOOKS (and there are plenty) written on wine to become more knowledgeable on the subject, but the best way to truly enhance your understanding of wine is to taste as many wines as possible. Reading covers the more academic side of wine, while tasting is more enjoyable and practical. A little of each will do you the most good.

The following are the necessary steps for tasting wine. You may wish to follow them with a glass of wine in hand.

Wine tasting can be broken down into five basic steps: Color, Swirl, Smell, Taste, and Savor.

Color

The best way to get an idea of a wine's color is to get a white background—a napkin or tablecloth—and hold the glass of wine on an angle in front of it. The range of colors that you may see depends, of course, on whether you're tasting a white or red wine. Here are the colors for both, beginning with the youngest wine and moving to an older wine:

WHITE WINE			RED WINE
Pale yellow-green			Purple
Straw yellow			
			Ruby
Yellow-gold			
Gold			Red
Old gold			
			Brick red
Yellow-brown			
Maderized			Red-brown
Brown			Brown

Color tells you a lot about the wine. Since we start with the white wines, let's consider three reasons why a white wine may have more color:

1. It's older.
2. Different grape varieties give different color. (For example, Chardonnay usually gives off a deeper color than does Sauvignon Blanc.)
3. The wine was aged in wood.

In class, I always begin by asking my students what color the wine is. It's not unusual to hear that some believe that the wine is pale yellow-green, while others say it's gold. Everyone begins with the same wine, but color perceptions vary. There are no right or wrong answers, because perception is subjective. So you can imagine what happens when we actually taste the wine!

Swirl

Why do we swirl wine? To allow oxygen to get into the wine: Swirling releases the esters, ethers, and aldehydes that combine with oxygen to yield a wine's bouquet. In other words, swirling aerates the wine and releases more of the bouquet and aroma.

SOME WINE experts say that if you put your hand over the glass while you swirl, you will get a better bouquet and aroma.

Smell

This is the most important part of wine tasting. You can perceive just four tastes—sweet, sour, bitter, and salt—but the average person can identify more than two thousand different scents, and wine has more than two hundred of its own. Now that you've swirled the wine and released the bouquet, I want you to smell the wine at least three times. You will find that the third smell will give you more information than the first smell did. What does the wine smell like? What type of nose does it have? Smell is the most important step in the tasting process and most people simply don't spend enough time on it.

Pinpointing the nose of the wine helps you to identify certain characteristics. The problem here is that many people in class want me to tell them what the wine smells like. Since I prefer not to use pretentious words, I may say that the wine smells like a French white Burgundy. Still, I find that this doesn't satisfy the majority of the class. They want to know more. I ask these people to describe what steak and onions smell like. They answer, "Like steak and onions." See what I mean?

The best way to learn what your own preferences are for styles of wine is

BOUQUET IS the total smell of the wine.

AROMA IS the smell of the grapes.

"NOSE" IS a word that wine tasters use to describe the bouquet and aroma of the wine.

THIS JUST IN: It is now known that each nostril can detect different smells.

THE OLDEST part of the human brain is the olfactory region.

THE 2004 NOBEL PRIZE for medicine was awarded to two scientists for their research on the olfactory system and the discovery that there are more than 10,000 different smells!

to "memorize" the smell of the individual grape varieties. For white, just try to memorize the three major grape varieties: Chardonnay, Sauvignon Blanc, and Riesling. Keep smelling them, and smelling them, and smelling them until you can identify the differences, one from the other. For the reds it's a little more difficult, but you still can take three major grape varieties: Pinot Noir, Merlot, and Cabernet Sauvignon. Try to memorize those smells without using flowery words, and you'll understand what I'm talking about.

For those in the wine school who remain unconvinced, I hand out a list of five hundred different words commonly used to describe wine. Here is a small excerpt:

acetic	character	legs	seductive
aftertaste	corky	light	short
aroma	delicate	maderized	soft
astringent	developed	mature	stalky
austere	earthy	metallic	sulfury
baked-burnt	finish	moldy	tart
balanced	flat	nose	thin
big-full-heavy	fresh	nutty	tired
bitter	grapey	off	vanilla
body	green	oxidized	woody
bouquet	hard	pétillant	yeasty
bright	hot	rich	young

You're also more likely to recognize some of the defects of a wine through your sense of smell.

Following is a list of some of the negative smells in wine:

SMELL	WHY
Vinegar	Too much acetic acid in wine
Sherry*	Oxidation
Dank, wet-mold, cellar smell	Wine absorbs the taste of a defective cork (referred to as "corked wine")
Sulfur (burnt matches)	Too much sulfur dioxide

* Authentic Sherry, from Spain, is intentionally made through controlled oxidation.

Sulfur dioxide is used in many ways in winemaking. It kills bacteria in wine, prevents unwanted fermentation, and acts as a preservative. It sometimes causes a burning and itching sensation in your nose.

WHAT KIND of wine do I like? I like my wine bright, rich, mature, developed, seductive, and with nice legs!

OXYGEN CAN be the best friend of a wine, but it can also be its worst enemy. A little oxygen helps release the smell of the wine (as with swirling), but prolonged exposure can be harmful, especially to older wines.

EVERY WINE contains a certain amount of sulfites. They are a natural by-product of fermentation.

EACH PERSON has a different threshold for sulfur dioxide and although most people do not have an adverse reaction, it can be a problem for individuals with asthma. To protect those who are prone to bad reactions to sulfites, federal law requires winemakers to label their wines with the warning that the wine contains sulfites.

Taste

To many people, tasting wine means taking a sip and swallowing immediately. To me, this isn't tasting. Tasting is something you do with your taste buds. You have taste buds all over your mouth—on both sides of the tongue, underneath, on the tip, and extending to the back of your throat. If you do what many people do, you take a gulp of wine and bypass all of those important taste buds. When I taste wine I leave it in my mouth for three to five seconds before swallowing.

What should you think about when tasting wine?

Be aware of the most important sensations of taste and your own personal thresholds to those tastes. Also, pay attention to where they occur on your tongue and in your mouth. As I mentioned earlier, you can perceive just four tastes: sweet, sour, bitter, and salt (but there's no salt in wine, so we're down to three). Bitterness in wine is usually created by high alcohol and high tannin. Sweetness occurs only in wines that have some residual sugar left over after fermentation. Sour (sometimes called "tart") indicates the acidity in wine.

Sweetness: The highest threshold is on the tip of the tongue. If there's any sweetness in a wine whatsoever, you'll get it right away.

Acidity: Found at the sides of the tongue, the cheek area, and the back of the throat. White wines and some lighter-style red wines usually contain a higher degree of acidity.

Bitterness: Tasted in the back of the tongue.

Tannin: The sensation of tannin begins in the middle of the tongue. Tannin frequently exists in red wines or white wines aged in wood. When the wines are too young, tannin dries the palate to excess. If there's a lot of tannin in the wine, it can actually coat your whole mouth, blocking the fruit. Remember, tannin is not a taste: It is a tactile sensation.

Fruit and varietal characteristics: These are not tastes, but smells. The weight of the fruit (the "body") will be felt in the middle of the tongue.

Aftertaste: The overall taste and balance of the components of the wine that lingers in your mouth. How long does the balance last? Usually a sign of a high-quality wine is a long, pleasing aftertaste. The taste of many of the great wines lasts anywhere from one to three minutes, with all their components in harmony.

THE AVERAGE person has 5,000 taste buds.

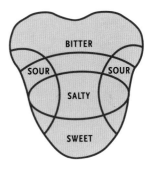

THERE IS now evidence that people may perceive five tastes: sweet, sour, bitter, salt, and possibly umami—aka MSG.

OTHER SENSATIONS associated with wine include numbing, tingling, drying, cooling, warmth, and coating.

"The key to great wine is balance, and it is the sum of the different parts that make a wine not only delicious but complete and fascinating as well as worthy of aging."
—FIONA MORRISON, M.W.

WINE TEXTURES:
Light—skim milk
Medium—whole milk
Full—heavy cream

"One not only drinks wine, one smells it, observes it, tastes it, sips it, and—one talks about it."
—KING EDWARD VII of England

"A wine goes in my mouth, and I just see it. I see it in three dimensions. The textures. The flavors. The smells. They just jump out at me. I can taste with a hundred screaming kids in a room. When I put my nose in a glass, it's like tunnel vision. I move into another world, where everything around me is just gone, and every bit of mental energy is focused on that wine."
—ROBERT M. PARKER JR., author and wine critic, in The Atlantic Monthly

Savor

After you've had a chance to taste the wine, sit back for a few moments and savor it. Think about what you just experienced, and ask yourself the following questions to help focus your impressions. Was the wine light, medium, or full-bodied?

- For a white wine: How was the acidity? Very little, just right, or too much?

- For a red wine: Is the tannin in the wine too strong or astringent? Does it blend with the fruit or overpower it?

- What is the strongest component (residual sugar, fruit, acid, tannin)?

- How long did the balance of the components last? (Ten seconds, sixty seconds, etc.)

- Is the wine ready to drink? Or does it need more time to age? Or is it past its prime?

- What kind of food would you enjoy with the wine?

- To your taste, is the wine worth the price?

- This brings us to the most important point. The first thing you should consider after you've tasted a wine is whether or not you like it. Is it your style?

You can compare tasting wine to browsing in an art gallery. You wander from room to room looking at the paintings. Your first impression tells whether or not you like something. Once you decide you like a piece of art, you want to know more: Who was the artist? What is the history behind the work? How was it done? And so it is with wine. Usually, once oenophiles (wine aficionados) discover a wine that they like, they want to learn everything about it: the winemaker; the grapes; exactly where the vines were planted; the blend, if any; and the history behind the wine.

How do you know if a wine is good or not?

The definition of a good wine is one that you enjoy. I cannot emphasize this enough. Trust your own palate and do not let others dictate taste to you!

When is a wine ready to drink?

This is one of the most frequently asked questions in my wine school. The answer is very simple: when all components of the wine are in balance to your particular taste.

The 60-Second Wine Expert

Over the last few years I have insisted that my students spend one minute in silence after they swallow the wine. I use a "60-second wine expert" tasting sheet in my classes for students to record their impressions. The minute is divided into four sections: 0 to 15 seconds, 15 to 30 seconds, 30 to 45 seconds, and the final 45 to 60 seconds. Try this with your next glass of wine.

Please note that the first taste of wine is a shock to your taste buds. This is due to the alcohol content and acidity of wine. The higher the alcohol or acidity, the more of a shock. For the first wine in any tasting, it is probably best to take a sip and swirl it around in your mouth, but don't evaluate it. Wait another thirty seconds, try it again and then begin the sixty-second wine expert.

0 to 15 seconds: If there is any residual sugar/sweetness in the wine, I will experience it now. If there is no sweetness in the wine, the acidity is usually at its strongest sensation in the first fifteen seconds. I am also looking for the fruit level of the wine and its balance with the acidity or sweetness.

15 to 30 seconds: After the sweetness or acidity, I am looking for great fruit sensation. After all, that is what I am paying for! By the time I reach thirty seconds, I am hoping for balance of all the components. By this time, I can identify the weight of the wine. Is it light, medium, or full-bodied? I am now starting to think about what kind of food I can pair with this wine (see page 173).

30 to 45 seconds: At this point I am beginning to formulate my opinion of the wine, whether I like it or not. Not all wines need sixty seconds of thought. Lighter-style wines, such as Rieslings, will usually show their best at this point. The fruit, acid, and sweetness of a great German Riesling should be in perfect harmony from this point on. For quality red and white wines, acidity—which is a very strong component (especially in the first thirty seconds)—should now be in balance with the fruit of the wine.

45 to 60 seconds: Very often wine writers use the term "length" to describe how long the components, balance, and flavor continue in the mouth. I

"Wine makes daily living easier, less hurried, with fewer tensions and more tolerance."
—Benjamin Franklin

Step One: Look at the color of the wine.
Step Two: Smell the wine three times.
Step Three: Put the wine in your mouth and leave it there for three to five seconds.
Step Four: Swallow the wine.
Step Five: Wait and concentrate on the wine for 60 seconds before discussing it.

THE CELEBRATION OF WINE AND LIFE: THE TOAST

To complete the five senses (sight, hearing, smell, taste, and touch), don't forget to toast your family and friends with the clinking of the glasses. This tradition started in ancient times when the Greeks, afraid of being poisoned by their enemies, shared a little of their wine with one another. If someone had added something to the wine, it would be a short evening for everyone! The clinking of the glasses also is said to drive away the "bad spirits" that might exist and cause the next-day hangover!

I WILL MAKE my decision about whether or not I like the style of a wine within 45 to 60 seconds.

"Wine is the best of all beverages . . . because it is purer than water, safer than milk, plainer than soft drinks, gentler than spirits, nimbler than beer, and ever so much more pleasant to the educated senses of sight, smell, and taste than any of the drinkable liquids known to us."
—ANDRE L. SIMON, author and founder of the Wine & Food Society

concentrate on the length of the wine in these last fifteen seconds. In big, full-bodied red wines from Bordeaux and the Rhône Valley, Cabernets from California, Barolos and Barbarescos from Italy, and even some full-bodied Chardonnays, I am concentrating on the level of tannin in the wine. Just as the acidity and fruit balance are my major concerns in the first thirty seconds, it is now the tannin and fruit balance I am looking for in the last thirty seconds. If the fruit, tannin, and acid are all in balance at sixty seconds, then I feel that the wine is probably ready to drink. Does the tannin overpower the fruit? If it does at the sixty-second mark, I will then begin to question whether I should drink the wine now or put it away for more aging.

It is extremely important to me that if you want to learn the true taste of the wine, you take at least one minute to concentrate on all of its components. In my classes it is amazing to see more than a hundred students silently taking one minute to analyze a wine. Some close their eyes, some bow their heads in deep thought, others write notes.

One final point: Sixty seconds to me is the minimum time to wait before making a decision about a wine. Many great wines continue to show balance well past 120 seconds. The best wine I ever tasted lasted more than three minutes—that's three minutes of perfect balance of all components!

FOR FURTHER READING

I recommend Michael Broadbent's *Pocket Guide to Wine Tasting*; Jancis Robinson's *Vintage Timecharts*; and Alan Young's *Making Sense of Wine.*

White Grapes of the World

NOW THAT YOU KNOW THE BASICS of how wine is made and how to taste it, you're almost ready to begin the first three classes on white wines.

Before you do, simplify your journey by letting me answer the question most frequently asked by my wine students on what will help them most in learning about wine. The main thing is to understand the major grape varieties and where they are grown in the world.

The purpose of this book is not to overwhelm you with information about every grape under the sun. My job as a wine educator is to try to narrow down this over-abundance of data. So let's start off with the three major grapes you need to know to understand white wine. More than 90 percent of all quality white wine is made from these three grapes. They are listed here in order from the lightest style to the fullest:

Riesling **Sauvignon Blanc** **Chardonnay**

This is not to say that world-class white wine comes from only these grapes, but knowing these three is a good start.

One of the first things I show my students in Class One is a list indicating where these three grape varieties grow best. It looks something like this:

GRAPES	WHERE THEY GROW BEST
Riesling	Germany; Alsace, France; New York State; Washington State
Sauvignon Blanc	Bordeaux, France; Loire Valley, France; New Zealand; California (Fumé Blanc)
Chardonnay	Burgundy, France; Champagne, France; California; Australia

There are world-class Rieslings, Sauvignon Blancs, and Chardonnays made in other countries, but in general the above regions are best known for wine made from these grapes.

COMMON AROMAS		
Riesling	**Sauvignon Blanc**	**Chardonnay**
Fruity,	Grapefruit,	Apple, Butter, Citrus,
Lychee nut,	Grass, Herbs,	Grapefruit, Melon, Oak,
Sweet	Cat pee	Pineapple, Toast, Vanilla

ON AVERAGE it takes 30 pounds of grapes to produce one case of wine.

MORE THAN 50 major white wine grape varieties are grown throughout the world. In California alone, more than 24 white grape varieties are planted.

OTHER WHITE GRAPES and regions you may wish to explore:

GRAPES	WHERE THEY GROW BEST
Albariño	Spain
Chenin Blanc	Loire Valley, France; California
Gewürztraminer, Pinot Blanc, Pinot Gris	Alsace, France
Pinot Grigio (aka Pinot Gris)	Italy; California; Oregon
Sémillon	Bordeaux (Sauternes); Australia
Viognier	Rhône, France; California

NEW WORLD VS. OLD WORLD

Wines from the United States, Australia, Chile, Argentina, New Zealand, and South Africa usually list the grape variety on the label. French, Italian, and Spanish wines usually list the region, village, or vineyard where the wine is made—but not the grape.

The White Wines of France

UNDERSTANDING FRENCH WINE • ALSACE • LOIRE VALLEY •

WHITE WINES OF BORDEAUX • GRAVES • SAUTERNES/BARSAC •

WHITE WINES OF BURGUNDY • CHABLIS • CÔTE DE BEAUNE •

CÔTE CHÂLONNAISE • MÂCONNAIS

Vineyards and fields in Chablis, early autumn
(Owen Frunken/Corbis)

FRANCE

CHAMPAGNE

Paris ★

LOIRE VALLEY

ALSACE

Atlantic Ocean

BURGUNDY

BORDEAUX

CÔTES DU RHÔNE

LANGUEDOC-ROUSILLON

PROVENCE

0 Miles 100 200

0 Kilometers 200

Mediterranean Sea

THE 2003 HARVEST in France was the smallest since 1997.

Understanding French Wine

B EFORE WE BEGIN OUR FIRST CLASS, "The White Wines of France," I think you should know a few important points about all French wines. Take a look at a map of France to get familiar with the main wine-producing areas. As we progress, you'll understand why geography is so important.

Here's a quick rundown of which areas produce which kinds of wine:

WINE REGIONS	MAJOR GRAPES
Champagne—sparkling wine	Pinot Noir, Chardonnay
Loire Valley—mostly white	Sauvignon Blanc, Chenin Blanc, Cabernet Franc
Alsace—mostly white	Riesling, Gewürztraminer
Burgundy—red and white	Pinot Noir, Gamay, Chardonnay
Bordeaux—red and white	Sauvignon Blanc, Sémillon, Merlot, Cabernet Sauvignon, Cabernet Franc
Côtes du Rhône—mostly red	Syrah, Grenache
Languedoc-Roussillon—red and white	Merlot, Cabernet Sauvignon, Sauvignon Blanc, Chardonnay
Provence—red, white, and rosé	Grenache, Syrah

IN THE SOUTHERN French region of Provence, look for these producers:
Domaine Tempier
Château Routas

PRODUCT OF FRANCE

MARQUE DÉPOSÉE

MOREAU
BLANC RESERVE

VIN DE TABLE FRANCAIS
MIS EN BOUTEILLE PAR
J. MOREAU & FILS
NEGOCIANT A 89800 . FRANCE

750 ml.   Alc. 11% by vol.

AOC

Established in the 1930s, the Appellation d'Origine Contrôlée laws set minimum requirements for each wine-producing area in France. These laws also can help you decipher French wine labels, since the AOC controls the following:

	EXAMPLE	EXAMPLE
1. Geographic origin	Chablis	Pommard
2. Grape variety: Which grapes can be planted where.	Chardonnay	Pinot Noir
3. Minimum alcohol content: This varies depending upon the particular area where the grapes are grown.	10%	10.5%
4. Vine-growing practices: For example, a vintner can produce only so much wine per acre.	40 hectoliters/acre	35 hectoliters/acre

FAMOUS NON-AOC French wines that are available in the United States include: Valbon, Moreau, Boucheron, Chantefleur, and René Junot.

ONLY 35% OF all French wines are worthy of the AOC designation.

THERE ARE more than 465 AOC French wines.

HECTARE—metric measure
1 hectare = 2.471 acres

HECTOLITER—metric measure
1 hectoliter = 26.42 U.S. gallons

THE REGION most active in the production of Vin de Pays varietal wines is the Midi, also called Languedoc-Roussillon, in southwest France. Called in the past the "wine lake" because of the vast quantities of anonymous wine made there, the Languedoc has more than 700,000 acres of vineyards, almost twice as many as California, and produces more than 200 million cases a year, about a third of the total French crop.

WHY WOULD Georges Duboeuf, Louis Latour, and many other famous winemakers start wineries in the Midi? For one thing, Midi vineyard land is much cheaper than land in places such as Burgundy or Bordeaux, so the winemakers can produce moderately priced wines and still get a good return on their investment.

CHAMPAGNE IS another major white wine producer, but that's a chapter in itself.

Anyone who is interested in wine is bound to encounter French wine at one time or another. Why? Because of thousands of years of history and wine-making tradition, because of the great diversity and variety of wines from the many different regions, and because French wines have the reputation of being among the best in the world. There's a reason for this, and it goes back to quality control.

French winemaking is regulated by strict government laws that are set up by the **Appellation d'Origine Contrôlée**. If you don't want to say "Appellation d'Origine Contrôlée" all the time, you can simply say "AOC." This is the first of many wine lingo abbreviations you'll learn in this book.

Vins de Pays—This is a category that's growing in importance. A 1979 French legal decision liberalized the rules for this category, permitting the use of nontraditional grapes in certain regions and even allowing vintners to label wines with the varietal rather than the regional name. For exporters to the American market, where consumers are becoming accustomed to buying wines by grape variety—Cabernet Sauvignon or Chardonnay, for example—this change makes their wines much easier to sell.

Vins de Table—These are ordinary table wines and represent almost 35 percent of all wines produced in France.

Most French wine is meant to be consumed as a simple beverage. Many of the *vins de table* are marketed under proprietary names and are the French equivalent of California jug wines. Don't be surprised if you go into a grocery store in France to buy wine and find it in a plastic wine container with no label on it! You can see the color through the plastic—red, white, or rosé—but the only marking on the container is the alcohol content, ranging from 9 to 14 percent. You choose your wine depending on what you have to do during the rest of the day!

When you buy wines, keep these distinctions in mind, because there's not only a difference in quality but also in price.

What are the four major white wine–producing regions of France?

ALSACE   LOIRE VALLEY   BORDEAUX   BURGUNDY

Let's start with Alsace and the Loire Valley, because these are the two French regions that specialize in white wines. As you can see from the map at the beginning of this chapter, Alsace, the Loire Valley, and Chablis (a white wine–producing region of Burgundy) have one thing in common: They're all located in the northern region of France. These areas produce white wines predominantly, because of the shorter growing season and the cooler climate, both of which are best suited for growing white grapes.

ALSACE

I OFTEN FIND THAT PEOPLE are confused about the difference between wines from Alsace and those from Germany. Why do you suppose this is?

First of all, Alsace and Germany grow the same grape varieties. When you think of Riesling, what are your associations? You'll probably answer "Germany" and "sweetness." That's a very typical response. However, after the winemaker from Alsace harvests his Riesling, he makes his wine much differently than does his German counterpart. The winemaker from Alsace ferments every bit of the sugar in the grapes, while in Germany the winemaker adds a small amount of the naturally sweet unfermented grape juice back into the wine, to create the distinctive German Riesling. Ninety-nine percent of all Alsace wines are totally dry.

Another fundamental difference between wine from Alsace and wine from Germany is the alcohol content. Wine from Alsace has 11 to 12 percent alcohol, while most German wine has a mere 8 to 9 percent.

Just to confuse you a bit more, both wines are bottled in similarly shaped bottles that are tall with a tapering neck.

What are the white grapes grown in Alsace?

The four grapes you should know are:

Riesling: accounts for 23 percent

Gewürztraminer: accounts for 19 percent

Pinot Blanc: accounts for 20 percent

Pinot Gris: accounts for 7 percent

FROM 1871 TO 1919, Alsace was part of Germany.

ALL WINES produced in Alsace are AOC-designated and represent nearly 20% of all AOC white wines in France.

ALSACE PRODUCES 8% of its red wines from the Pinot Noir grape. These generally are consumed in the region and are rarely exported.

WINE LABELING in Alsace is different from other French regions administered by the AOC, because Alsace is the only region that labels its wine by varietal. All Alsace wines that put the name of the grape on the label must be made entirely from that grape.

GREAT SWEET (LATE HARVEST) WINES FROM ALSACE

Vendange Tardive
Seléction de Grains Nobles

IN THE LAST 10 years, there have been more Pinot Blanc and Riesling grapes planted in Alsace than any other variety.

THERE ARE 35,000 acres of grapes planted in Alsace, but the average plot of land for each grower is only 5 acres.

THE ALSACE region has little rainfall, especially during the grape harvest, and the town of Colmar—the Alsace wine center—is the second driest in France. That's why they say a "one-shirt harvest" will be a good vintage.

SOMETIMES YOU'LL see "Grand Cru" on an Alsace label. This wine can be made only from the best grape varieties of Alsace. There are more than 50 different vineyards entitled to be called Grand Cru.

What type of wine is produced in Alsace?

As mentioned earlier, virtually all the Alsace wines are dry. Riesling is the major grape planted in Alsace, and it is responsible for the highest-quality wines of the region. Alsace is also known for its Gewürztraminer, which is in a class by itself. Most people either love it or hate it, because Gewürztraminer has a very distinctive style. *Gewürz* is the German word for "spice," which aptly describes the wine.

Pinot Blanc and Pinot Gris are becoming increasingly popular among the growers of Alsace.

How should I select an Alsace wine?

Two factors are important in choosing a wine from Alsace: the grape variety and the reputation and style of the shipper. Some of the most reliable shippers are:

DOMAINE MARCEL DEISS	F. E. TRIMBACH
DOMAINE WEINBACH	HUGEL & FILS
DOMAINE ZIND-HUMBRECHT	LÉON BEYER
DOPFF "AU MOULIN"	

Why are the shippers so important?

The majority of the landholders in Alsace don't grow enough grapes to make it economically feasible to produce and market their own wine. Instead, they sell their grapes to a shipper who produces, bottles, and markets the wine under his own name. The art of making high-quality wine lies in the selection of grapes made by each shipper.

What are the different quality levels of Alsace wine?

The vast majority of the wine is a shipper's varietal; a very small percentage is labeled with a specific vineyard's name, especially in the appellation "Alsace Grand Cru." Some wines are also labeled "Réserve" or "Réserve Personelle," terms that are not legally defined. Their importance is determined by the shipper's reputation.

Should I lay down my Alsace wines for long aging?

In general, most Alsace wines are made to be consumed young—that is, one to five years after they're bottled. As in any fine-wine area, there is a small percentage of great wines produced in Alsace that may be aged for ten years or more.

What are the recent trends in Alsace wine?

What I've learned over the last twenty years is that the more I drink Alsace wines, the more I like them. They're fresh, they're "clean," they're easy to drink, they're very compatible with food.

I think Riesling is still the best grape, but Pinot Blanc, which is lighter in style, is a perfect apéritif wine at a very good price.

Most Alsace wines are very affordable, of good quality, and are available in most markets.

BEST BETS FOR RECENT VINTAGES OF ALSACE

2000* 2001* 2002* 2003*

*Note: * signifies exceptional vintage*

FOR FURTHER READING

I recommend *Alsace* by S. F. Hallgarten and *Alsace* by Pamela Van Dyke Price.

ALSACE is also known for its fruit brandies, or eaux-de-vie:

Fraise: Strawberries
Framboise: Raspberries
Kirsch: Cherries
Mirabelle: Yellow plums
Poire: Pears

FOR THE TOURISTS

Visit the beautiful wine village of Riquewihr, whose buildings date from the 15th and 16th centuries.

WINE AND FOOD

During a visit to Alsace, I spoke with two of the region's best-known producers to find out which types of food they enjoy with Alsace wines. Here's what they prefer:
ÉTIENNE HUGEL: *"Alsace wines are not only suited to classic Alsace and other French dishes. For instance, I adore Riesling with such raw fish specialties as Japanese sushi and sashimi, while our Gewürztraminer is delicious with smoked salmon and brilliant with Chinese, Thai, and Indonesian food."*

Mr. Hugel describes Pinot Blanc as "round, soft, not aggressive . . . an all-purpose wine . . . can be used as an apéritif, with all kinds of pâté and

charcuterie, and also with hamburgers. Perfect for brunch—not too sweet or flowery."
HUBERT TRIMBACH: *"Riesling with fish—blue trout with a light sauce."* He recommends Gewürztraminer as an apéritif, or with foie gras or any pâté at the end of the meal; with Muenster cheese, or a stronger cheese such as Roquefort.

FOR THE FOODIES

Alsace boasts three Michelin three-star restaurants within a 30-mile radius.

IN THE Loire Valley, 56% of the AOC wines produced are white, and 96% of those are dry.

THE LOIRE Valley is famous not only for its wines, but also as a summer retreat for royalty. Elegant and sometimes enormous châteaus embellish the countryside.

FOR RED wine look to Bourgueil, Chinon, and Saumur, all made from the Cabernet Franc grape.

THE DISTINCT nose, or bouquet, of Pouilly-Fumé comes from a combination of the Sauvignon Blanc grape and the soil of the Loire Valley.

MOST POUILLY-FUMÉ and Sancerre wines are not aged in wood.

IF YOU see the phrase "sur lie" on a Muscadet wine label, it means that the wine was aged on its lees (sediment).

OTHER SAUVIGNON BLANC wines from the Loire to look for: Menetou-Salon and Quincy. For Chenin Blanc try Savennières.

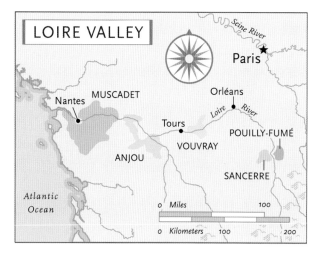

LOIRE VALLEY

STARTING AT THE CITY OF NANTES, a bit upriver from the Atlantic Ocean, this valley stretches inland for six hundred miles along the Loire River.

There are two white grape varieties you should be familiar with:

SAUVIGNON BLANC   CHENIN BLANC

Rather than choosing by grape variety and shipper, as you would in Alsace, choose Loire Valley wines by style and vintage. Here are the main styles:

Pouilly-Fumé: A dry wine that has the most body and concentration of all the Loire Valley wines. It's made with 100 percent Sauvignon Blanc.

Muscadet: A light, dry wine, made from 100 percent Melon grape.

Sancerre: Striking a balance between full-bodied Pouilly-Fumé and light-bodied Muscadet, it's made with 100 percent Sauvignon Blanc.

Vouvray: The "chameleon"; it can be dry, semisweet, or sweet. It's made from 100 percent Chenin Blanc.

How did Pouilly-Fumé get its name, and what does *fumé* mean?

Many people ask me if Pouilly-Fumé is smoked, because they automatically associate the word *fumé* with smoke. One of the many theories about the origin of the word comes from the white morning mist that blankets the area. As the sun burns off the mist, it looks as if smoke is rising.

When are the wines ready to drink?

Generally, Loire Valley wines are meant to be consumed young. The exception is a sweet Vouvray, which can be laid down for a longer time.

Here are more specific guidelines:

Pouilly-Fumé: Three to five years

Sancerre: Two to three years

Muscadet: One to two years

What's the difference between Pouilly-Fumé and Pouilly-Fuissé?

My students are often ask me this, expecting similarly named wines to be related. But Pouilly-Fumé is made from 100% Sauvignon Blanc and comes from the Loire Valley, while Pouilly-Fuissé is made from 100% Chardonnay and comes from the Mâconnais region of Burgundy.

What are the most recent trends in Loire Valley wines?

When I started in the wine business, the most important Loire Valley wine was Pouilly-Fumé. Back then, Sancerre played a minor role and cost much less than Pouilly-Fumé. Over the last twenty years, Sancerre's popularity has grown. Today, Sancerre is sometimes even more expensive than its neighbor. Both wines are made from the same grape variety, 100 percent Sauvignon Blanc, and have a similar style, most being unoaked and medium-bodied with great acidity and fruit balance.

Muscadet, on the other hand, remains a good value. In fact, these wines are being made even better than they were twenty years ago.

BEST BETS FOR RECENT VINTAGES OF LOIRE VALLEY
2002* 2003
Note: * signifies exceptional vintage

KEVIN ZRALY'S FAVORITE PRODUCERS

Sancerre: Archambault, Roblin, Lucien Crochet, Jean Vacheron, Château de Sancerre, Domaine Fournier, Henri Bourgeois

Pouilly-Fumé: Guyot, Michel Redde, Ch. de Tracy, Dagueneau, Ladoucette, Colin, Jolivet

Vouvray: Huet

Muscadet: Marquis de Goulaine, Sauvion, Métaireau

Savennières: Nicolas Joly

WINE AND FOOD

BARON PATRICK LADOUCETTE, *whose winery is the largest producer of Pouilly-Fumé, suggests the following combinations:*
Pouilly-Fumé: "Smoked salmon; turbot with hollandaise; white meat chicken; veal with cream sauce."
Sancerre: "Shellfish, simple food of the sea, because Sancerre is drier than Pouilly-Fumé."
Muscadet: "All you have to do is look at the map to see where Muscadet is made: by the sea where the main fare is shellfish, clams, and oysters."
Vouvray: "A nice semidry wine to have with fruit and cheese."

MARQUIS ROBERT DE GOULAINE *suggests these combinations:*
Muscadet: "Muscadet is good with a huge variety of excellent and fresh 'everyday' foods, including all the seafood from the Atlantic Ocean, the fish from the river—pike, for instance—game, poultry, and cheese (mainly goat cheese). Of course, there is a must in the region of Nantes: freshwater fish with the world-famous butter sauce, the beurre blanc, invented at the turn of the century by Clémence, who happened to be the chef at Goulaine. If you prefer, try Muscadet with a dash of crème de cassis (black currant); it is a wonderful way to welcome friends!"

THE LOIRE VALLEY also produces the world-famous Anjou Rosé.

GRAND CRU CLASSÉ DE GRAVES
1995

Château Olivier

PESSAC-LÉOGNAN
APPELLATION PESSAC-LÉOGNAN CONTROLÉE

GROUPEMENT FONCIER AGRICOLE DU CHATEAU OLIVIER
J.-J. DE BETHMANN · PROPRIÉTAIRE
LÉOGNAN · 33850 · GIRONDE · FRANCE

MIS EN BOUTEILLE AU CHATEAU

12,5% vol   PRODUCE OF FRANCE   75 cl

BORDEAUX PRODUCTION:
  84% red
  16% white

THE NAME "Graves" means "gravel"—the type of soil found in the region.

WHEN PEOPLE think of dry white Bordeaux wines, they normally think of the major areas of Graves or Pessac-Léognan, but some of the best value/quality white wines produced in Bordeaux come from the area called Entre-Deux-Mers.

CLASSIFIED WHITE château wines are hard to find, since they make up only 3% of the total production of white Graves.

THE WHITE WINES OF BORDEAUX

Doesn't Bordeaux always mean red wine?

That's a misconception. Actually, two of the five major areas of Bordeaux are known for their excellent white wines—Graves and Sauternes. Sauternes is world-famous for its sweet white wine.

The major white grape varieties used in both areas are:

SAUVIGNON BLANC   SÉMILLON

GRAVES

How are the white Graves wines classified?

There are two levels of quality:

GRAVES   PESSAC-LÉOGNAN

The most basic Graves is simply called "Graves." The best wines are produced in Pessac-Léognan. Those labeled "Graves" are from the southern portion of the region closest to Sauternes, while Pessac-Léognan is in the northern half of the region, next to the city of Bordeaux. The best wines are known by the name of a particular château, a special vineyard that produces the best-quality grapes. The grapes grown for these wines enjoy better soil and better growing conditions overall. The classified château wines and the regional wines of Graves are always dry.

BORDEAUX

Gironde River

Atlantic Ocean

0 Miles   25   50

0 Kilometers   50   100

MÉDOC

Bordeaux

POMEROL
ST-ÉMILION

Dordogne River

PESSAC-LÉOGNAN

ENTRE-DEUX-MERS

GRAVES

Garonne River

SAUTERNES

How should I select a Graves wine?

My best recommendation would be to purchase a classified château wine. The châteaus are:

CHÂTEAU HAUT-BRION
CHÂTEAU CARBONNIEUX*
CHÂTEAU COUHINS-LURTON
CHÂTEAU LA TOUR-MARTILLAC
CHÂTEAU MALARTIC-LAGRAVIÈRE
CHÂTEAU SMITH-HAUT-LAFITTE

CHÂTEAU BOUSCAUT*
DOMAINE DE CHEVALIER
CHÂTEAU LA LOUVIÈRE*
CHÂTEAU LAVILLE-HAUT-BRION
CHÂTEAU OLIVIER*

The largest producers and the easiest to find.

What are the most recent trends in the white wines of Bordeaux?

In the last twenty years, out of all of the white wines of France, the most significant shifts have occurred in Bordeaux. The winemakers have changed the style with more modern winemaking techniques, as well as by being more careful with their selection in the vineyard, thus resulting in much higher quality white Bordeaux wines.

THE STYLE of classified white château wines varies according to the ratio of Sauvignon Blanc and Sémillon used. Château Olivier, for example, is made with 65% Sémillon, and Château Carbonnieux with 65% Sauvignon Blanc.

BEST BETS FOR RECENT VINTAGES OF WHITE GRAVES

2000* 2001 2002 2003

*Note: * signifies exceptional vintage*

WINE AND FOOD

DENISE LURTON-MOULLE (*Château La Louvière, Château Bonnet*): With Château La Louvière Blanc: *grilled sea bass with a beurre blanc, shad roe, goat cheese soufflé. With Château Bonnet Blanc: oysters on the half-shell, fresh crab salad, mussels, and clams.*

JEAN-JACQUES DE BETHMANN (*Château Olivier*): *"Oysters, lobster, Rouget du Bassin d'Arcachon."*

ANTONY PERRIN (*Château Carbonnieux*): *"With a young Château Carbonnieux Blanc: chilled lobster consommé, or shellfish, such as oysters, scallops, or grilled shrimp. With an older Carbonnieux: a traditional sauced fish course or a goat cheese."*

WHEN BUYING regional Sauternes look for these reputable shippers: Baron Philippe de Rothschild and B&G.

THERE ARE more Sémillon grapes planted in Bordeaux than there are Sauvignon Blanc.

OTHER SWEET-wine producers in Bordeaux: Ste-Croix-du-Mont, Loupiac.

SAUTERNES IS expensive to produce because several pickings must be completed before the crop is entirely harvested. The harvest can last into November.

SAUTERNES/BARSAC

FRENCH SAUTERNES ARE ALWAYS SWEET, meaning that not all the grape sugar has turned into alcohol during fermentation. A dry French Sauternes doesn't exist. The Barsac district, adjacent to Sauternes, has the option of using Barsac or Sauternes as its appellation.

What are the two different quality levels in style?

1. Regional ($)
2. Classified château ($$$)/($$$$)

Sauternes is still producing one of the best sweet wines in the world. With the great vintages of 2001, 2002, and 2003, you'll be able to find excellent regional Sauternes, if you buy from the best shippers. These wines represent good value for your money, considering the labor involved in production, but they won't have the same intensity of flavor as a classified château.

What are the main grape varieties in Sauternes?

SÉMILLON   **SAUVIGNON BLANC**

If the same grapes are used for both the dry Graves and the sweet Sauternes, how do you explain the extreme difference in styles?

First and most important, the best Sauternes is made primarily with the Sémillon grape. Second, to make Sauternes, the winemaker leaves the grapes on the vine longer. He waits for a mold called *Botrytis cinerea* ("noble rot") to form. When noble rot forms on the grapes, the water within them evaporates and they shrivel. Sugar becomes concentrated as the grapes "raisinate." Then, during the winemaking process, not all the sugar is allowed to ferment into alcohol: hence, the high residual sugar.

How are Sauternes classified?

FIRST GREAT GROWTH—GRAND PREMIER CRU

Château d'Yquem*

FIRST GROWTH—PREMIERS

Château La Tour Blanche*
Clos Haut-Peyraguey*
Château Suduiraut*
Château Climens* (Barsac)
Château Rieussec*
Château Sigalas-Rabaud*

Château Lafaurie-Peyraguey*
Château de Rayne-Vigneau*
Château Coutet* (Barsac)
Château Guiraud*
Château Rabaud-Promis

SECOND GROWTHS—DEUXIÈMES CRUS

Château Myrat (Barsac)
Château Doisy-Védrines* (Barsac)
Château d'Arche
Château Broustet (Barsac)
Château Caillou (Barsac)
Château de Malle*
Château Lamothe

Château Doisy-Daëne (Barsac)
Château Doisy-Dubroca (Barsac)
Château Filhot*
Château Nairac* (Barsac)
Château Suau (Barsac)
Château Romer du Hayot*
Château Lamothe-Guignard

These are the châteaus most readily available in the United States.

BEST BETS FOR VINTAGES OF SAUTERNES

1986* 1988* 1989* 1990* 1995 1996 1997*
1998 1999 2000 2001* 2002* 2003*

*Note: * signifies exceptional vintage*

JUST DESSERTS

My students always ask me, "What do you serve with Sauternes?" Here's a little lesson I learned when I first encountered the wines of Sauternes.

Many years ago, when I was visiting the Sauternes region, I was invited to one of the châteaus for dinner. Upon arrival, my group was offered appetizers of foie gras, and, to my surprise, Sauternes was served with it. All the books I had ever read said you should serve drier wines first and sweeter wines later. But since I was a guest, I thought it best not to question my host's selection.

When we sat down for the first dinner course (fish), we were once again served a Sauternes. This continued through the main course—which happened to be rack of lamb—when another Sauternes was served.

DOESN'T CHÂTEAU d'Yquem make a dry white wine? Yes, it does, and it's simply called "Y." By law, dry wine made in Sauternes cannot be called Appellation Sauternes. It can only be called Appellation Bordeaux.

NOT CLASSIFIED, but of outstanding quality: Château Fargues, Château Gilette, Château Raymond Lafon.

CHÂTEAU RIEUSSEC is owned by the same family as Château Lafite-Rothschild.

WORLD RECORD

One bottle of Château d'Yquem 1847 sold for $71,675 at the Zachy's wine auction in 2004.

Continued . . .

SAUTERNES IS a wine you can age.
In fact, most classified château wines
in good vintages can easily age for
10 to 30 years.

I thought for sure our host would serve a great old red Bordeaux with the cheese course, but I was wrong again. With the Roquefort cheese was served a very old Sauternes.

With dessert soon on its way, I got used to the idea of having a dinner with Sauternes, and waited with anticipation for the final choice. You can imagine my surprise when a dry red Bordeaux—Château Lafite-Rothschild—was served with dessert!

Their point was that Sauternes doesn't have to be served only with dessert. All the Sauternes went well with the courses, because all the sauces complemented the wine and food.

By the way, the only wine that didn't go well with dinner was the Château Lafite-Rothschild with dessert, but we drank it anyway!

Perhaps this anecdote will inspire you to serve Sauternes with everything. Personally, I prefer to enjoy Sauternes by itself; I'm not a believer in the "dessert wine" category. This dessert wine is dessert in itself.

THE WHITE WINES OF BURGUNDY

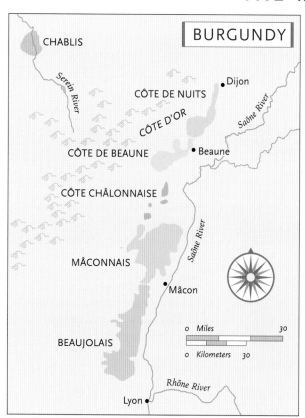

Where is Burgundy?

Burgundy is a region located in central eastern France. Its true fame is as one of the most famous wine-producing areas in the world.

What is Burgundy?

Burgundy is one of the major wine-producing regions that holds an AOC designation in France. However, over the years, I have often found that people are confused about what a Burgundy really is, because the name has been borrowed so freely.

Burgundy is *not* a synonym for red wine, even though the color known as burgundy is obviously named after red wine. Many of the world's most renowned (and expensive) white wines come from Burgundy. Adding to the confusion (especially going back twenty years) is that many red wines were simply labeled "Burgundy" even though they were ordinary table wines. There are still some wineries, especially in the United States, that continue to label their wine as Burgundy, but these wines have no resemblance to the style of authentic French Burgundy wine.

What are the main areas of Burgundy?

**CHABLIS   CÔTE D'OR}   CÔTE DE NUITS
                            CÔTE DE BEAUNE**

CÔTE CHÂLONNAISE   MÂCONNAIS   BEAUJOLAIS

Before we explore Burgundy region by region, it's important to know the types of wine that are produced there. Take a look at the chart below: It breaks down the types of wine and tells you the percentage of reds to whites.

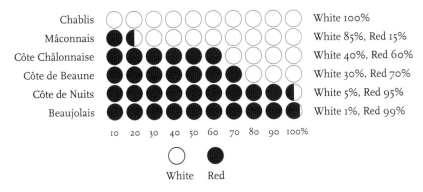

Chablis		White 100%
Mâconnais		White 85%, Red 15%
Côte Châlonnaise		White 40%, Red 60%
Côte de Beaune		White 30%, Red 70%
Côte de Nuits		White 5%, Red 95%
Beaujolais		White 1%, Red 99%

10 20 30 40 50 60 70 80 90 100%

○ White   ● Red

Burgundy is another region so famous for its red wines that people may forget that some of the finest white wines of France are also produced there. The three areas in Burgundy that produce world-famous white wines are:

CHABLIS   CÔTE DE BEAUNE   MÂCONNAIS

If it's any comfort to you, you need to know only one
white grape variety: Chardonnay. All the great white Burgundies
are made from 100 percent Chardonnay.

Is there only one type of white Burgundy?

Although Chardonnay is used to make all the best French white Burgundy wines, these three areas produce many different styles. Much of this has to do with where the grapes are grown and the vinification procedures. For example, the northerly climate of Chablis produces wines with more acidity than those of the southern region of Mâconnais.

THE LARGEST city in Burgundy is known not for its wines but for another world-famous product. The city is Dijon, and the product is mustard.

ALTHOUGH CHABLIS is part of the Burgundy region, it is a three-hour drive south from there to the Mâconnais area.

CÔTE D'OR PRODUCTION:
    78% red
    22% white

ANOTHER WHITE grape found in the Burgundy region is the Aligoté. It is a lesser grape variety and the grape name usually appears on the label.

With regard to vinification procedures, after the grapes are harvested in the Chablis and Mâconnais areas, 95 percent are fermented and aged in stainless-steel tanks. In the Côte de Beaune, after the grapes are harvested, a good percentage of the wines are fermented in small oak barrels and also aged in oak barrels. The wood adds complexity, depth, body, flavor, and longevity to the wines.

White Burgundies have one trait in common: They are dry.

How are the white wines of Burgundy classified?

The type of soil and the angle and direction of the slope are the primary factors determining quality. Here are the levels of quality:

Village Wine: Bears the name of a specific village. ($ = good)

Premier Cru: From a specific vineyard with special characteristics, within one of the named villages. Usually a Premier Cru wine will list the village first and the vineyard second. ($$ = better)

Grand Cru: From a specific vineyard that possesses the best soil and slope in the area and meets or exceeds all other requirements. In most areas of Burgundy, the village doesn't appear on the label—only the vineyard name is used. ($$$$ = best)

ALSO LOOK for regional Burgundy wine, such as Bourgogne Blanc or Bourgogne Rouge.

MOST PREMIER Cru wines give you the name of the vineyard on the label, but others are simply called "Premier Cru," which is a blend of different cru vineyards.

THE AVERAGE yield for a village wine in Burgundy is 360 gallons per acre. For the Grand Cru wines it is 290 gallons per acre, a noticeably larger concentration, which produces a more flavorful wine.

THE STORY OF KIR

The apéritif Kir has been popular from time to time. It is a mixture of white wine and crème de cassis (made from black currants). It was the favorite drink of the former mayor of Dijon, Canon Kir, who originally mixed the sweet cassis to balance the acidity of the local white wine made from the Aligoté grape.

A NOTE ON THE USE OF WOOD

Each wine region in the world has its own way of producing wines. Wine was always fermented and aged in wood—until the introduction of cement tanks, glass-lined tanks, and, most recently, stainless-steel tanks. Despite these technological improvements, many winemakers prefer to use the more traditional methods. For example, some of the wines from the firm of Louis Jadot are fermented in wood as follows:

> *One-third of the wine is fermented in new wood.*
> *One-third of the wine is fermented in year-old wood.*
> *One-third of the wine is fermented in older wood.*

Jadot's philosophy is that the better the vintage, the newer the wood: Younger wood imparts more flavor and tannin, which might overpower wines of lesser vintage. Thus, younger woods are generally reserved for aging the better vintages.

CHABLIS

CHABLIS IS THE NORTHERNMOST AREA in Burgundy, and it produces only white wine.

Isn't Chablis just a general term for white wine?

The name "Chablis" suffers from the same misinterpretation and overuse as does the name "Burgundy." Because the French didn't take the necessary precautions to protect the use of the name, "Chablis" is now randomly applied to many ordinary bulk wines from other countries. Chablis has come to be associated with some very undistinguished wine, but this is not the case with French Chablis. In fact, the French take their Chablis very seriously. There is a special classification of Chablis.

What are the quality levels of Chablis?

Petit Chablis: The most ordinary Chablis; rarely seen in the United States.

Chablis: A wine that comes from grapes grown anywhere in the Chablis district.

Chablis Premier Cru: A very good quality of Chablis that comes from specific high-quality vineyards.

Chablis Grand Cru: The highest classification of Chablis, and the most expensive because of its limited production. There are only seven vineyards in Chablis entitled to be called Grand Cru.

ALL FRENCH Chablis is made of 100% Chardonnay grapes.

THERE ARE more than 250 grape growers in Chablis, but only a handful age their wine in wood

OF THESE quality levels, the best price/value wine is a Chablis Premier Cru.

THERE ARE only 245 acres planted in Grand Cru vineyards.

VILLAGE $

PREMIER CRU $$

GRAND CRU $$$

THE WINTER temperatures in some parts of Chablis can match those of Norway.

If you're interested in buying only the best Chablis, here are the seven Grands Crus and the most important Premiers Crus vineyards:

THE GRAND CRU VINEYARDS OF CHABLIS

Blanchots	Preuses
Bougros	Valmur
Grenouilles	Vaudésir
Les Clos	

THE TOP PREMIER CRU VINEYARDS OF CHABLIS

Côte de Vaulorent	Montmains
Fourchaume	Monts de Milieu
Lechet	Vaillon
Montée de Tonnerre	

What has been the most important recent change in Chablis?

The cold, northerly climate of Chablis poses a threat to the vines. Back in the late 1950s, Chablis almost went out of business because the crops were ruined by frost. Through modern technology, and with improved methods of frost protection, vintners have learned to control this problem, so more and better wine is being produced.

How should I buy Chablis?

The two major aspects to look for in Chablis are the shipper and the vintage. Here is a list of the most important shippers of Chablis to the United States:

A. REGNARD & FILS	JOSEPH DROUHIN
ALBERT PIC & FILS	LA CHABLISIENNE
DOMAINE LAROCHE	LOUIS JADOT
FRANÇOIS RAVENEAU	LOUIS MICHEL
GUY ROBIN	RENÉ DAUVISSAT
J. MOREAU & FILS	ROBERT VOCORET
JEAN DAUVISSAT	WILLIAM FÈVRE

BEST BETS FOR RECENT VINTAGES OF CHABLIS

1999   2000*   2001   2002*   2003

*Note: * signifies exceptional vintage*

When should I drink my Chablis?

Chablis: Within two years of the vintage.
Premier Cru: Between two and four years.
Grand Cru: Between three and eight years.

CÔTE DE BEAUNE

THIS IS ONE OF THE TWO major areas of the Côte d'Or. The wines produced here are some of the finest examples of dry white Chardonnay produced in the world and are considered a benchmark for winemakers everywhere.

CÔTE DE BEAUNE

Here is a list of my favorite white wine–producing villages and vineyards in the Côte de Beaune.

VILLAGE	PREMIER CRU VINEYARDS	GRAND CRU VINEYARDS
Aloxe-Corton		Corton-Charlemagne
		Charlemagne
Beaune	Clos des Mouches	None
Meursault	Les Perrières	None
	Les Genevrières	
	La Goutte d'Or	
	Les Charmes	
	Blagny	
	Poruzots	
Puligny-Montrachet	Les Combettes	Montrachet*
	Les Caillerets	Bâtard-Montrachet*
	Les Pucelles	Chevalier-Montrachet
	Les Folatières	Bienvenue-Bâtard-Montrachet
	Clavoillons	
	Les Referts	
Chassagne-Montrachet	Les Ruchottes	Montrachet*
	Morgeot	Bâtard-Montrachet*
		Criots-Bâtard-Montrachet

* The vineyards of Bâtard-Montrachet and Montrachet overlap between the villages of Puligny-Montrachet and Chassagne-Montrachet.

THE LARGEST Grand Cru, in terms of production, is Corton-Charlemagne, which represents more than 50% of all white Grand Cru wines.

The three most important white wine–producing villages of the Côte de Beaune are Meursault, Puligny-Montrachet, and Chassagne-Montrachet. All three produce their white wine from the same grape—100 percent Chardonnay.

What makes each Burgundy wine different?

"The difference between the Village wine, Puligny-Montrachet, and the Grand Cru Montrachet, is not in the type of wood used in aging or how long the wine is aged in wood. The primary difference is in the location of the vineyards, i.e., the soil and the slope of the land."

—ROBERT DROUHIN

THE BIGGEST harvest ever for white Burgundy was the 1999 vintage.

In Burgundy, one of the most important factors in making a good wine is soil. The quality of the soil is the main reason why there are three levels and price points between a Village, a Premier Cru, and a Grand Cru wine. Another major factor that differentiates each wine is the vinification procedure the winemaker uses—the recipe. It's the same as if you were to compare the chefs at three gourmet restaurants: They may start out with the same ingredients, but it's what they do with those ingredients that matters.

BEST BETS OF CÔTE DE BEAUNE WHITE

1995*　1996*　1999　2000*　2001　2002*　2003　2004

*Note: * signifies exceptional vintage*

CÔTE CHÂLONNAISE

THE CÔTE CHÂLONNAISE IS THE LEAST known of the major wine districts of Burgundy. Although the Châlonnaise produces such red wines as Givry and Mercurey (see Class Four, "The Red Wines of of Burgundy and the Rhône Valley"), it also produces some very good white wines that not many people are familiar with, which means value for you. I'm referring to the wines of Montagny and Rully. These wines are of the highest quality produced in the area, similar to the white wines of the Côte d'Or.

Look for the wines of Antonin Rodet, Faiveley, Louis Latour, Moillard, and Olivier Leflaive.

MÂCONNAIS

THE SOUTHERNMOST WHITE WINE–PRODUCING AREA in Burgundy, the Mâconnais has a climate warmer than that of the Côte d'Or and Chablis. Mâcon wines are, in general, pleasant, light, uncomplicated, reliable, and a great value.

What are the quality levels of Mâconnais wines?

From basic to best:

1. MÂCON BLANC	4. ST-VÉRAN
2. MÂCON SUPÉRIEUR	5. POUILLY-VINZELLES
3. MÂCON-VILLAGES	6. POUILLY-FUISSÉ

Of all Mâcon wines, Pouilly-Fuissé is unquestionably one of the most popular. It is among the highest-quality Mâconnais wines, fashionable to drink in the United States long before most Americans discovered the splendors of wine. As wine consumption increased in America, Pouilly-Fuissé and other famous areas such as Pommard, Nuits-St-Georges, and Chablis became synonymous with the best wines of France, and could always be found on any restaurant's wine list.

In my opinion, Mâcon-Villages is the best value. Why pay more for Pouilly-Fuissé—sometimes three times as much—when a simple Mâcon will do just as nicely?

BEST BETS OF RECENT VINTAGES OF MÂCON WHITE

2002*   2003   2004

*Note: * signifies exceptional vintage*

MORE THAN four-fifths of the wines from the Mâconnais are white.

THERE IS a village named Chardonnay in the Mâconnais area, where the grape's name is said to have originated.

IN AN average year, around 450,000 cases of Pouilly-Fuissé are produced—not nearly enough to supply all the restaurants and retail shops for worldwide consumption.

SINCE MÂCON wines are usually not aged in oak, they are ready to drink after one to three years.

IF YOU'RE taking a client out on a limited expense account, a safe wine to order is a Mâcon. If the sky's the limit, go for the Meursault!

ESTATE-BOTTLED wine: The wine is made, produced, and bottled by the owner of the vineyard.

DOMAINE LEFLAIVE'S wines are named for characters and places in a local medieval tale. The Chevalier of Puligny-Montrachet, lonely for his son who was off fighting in the Crusades, amused himself in the ravinelike vineyards (Les Combettes) with a local maiden (Pucelle), only to welcome the arrival of another son (Bâtard-Montrachet) nine months later.

OVERVIEW

Now that you're familiar with the many different white wines of Burgundy:

How do you choose the right one for you?

First look for the vintage year. With Burgundy, it's especially important to buy a good year. After that, your choice becomes a matter of taste and cost. If price is no object, aren't you lucky?

Also, after some trial and error, you may find that you prefer the wines of one shipper over another. Here are some of the shippers to look for when buying white Burgundy:

BOUCHARD PÈRE & FILS
CHARTRON ET TRÉBUCHET
JOSEPH DROUHIN
LABOURÉ-ROI
LOUIS JADOT
LOUIS LATOUR
MOMMESSIN
OLIVIER LEFLAIVE FRÈRES
PROSPER MAUFOUX
ROPITEAU FRÈRES

Although 80 percent of Burgundy wines are sold through shippers, some fine estate-bottled wines are available in limited quantities in the United States. The better ones include:

CHÂTEAU FUISSÉ (POUILLY-FUISSÉ)
DOMAINE BACHELET-RAMONET (CHASSAGNE-MONTRACHET)
DOMAINE BOILLOT (MEURSAULT)
DOMAINE BONNEAU DU MARTRAY (CORTON-CHARLEMAGNE)
DOMAINE COCHE-DURY (MEURSAULT, PULIGNY MONTRACHET)
DOMAINE DES COMTES LAFON (MEURSAULT)
DOMAINE ÉTIENNE SAUZET (CHASSAGNE-MONTRACHET,
   PULIGNY-MONTRACHET)
DOMAINE LEFLAIVE (MEURSAULT, PULIGNY-MONTRACHET)
DOMAINE MATROT (MEURSAULT)

What are the recent trends in white Burgundy?

If anything, white Burgundy wines have gotten better over the last twenty years. Since 1995—and especially with the vintage 2002—Burgundy has made some of its best wines ever. Mâcon wines remain one of today's great values in the world of wine, being made from 100 percent Chardonnay grapes, yet usually priced around ten dollars a bottle.

One of the most interesting things I have seen on the labels of French wines in the U.S. market, particularly from the Mâconnais, is the inclusion of the grape variety. French winemakers have finally realized that Americans buy wines by grape varieties.

I have also found that the major shippers have continued to make high-quality wines.

FOR FURTHER READING

I recommend *Burgundy* by Anthony Hanson; *Burgundy* by Robert M. Parker Jr.; *The Great Domaines of Burgundy* by Remington Norman; and *Making Sense of Burgundy* by Matt Kramer.

WINE AND FOOD

When you choose a white Burgundy wine, you have a whole gamut of wonderful food possibilities. Let's say that you decide upon a wine from the Mâconnais area: Very reasonably priced, Mâconnais wines are suitable for picnics, as well as for more formal dinners. Or, you might select one of the fuller-bodied Côte de Beaune wines that can even stand up to a hearty steak, or if you prefer, an all-purpose wine, Chablis. Here are some tempting combinations offered by the winemakers.

ROBERT DROUHIN: *With a young Chablis or St-Véran, Mr. Drouhin enjoys shellfish. "Fine Côte d'Or wines match well with any fish or light white meat such as veal or sweetbreads. But please, no red meat."*

CHRISTIAN MOREAU: *"A basic village Chablis is good as an apéritif and with hors d'oeuvres and salads. A great Premier Cru or Grand Cru Chablis needs something more special, such as lobster. It's an especially beautiful match if the wine has been aged a few years."*

PIERRE HENRY GAGEY *(Louis Jadot):* *"My favorite food combination with white Burgundy wine is, without doubt, homard grillé Breton (blue lobster). Only harmonious, powerful, and delicate wines are able to go with the subtle, thin flesh and very fine taste of the Breton lobster."*

Mr. Gagey says that Chablis is a great match for oysters, snails, and shellfish, but a "Grand Cru Chablis should be had with trout."

On white wines of the Côte de Beaune,

Mr. Gagey gets a bit more specific: "With Village wines, which should be had at the beginning of the meal, try a light fish or quenelles (light dumplings).

"Premier Cru and Grand Cru wines can stand up to heavier fish and shellfish such as lobster—but with a wine such as Corton-Charlemagne, smoked Scottish salmon is a tasty choice."

Mr. Gagey's parting words on the subject: "Never with meat."

LOUIS LATOUR: *"With Corton-Charlemagne, filet of sole in a light Floren-tine sauce. Otherwise, the Chardonnays of Burgundy complement roast chicken, seafood, and light-flavored goat cheese particularly well." Mr. Latour believes that one should have Chablis with oysters and fish.*

THE TOP FIVE WINE PRODUCERS OF THE WORLD

1. France
2. Italy
3. United States
4. Spain
5. Argentina

THE TOP FIVE WINE-CONSUMING COUNTRIES

Rank	Country
1.	France
2.	Italy
3.	United States
4.	Germany
5.	Spain

THE WORLD'S TOP PER CAPITA WINE-CONSUMING COUNTRIES

Rank	Country	Gallons/Person
1.	Luxembourg	16.0
2.	France	15.8
3.	Italy	14.3
4.	Portugal	13.0
5.	Croatia	12.4
↓		
33.	United States	3

TO LOOK at it another way, each American consumes only 15 bottles of wine per year, compared to 70 bottles for each Italian.

American Wine and Winemaking: A Short History

AMERICANS ARE DRINKING MORE WINE now than ever before. In 2004 Americans consumed three gallons of wine per person, the highest ever. The number of American wineries has doubled in the last two decades—to more than 4,000—and, for the first time in American history, all fifty states produce wine.

Still, wine has never been America's favorite beverage. In fact, 40 percent of all Americans don't drink alcohol at all, and another 30 percent don't drink wine. (They prefer beer or distilled spirits.) This leaves only 30 percent of Americans who drink one glass of wine each week, the definition of a "wine drinker" in the United States. In the final analysis, 86 percent of all wine is consumed by 12 percent of the population.

The leading beverage in the United States is soda, with the typical American consuming an average of fifty-four gallons per year. Beer is in second place with thirty-one gallons per person per year. According to Gallup, wine drinking has jumped by more than a third in the United States over the last twenty years, leading an overall increase in alcohol consumption.

Of the 30 percent of U.S. consumers who enjoy wine, the preference is decidedly for American wines: More than 75 percent of all wines consumed by Americans are produced in the United States; the rest are imported. Within the United States, California accounts for 90 percent of wine production. Another 8 percent comes from Washington, New York, and Oregon.

Because American wines are so dominant in the U.S. market, before we move to Class Two it makes sense to pause here and take a detailed look at winemaking in the United States. While we often think of the wine industry as "young" in America, in fact its roots go back some four hundred years.

We've All Gone to Look for America: A Personal Wine Journey

My own love affair with wine began in 1970 when, at the age of nineteen, I visited my first winery, Benmarl, which was—and still is—located in New York's Hudson Valley. That experience struck a nerve. I felt deeply connected to the earth, the grapes, the growers, and, of course, the wine. My soul was stirred; I knew after this first visit that I needed to learn more about wine, winemaking, and wine culture. I continued my early education by seeking out and visiting other wineries in New York State, beginning with wineries in the Hudson Valley and on to those in the Finger Lakes area. I made trip after trip, trekking from vineyard to vineyard.

But that wasn't enough. Each winery I visited provoked an urgent desire to see and learn more about wine. I had taken the first steps of what would become a lifelong journey. I began going to wine tastings as frequently as I could, sampling wines from all over the world. I studied grapes, learning each variety and its characteristics until I was able to identify most of the grapes used in the wines I tasted. And I became obsessive in my study of viticulture and wine tasting. The more I learned, the more I needed to know.

In the early '70s the Finger Lakes district of New York and the North Coast of California were the only two regions in America producing quality wine. I will never forget reading, in 1972, the cover of Time magazine. The headline read: AMERICAN WINE: THERE'S GOLD IN THEM THAR GRAPES, referring to the renaissance of California winemaking. So that summer I took a year off from college and hitchhiked west to California. I stayed for six months, visiting every major winery I'd heard of, tasting the wine and absorbing as much as I could about California wines and wine culture.

On that trip I discovered that although some California winemakers were committed to producing fine wine, top quality American wine was still hard to come by. I found only a very few California wines worthy of comparison to the quality European wine I'd tasted. The best California wine was yet to come.

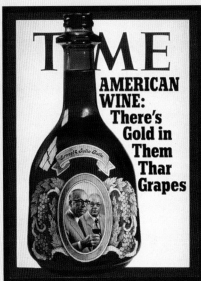

In 1974, after graduating from college, I traveled to Europe to tour the great vineyards of France, Spain, Italy, Germany, and Portugal. I was astounded by the extent to which each country possessed unique wine traditions, producing an impressive variety of superior-quality wines. What struck me most was the difference between the Old World and the New. European wine was like classical music—complex, yet soft and memorable, nurtured and matured over centuries

Continued . . .

Time & Life Pictures/Getty Images

IN 2004, WINE sales in the United States topped $22 billion.

CALIFORNIA PRODUCES nine-tenths of all wine made in the United States.

THE TOP 10 states in production of U.S. wines:

1. California
2. Washington
3. New York
4. Oregon
5. Ohio
6. Virginia
7. Pennsylvania
8. Texas
9. Missouri
10. Illinois

CALIFORNIA IS the leading wine consumer in the United States, with more than 42 million cases of wine sold. New York is a distant second, with 19 million cases sold.

THE TOP seven states in wine consumption:

1. California
2. New York
3. Florida
4. Texas
5. Illinois
6. New Jersey
7. Pennsylvania

of tradition. American wine, on the other hand, was like rock and roll—young, brash, and new—honoring no rules.

A year after I returned from Europe, fortune smiled on me: I became the first cellar master at Windows on the World—the world-class restaurant atop the newly built World Trade Center in New York City. When we opened, our customers favored European wines, primarily French Bordeaux and Burgundy, which was fine with me. My time abroad had taught me how to taste, what to buy, and how long to age each. However, I was still drawn to American wine, so, in the late '70s, I arranged for a return visit to California. To my delight, this time I found, just as Time had predicted, that California winemakers were beginning to produce more and higher quality wines, some of which were comparable to the finest European wines.

I came back to New York and immediately revised the Windows on the World wine list. My original wine list had been 90 percent French. My new wine list favored American wine by a three-to-one margin. Our customers were cautious, but adventurous enough to taste. Once they sampled and enjoyed the delicious Sonoma Chardonnays and Napa Valley Cabernet Sauvignons, they too became believers. By 1980, American consumers had begun to take California wine seriously.

But California wasn't the only state producing good wine. Other states and regions, such as Oregon, Washington, and Long Island, were developing excellent vineyards and wineries as well. Word on the street quickly spread, and in culinary circles conversation often began with: "Have you tried the Oregon Pinot Noir and Pinot Gris?" followed by, "What about Washington State Cabernet Sauvignon and Long Island Merlot?"

Fast-forward twenty-five years to 2005. Not only do California, New York, Oregon, and Washington State now produce great wines, but for the first time in its history America is becoming well known as a wine-producing nation. Today I can enjoy a meal accompanied by wines from Virginia, Pennsylvania, Texas, or any of the fifty states. This couldn't have happened without Americans rediscovering wine over the last twenty years. In fact, we are now the third-largest wine-consuming nation in the world, with projections indicating that within the next five years the United States will be the top wine consumer worldwide!

Finally, our time has arrived. Thanks to the conviction and determination of American producers, the demands of American consumers, and the savvy of American wine writers, and in spite of the many obstacles that prevented more rapid progress, I can proudly say that many of the best wines in the world are produced in the United States.

So why did it take more than four hundred years for American wines to reach this quality? What about the early days of winemaking in the United States?

The Pilgrims and early pioneers paved the way for American wine. Upon arriving in America, the early settlers, accustomed to drinking wine with meals, were delighted to find grapevines growing wild. These thrifty, self-reliant colonists thought they had found in this species (*Vitis labrusca*, primarily) a means of producing their own wine, which would end their dependency on costly wine from Europe. The early settlers cultivated the existing local grapevines, harvested the grapes, and made their first American wine. The taste of the new vintage was disappointing, however, for they discovered that wine made from New World grapes possessed an unfamiliar and entirely different flavor than did wine made from European grapes. Undaunted by this first failure and resolute in their determination, cuttings were ordered from Europe of the *Vitis vinifera* vine, which had for centuries produced the finest wines in the world. Soon ships arrived bearing the tender cuttings, and the colonists, having paid scarce, hard-earned money for these new vines, planted and tended them with great care. They were eager to taste their first wine made using European grapes.

The three major varieties of wine produced in the United States are made from the following species:

American: *Vitis labrusca,* such as the Concord, Catawba, and Delaware; and Vitis rotundifolia, commonly called Scuppernong.

European: *Vitis vinifera,* such as Riesling, Sauvignon Blanc, Chardonnay, Pinot Noir, Merlot, Cabernet Sauvignon, Zinfandel, and Syrah.

Hybrids: A cross between *vinifera* and *labrusca,* such as Seyval Blanc, Vidal Blanc, Baco Noir, and Chancellor.

What happened?

Nothing but problems! Despite their careful cultivation, few of the European vines thrived. Many died, and those that did survive produced few grapes whose meager yield resulted in very poor quality wine. Early settlers blamed the cold climate, but today we know that their European vines lacked immunity to the New World's plant diseases and pests. If the colonists had had access to modern methods of pest and disease control, the *Vitis vinifera* grapes would have thrived then, just as they do today. However, for the next two hundred years every attempt at establishing varieties of *vinifera*—either intact or through cross-

LEIF ERIKSSON, upon discovering North America, named it Vineland. In fact, there are more species of native grapes in North America than on any other continent.

THE FRENCH Huguenots established colonies in Jacksonville, Florida, in 1562 and produced wine using the wild Scuppernong grape. Evidence indicates that there was a flourishing wine industry in 1609 at the site of the early Jamestown settlements. In 2004 an old wine cellar was discovered in Jamestown with an empty bottle dating back to the 17th century.

WILLIAM PENN planted the first vineyard in Pennsylvania in 1683.

VITIS LABRUSCA, the "slip-skinned" grape, is native to both the Northeast and the Midwest and produces a unique flavor. It is used in making grape juice—the bottled kind you'll find on supermarket shelves. Wine produced from *labrusca* grapes tastes, well, more "grapey" (also described as "foxy") than European wines.

EARLY GERMAN immigrants imported Riesling grapes and called their finished wine Hock; the French called their wine Burgundy or Bordeaux; and the Italians borrowed the name "Chianti" for theirs.

breeding with native vines—failed. Left with no choice, growers throughout the Northeast and Midwest returned to planting *Vitis labrusca*, North America's vine, and a small wine industry managed to survive.

Americans never really got used to the taste of this wine, however, and European wine remained the preferred—though high-priced—choice. The failures of these early attempts to establish a wine industry in the United States, along with the high cost of imported wines, resulted in decreasing demand for wine. Gradually, American tastes changed and wine served at mealtime was reserved for special occasions; beer and whiskey had taken over wine's traditional place in American homes.

But when I think of American wines I think of California. How and when did wine arrive in the West?

Wine production in the West began with the Spanish. As the Spanish settlers began pushing northward from Mexico, the Catholic Church followed, and a great era of mission building began. Early missions were more than just churches; they were entire communities conceived as self-sufficient fortifications protecting Spanish colonial interests throughout the Southwest and along the Pacific Coast. Besides growing their own food and making their own clothing, these early settlers also made their own wine, produced primarily for use in the Church. Sacramental wine was especially important in early Church ritual. (Perhaps higher quality wine was an important factor in attracting congregants!) The demand for wine led Padre Junípero Serra to bring *Vitis vinifera* vines—brought to Mexico by the Spaniards—from Mexico to California in 1769. These vines took root, thriving in California due to its moderate climate. The first true California wine industry had been established, albeit on a small scale.

Two events occurred in the mid-1800s that resulted in an explosive growth of quality wine production. The first was the California Gold Rush, in 1849. With a huge rush of immigrants pushing steadily westward, California's population exploded. Along with their hopes of finding treasure, immigrants from Europe and the East Coast brought their winemaking traditions. Unsuccessful in finding gold nuggets, many discovered a different kind of gold: California's grapevines. They cultivated the vines and were soon producing good-quality commercial wine.

The second critical event occurred in 1861, when the governor of California, understanding the importance of viticulture to the state's growing economy, commissioned Count Agoston Haraszthy to select and import classic *Vitis*

THE EARLY missionaries established wineries in the southern parts of California. The first winery was established in what we know today as Los Angeles.

THE GRAPE variety the missionaries used to make their sacramental wine was actually called the Mission grape. Unfortunately, it did not have the potential to produce a great wine.

IN 1861, FIRST LADY Mary Todd Lincoln served American wines in the White House.

vinifera cuttings—such as Riesling, Zinfandel, Cabernet Sauvignon, and Chardonnay—from Europe. The count traveled to Europe, returning with more than 100,000 carefully selected vines. Due to the climatic conditions in California, not only did these grape varieties thrive, they also produced good-quality wine! Serious California winemaking was beginning in earnest. It was during this period that the Civil War broke out in the United States, leaving the fledgling wine industry with very little government attention or support. In spite of this, the quality of California wine improved dramatically over the next thirty years.

So, the rest, as they say, is history?

Not at all. In 1863, while California wines were flourishing, European vineyards were in trouble. Phylloxera—an aphid pest native to the East Coast that is very destructive to grape crops—began attacking European vineyards. This infestation, which arrived in Europe on cuttings from native American vines exported for experimental purposes, proved devastating. Over the next two decades, the phylloxera blight destroyed thousands of acres of European vines, severely diminishing European wine production just as demand was rapidly growing.

Since California was now virtually the only area in the world producing wine made from European grapes, demand for its wines skyrocketed. This helped develop, almost overnight, two huge markets for California wine. The first market clamored for good, inexpensive, yet drinkable wine produced on a mass scale. The second market sought higher-quality wines.

California growers responded to both demands, and by 1876 California was producing more than 2.3 million gallons of wine per year, some of remarkable quality. California was, for the moment, the new center of global winemaking.

Unfortunately, in that same year, phylloxera arrived in California and began attacking its vineyards. Once it got there, it spread as rapidly as it had in Europe. With thousands of vines dying, the California wine industry faced financial ruin. To this day, the phylloxera blight remains the most destructive crop epidemic of all time.

What happened next?

Luckily, other states had continued producing wine made from *labrusca* vines, and American wine production didn't grind to a complete halt. Meanwhile, after years of research, European winemakers finally found a defense against the pernicious phylloxera aphid. They were the first to successfully graft *Vitis*

THE THREE major wine-producing states in the 19th century were New York, Ohio, and Missouri.

WHEN ROBERT Louis Stevenson honeymooned in the Napa Valley in 1880, he described the efforts of local vintners to match soil and climate with the best possible varietals. "One corner of land after another . . . this is a failure, that is better, this is best. So bit by bit, they grope about for their Clos de Vougeot and Lafite . . . and the wine is bottled poetry."

FORTY DIFFERENT American wineries won medals at the 1900 Paris Exposition, including wines from California, New Jersey, New York, Ohio, and Virginia.

IN 1920 THERE were more than 700 wineries in California. By the end of Prohibition there were 160.

"Once, during Prohibition, I was forced to live for days on nothing but food and water."
—W. C. FIELDS

WELCH'S GRAPE JUICE

Welch's grape juice has been around since the late 1800s. It was originally produced by staunch prohibitionists and labeled "Dr. Welch's Unfermented Wine." In 1892 it was renamed "Welch's Grape Juice" and was successfully launched at the Columbian Exposition in Chicago in 1893.

vinifera vines onto the rootstock of *labrusca* vines (which were immune to the phylloxera), rescuing their wine industry.

Americans followed, and the California wine industry not only recovered but began producing better-quality wines than ever before. By the late 1800s, California wines were winning medals in international competition, gaining the respect and admiration of the world. And it only took three hundred years!

PROHIBITION: YET ANOTHER SETBACK

IN 1920, THE EIGHTEENTH AMENDMENT to the United States Constitution was enacted, creating yet another setback to the American wine industry. The National Prohibition Act, also known as the Volstead Act, prohibited the manufacture, sale, transportation, importation, exportation, delivery, or possession of intoxicating liquors for beverage purposes. Prohibition nearly destroyed what had become a thriving and national industry.

If Prohibition had lasted only four or five years, its impact on the wine industry might have been negligible. Unfortunately, it continued for thirteen years, during which grapes became important to the economy of the criminal world. One of the loopholes in the Volstead Act allowed for the manufacture and sale of sacramental wine, medicinal wines for sale by pharmacists with a doctor's prescription, and medicinal wine tonics (fortified wines) sold without prescription. Perhaps more important, Prohibition allowed anyone to produce up to 200 gallons yearly of fruit juice or cider. The fruit juice, which was sometimes made into concentrate, was ideal for making wine. Some of this yield found its way to bootleggers throughout America who did just that. But not for long, because the government stepped in and banned the sale of grape juice, preventing illegal wine production. Vineyards stopped being planted, and the American wine industry came to a halt.

The Roaring Twenties fostered more beer and distilled-spirit drinkers than wine drinkers, because the raw materials used in production were easier to come by. But fortified wine, or medicinal wine tonic—containing about 20 percent alcohol, which makes it more like a distilled spirit than regular wine—was still available and became America's number one wine. American wine was soon popular more for its effect than its taste; in fact, the word *wino* came into use during the Depression from the name given to those unfortunate souls who turned to fortified wine to forget their troubles.

ONE WAY TO GET AROUND PROHIBITION . . .

During Prohibition, people would buy grape concentrate from California and have it shipped to the East Coast. The top of the container was stamped in big, bold letters: CAUTION: DO NOT ADD SUGAR OR YEAST OR ELSE FERMENTATION WILL TAKE PLACE!

Of course, we know the formula: Sugar + Yeast = Alcohol. Do you want to guess how many people had the sugar and yeast ready the very moment the concentrate arrived?

Prohibition came to a close in 1933, but its impact would be felt for decades. By its end, Americans had lost interest in quality wine. During Prohibition, thousands of acres of valuable grapes around the country had been plowed under. Wineries nationwide shut down and the winemaking industry dwindled to a handful of survivors, mostly in California and New York. Many growers on the East Coast returned to producing grape juice—the ideal use for the American *labrusca* grape.

The federal government, in repealing Prohibition, empowered states to legislate the sale and transportation of alcohol. Some states handed control to counties and, occasionally, even municipalities—a tradition that continues today, varying from state to state and often from county to county.

SOME OF THE dilemmas facing winemakers after Prohibition:
    Locate on the East Coast or the West Coast?
    Make sweet wine or dry wine?
    Make high alcohol wine or low alcohol wine?
    Make inexpensive bulk wine or premium wine?

HARD TIMES FOR WINE: 1933—68

ALTHOUGH PROHIBITION WAS DEVASTATING to the majority of American wine producers, some endured by making sacramental wines. Beringer, Beaulieu, and the Christian Brothers are a few of the wineries that managed to survive this dry time. Since these wineries didn't have to interrupt production during Prohibition, they had a jump on those that had to start all over again in 1933.

From 1933 to 1968, grape growers and winemakers had little more than personal incentive to produce any wine of quality. Jug wines, which got their name from the containers in which they were bottled, were inexpensive, nondescript, and mass-produced. A few wineries, notably in California, were producing some good wines, but the majority of American wines produced during this period were ordinary.

THE BEST-SELLING wineries, from 1933–68, were Almaden, Gallo, and Paul Masson.

IN 1960 THERE were only 10 wineries in Napa Valley.

THE BEST-KNOWN wineries of California in the 1960s:

Almaden	Korbel
Beaulieu	Krug
Beringer	Martini
Concannon	Paul Masson
Inglenook	Wente

IN THE early 1970s, Chenin Blanc was the largest-selling white wine and Zinfandel the best-selling red.

IN 1933 MORE than 60% of wine sold in the United States contained over 20% alcohol.

SOME EXAMPLES of fortified wine may be familiar to consumers today. The list includes Thunderbird and Wild Irish Rose.

TODAY CALIFORNIA produces 565 million gallons of wine per year.

IN 2005, THERE were more than 4,000 wineries in the United States, up from 580 in 1975.

THE RENAISSANCE OF AMERICAN WINE

I CAN'T SAY WHEN, EXACTLY, the American wine renaissance began, but let's start in 1968, when, for the first time since Prohibition, table wines—wines with alcohol content between 7 and 14 percent—outsold fortified wines. Although American wines were improving, consumers still believed the best wines were made in Europe, especially France.

In the mid-sixties and early seventies, a small group of dedicated winemakers, determined that California could produce wines equal to the finest of France, began concentrating on making high-quality wine. Their early wines, though not world-class, demonstrated potential and began attracting the attention of astute wine writers and wine enthusiasts around the country.

As they continued to improve their product, these same winemakers began to realize that in order to market their wine successfully they had to find a way to differentiate their quality wines from California's mass-produced wines—which had such generic names as Burgundy, Chablis, or Chianti—and to ally their wines, at least in the minds of wine buyers and consumers, with European wines. Their solution was brilliant: They chose to label their best wines by varietal.

Varietal designation calls the wine by the name of the predominant grape used to produce it: Chardonnay, Cabernet Sauvignon, Pinot Noir, etc. The savvy consumer learned that a wine labeled Chardonnay would have the general characteristics of any wine made from that grape. This made wine buying easier for both wine buyers and sellers.

Varietal labeling quickly spread throughout the industry and became so successful that, in the eighties, varietal designation became an American industry standard, forcing the federal government to revise its labeling regulations.

Today, varietal labeling is the norm for the highest quality American wines, has been adopted by many other countries, and has helped bring worldwide attention to California wine. While California still produces 90 percent of American wine, its success has inspired winemakers in other areas of the United States to refocus on producing high-quality wine.

How does all this help me select and enjoy American wine?

This short history should help you understand and appreciate the trials and tribulations American grape growers and winemakers have endured for centuries. To buy American wine intelligently means having knowledge about and familiarity with each state whose wine you're interested in buying, as well as the regions within the state. Some states—or even regions within a state—may specialize in white wine, others in red, and, going further, there are even regions that specialize in wine made from a specific grape variety. Therefore, it is helpful to know the defined grape-growing areas within each state or region, which are called American Viticultural Areas (AVAs).

What is an AVA?

An AVA, or American Viticultural Area, is a specific grape-growing area within a state or a region recognized by and registered with the federal government. AVA designation began in the 1980s and is a system styled after the European regional system. In France, Bordeaux and Burgundy are strictly enforced regional appellations (marked *Appellation d'Origine Contrôlée,* or AOC); in Italy, Tuscany and Piedmont are recognized as zones (marked *Denominazione di Origine Controllata,* or DOC). The Napa Valley, for example, is a defined viticultural area in the state of California. Yakima is an AVA

WINERIES IN the United States are opening at the rate of 300 per year.

IN 2004, 35 new applications for AVAs were submitted—18 in California, 8 in Oregon, 2 in Illinois, 2 in Texas, and 1 each in Minnesota, New Jersey, New York, Oklahoma, and Washington.

2001

COLUMBIA WINERY

COLUMBIA VALLEY

SYRAH

THE UNITED STATES

Pacific Ocean

CANADA

Washington 323/6
Montana 8
North Dakota 2
Minnesota 19
Wisconsin 20/1
Michigan 90/4
Maine 10
Vermont 6
New Hampshire 2
New York 203/8
Mass. 29/2
R.I. 3/1
Conn. 15/2
New Jersey 33/2
Delaware 1
Maryland 19/3

Oregon 228/7
Idaho 27
Wyoming 1
South Dakota 4
Iowa 27
Illinois 62
Indiana 35/1
Ohio 100/6
Pennsylvania 99/4
W.V. 14/2
Virginia 97/6

Nevada 2
Utah 4
Colorado 54/2
Nebraska 8
Kansas 12
Missouri 67/4
Kentucky 31/1
Tennessee 29/1
North Carolina 48/1
South Carolina 3

California 1689/92
Arizona 17/1
New Mexico 37/3
Oklahoma 17/1
Arkansas 7/3
Mississippi 1/1
Alabama 5
Georgia 17

Atlantic Ocean

0 Miles 250 500
0 Kilometers 500

Hawaii 5
Alaska 6

Texas 91/7
Louisiana 6/1

Florida 34

MEXICO

Gulf of Mexico

67 Number of wineries in state
4 Number of AVAs in state

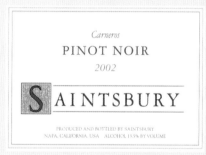

located in Washington State; both Oregon's Willamette Valley and New York's Finger Lakes district are similarly identified.

Vintners are discovering, as their European counterparts did years ago, which grapes grow best in which particular soils and climatic conditions. There are more than 145 viticultural areas in the United States, 92 of which are located in California. I believe the AVA concept is important to wine buying and will continue to be so as individual AVAs become known for certain grape varieties or wine styles. If an AVA is listed on the label, at least 85 percent of the grapes must come from that region.

For example, let's look at Napa Valley, which is probably the best known AVA in the United States, renowned for its Cabernet Sauvignon. Within Napa, there is a smaller inner district called Carneros, which has a cooler climate. Since Chardonnay and Pinot Noir need a cooler growing season to mature properly, these grape varieties are especially suited to that AVA. In New York, the Finger Lakes region is noted for Riesling. And those of you who have seen the movie *Sideways* know that Santa Barbara is a great place for Pinot Noir.

Although not necessarily a guarantee of quality, an AVA designation identifies a specific area well known and established for its wine. It is a point of reference for winemakers and consumers. Any wine can be understood by its provenance, or where it came from. The more knowledge you have about a wine's origin, by region and grape, the easier it is to buy even unknown brands with confidence.

How do I choose an American wine?

The essence of this book is to simplify wine for those who are buying or selling it. Do you prefer lighter or heavier wines; red wine or white; sweet wine or dry? You must learn the general characteristics of the major red and white grapes (see pages 15 and 87). Understanding these fundamental differences makes selecting an appropriate wine less difficult, as they help define the wine's style—and selecting the style of wine you want is the first decision you'll need to make.

Next, determine your price range. Are you looking for a nice, everyday wine for under ten dollars? Or are you in the market for a twenty-five- or one-hundred-dollar wine? Set your limit and stick to it. You'll find the style of wine you're looking for at almost any price.

Finally, learn how to read the label (see page 67). Some of the highest quality wines in the United States come from individual vineyards. The general rule is: The more specific the label, the better the quality of wine. All the important information about any American wine appears on the label. Since the federal government controls wine labeling and has established standards, all American wine labels, regardless of where in the United States the wine was produced, contain essential information that conforms to national standards. This standardization can assist you in making informed decisions about the wine you're about to purchase or pour.

Is that all I need to know?

There is more: An even higher quality of wine is now given a "proprietary" name.

The most recent worldwide trend is to ignore all existing standards by giving the highest-quality wines a proprietary name. A proprietary name helps high-end wineries differentiate their best wines from other wines from the same AVA, from similar varietals, and even from their own other offerings. In the United States, many of these proprietary wines fall under the category called Meritage (see page 130). Some examples of American proprietary wines are Dominus, Opus One, and Rubicon.

Federal laws governing standards and labels are another reason select wineries are increasingly using proprietary names. Federal law mandates, for example, that if a label lists a varietal, at least 75 percent of the grapes used to make the wine must be of that varietal.

Imagine a talented, innovative winemaker in the Columbia Valley region of Washington State. This winemaker is determined to produce an outstanding, full-bodied Bordeaux-style wine consisting of 60 percent Cabernet Sauvignon blended with several other grapes. Our ambitious winemaker has used his best soil for the vines, nurturing them with care and love. He has invested considerable time and labor to produce a really great wine: a wine suitable for aging that will be ready to drink in five years—but will be even better in ten.

After five years, our winemaker tastes the fruits of his labor and voilà! It is delicious, with all the promise of a truly outstanding wine. But how does he distinguish this wine; how can he attract buyers willing to pay a premium price for an unknown wine? He can't label it Cabernet Sauvignon, because less than 75 percent of the grapes used are of that type. For this reason, many producers of fine wine are beginning to use proprietary names. It's indicative of the healthy state of the American wine industry as well. More and more winemakers are turning out better and better wines, and the very best is yet to come!

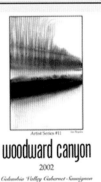

The Wines of Washington, Oregon, and New York

The White Wines of California

WASHINGTON STATE · OREGON · NEW YORK · NATIVE AMERICAN, EUROPEAN,

AND FRENCH AMERICAN VARIETIES · INTRODUCTION TO CALIFORNIA WINES ·

THE WHITE WINES OF CALIFORNIA

Napa Valley vineyards
(Charles O'Rear/Corbis)

The "Big Four" of U.S. Winemaking

PACIFIC NORTHWEST

WASHINGTON

• Seattle
★ Tacoma
Olympia
Yakima

Spokane

Richland

Vancouver
Portland •
Salem ★   OREGON

• Eugene

• Medford

Pacific Ocean

o Miles   100
o Kilometers   200

OREGON
☐ Applegate Valley
☐ Columbia Valley
☐ Rogue Valley
☐ Umpqua Valley
☐ Walla Walla Valley
☐ Willamette Valley

WASHINGTON
☐ Columbia Valley
☐ Puget Sound
☐ Red Mountain
☐ Walla Walla Valley
☐ Columbia Gorge
☐ Yakima Valley

THE PACIFIC NORTHWEST winegrowing region includes Washington, Oregon, British Columbia, and Idaho.

WASHINGTON STATE has more Riesling planted than any other state.

NOW THAT WE HAVE LOOKED at the history and "big picture" of American winemaking, we can turn our attention to the wines themselves. Before we tackle the exciting world of California wines, I'd like to talk about three other major winemaking regions in the United States: Washington, Oregon, and New York.

WASHINGTON STATE

IN WASHINGTON, THE CLIMATIC CONDITIONS are a little cooler and rainier than in California, but it's neither too cold nor too wet to make great wine. The winegrowing regions are protected from Washington's famous rains by the Cascade Mountains. The earliest record of grape growing in Washington can be traced back to 1825, while the beginning of its modern winemaking industry can be dated to 1967, with the first wine produced under the Chateau Ste. Michelle label.

The four major white grapes grown in Washington are Chardonnay, Riesling, Gewürztraminer, and Sauvignon Blanc. In the 1960s and 1970s, Washington was known only for white wines, but now Washington State has become known as one of the great American states for the production of red wines, especially Merlot and Cabernet Sauvignon. (As it turns out, the state's Columbia Valley is on the same latitude as Bordeaux, France). Over the last ten years Washington winemakers have increased their plantings of Syrah, and the recent vintages are turning out to be of very high quality.

There are six AVAs: Columbia Valley, Yakima, Walla Walla, Puget Sound, Red Mountain, and Columbia Gorge.

AVA (DATE AVA ESTABLISHED)	NUMBER OF WINERIES
Yakima (1983)	40
Walla Walla (1984)	55
Columbia Valley* (1984)	150+
Puget Sound (1995)	35
Red Mountain (2001)	10
Columbia Gorge (2004)	8

* Largest viticultural area, responsible for 95 percent of production.

Some of the wineries to look for include Columbia Crest, Columbia Winery, Hogue Cellars, L'Ecole No. 41, Leonetti Cellars, Woodward Canyon Winery, Andrew Will, Canoe Ridge, Seven Hills, Cayuse, McCrea Cellars, and the largest winery, Chateau Ste. Michelle.

WASHINGTON BEST BETS
2001*   2002*   2004*

Note: * signifies exceptional vintage

OREGON

ALTHOUGH GRAPES WERE PLANTED and wine was made as early as 1847 in Oregon, the modern era began in the early 1960s. Today, Oregon, because of its climate, is becoming well known for Burgundian-style wines. By Burgundian style I'm referring to Chardonnay and Pinot Noir, which are the major grapes planted in Oregon. Many critics feel the best Pinot Noir grown in the United States is grown in Oregon. Another success in Oregon is Pinot Gris (aka Pinot Grigio), which has recently overtaken Chardonnay as the most widely planted white grape in the state.

The major AVA in Oregon is the Willamette Valley, near Portland. Other AVAs include Rogue Valley, Umpqua, and Applegate Valley. Two others, the Columbia Valley and Walla Walla, are AVAs of both Oregon and Washington State.

Wineries to look for include Adelsheim, Eyrie Vineyards, Erath, Ponzi Vineyards, Rex Hill, Cristom, King Estate, Sokol Blosser, Tualatin, Archery Summit,

IN 1990 IN Washington, there were fewer than 70 wineries, which turned out less than 2 million cases. Today, there are more than 300 wineries, which produced more than 7 million cases. Acreage has increased from 10,000 acres to more than 30,000.

IN 2004, WASHINGTON STATE'S wine production was 57% red versus 43% white.

CHATEAU STE. MICHELLE has formed a winemaking partnership with the famous German wine producer Dr. Loosen. The new Riesling wine is called Eroica.

VITAL STATISTICS

Oregon
11,100 acres
228 wineries

Washington
More than 30,000 acres
323 wineries

Napa Valley
42,929 acres
250 wineries

THE LARGEST producer of Pinot Gris (Grigio) in the United States is King Estate in Oregon.

ABOUT 70% OF Oregon's wineries are located in the Willamette Valley.

One of the great wine festivals in the United States is the International Pinot Noir Celebration, which was started in Oregon in 1987.

THE 2002 VINTAGE is Oregon's best ever.

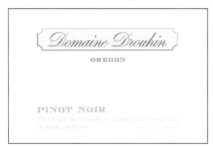

NEW YORK'S Hudson Valley is one of America's oldest wine-growing regions. Grapevines were planted by the French Huguenots in the 1600s. It also boasts the oldest active winery in the United States— Brotherhood, which recorded its first vintage in 1839.

THE FIRST winery on Long Island was started in 1973 by Alex and Louisa Hargrave.

THE CLIMATE on Long Island has more than 200 days of sunshine and a longer growing season, making it perfect for Merlot and Bordeaux style wines.

THERE ARE 33 wineries on Long Island, and the three AVAs are the North Fork, the Hamptons, and Long Island.

THERE ARE more than 200 wineries in New York State. In the three major regions, the Finger Lakes region has 73, the Hudson Valley has 28, and Long Island has 29.

Bethel Heights, St. Innocent, Beaux Frères, Domaine Serene, and Ken Wright. Also, the famous Burgundy producer Joseph Drouhin owns a winery in Oregon called Domain Drouhin, producing, not surprisingly, Burgundy-style wines.

OREGON BEST BETS

1999*   2001   2002**   2003   2004*

*Note: * signifies exceptional vintage   ** one of the best vintages ever for Pinot Noir in Oregon*

FOR FURTHER READING

I recommend *The Oxford Companion to the Wines of North America* by Bruce Cass and Jancis Robinson; *The Wines of the Pacific Northwest* by Lisa Shara Hall; and *The Northwest Wine Guide* by Andy Perdue.

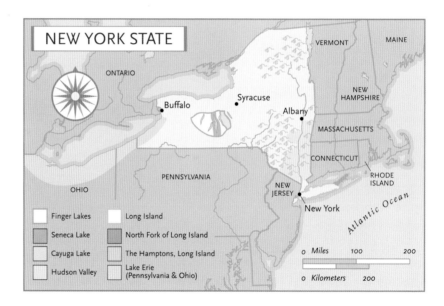

NEW YORK STATE

NEW YORK IS THE THIRD LARGEST wine-producing state in the United States, with eight AVAs. The three premium wine regions in New York are:

Finger Lakes: With the largest wine production east of California.
Hudson Valley: Concentrating on premium farm wineries.
Long Island: New York's fastest-growing wine region.

Which grapes grow in New York State?

There are three main categories:

Native American (*Vitis labrusca*)
European (*Vitis vinifera*)
French-American (hybrids)

SINCE 1995 VINE-PLANTED acreage on the North Fork has doubled, with over 3,000 acres and over 500,000 cases of wine.

TODAY, MORE than 80 of the 203 New York State wineries produce *vinifera* wines.

NATIVE AMERICAN VARIETIES

THE *VITIS LABRUSCA* ARE VERY POPULAR among grape growers in New York because they are hardy grapes that can withstand cold winters. Among the most familiar grapes of the *Vitis labrusca* family are Concord, Catawba, and Delaware. Until the last decade, these were the grapes that were used to make most New York wines. In describing these wines, words such as "foxy," "grapey," "Welch's," and "Manischewitz" are often used. These words are a sure sign of *Vitis labrusca*.

EUROPEAN VARIETIES

FORTY YEARS AGO, some New York wineries began to experiment with the traditional European (*Vitis vinifera*) grapes. Dr. Konstantin Frank, a Russian viticulturist skilled in cold-climate grape growing, came to the United States and catalyzed efforts to grow *Vitis vinifera* in New York. This was unheard of—and laughed at—back then. Other vintners predicted that he'd fail, that it was impossible to grow *vinifera* in New York's cold and capricious climate.

"What do you mean?" Dr. Frank replied. "I'm from Russia—it's even colder there."

Most people were still skeptical, but Charles Fournier of Gold Seal Vineyards was intrigued enough to give Konstantin Frank a chance to prove his theory. Sure enough, Dr. Frank was successful with the *vinifera* and has produced some world-class wines, especially his Riesling and Chardonnay. So have many other New York wineries, thanks to the vision and courage of Dr. Frank and Charles Fournier.

EXAMPLES OF *Vitis vinifera* grapes are Pinot Grigio, Riesling, Sauvignon Blanc, Chardonnay, Pinot Noir, Merlot, Cabernet Sauvignon, and Syrah.

"IT'S NOT YOUR FATHER'S KOSHER WINE"

Kosher wines around the world have vastly improved in quality. For years, kosher wines were thought of only as sweet wines. Today you can buy great examples of American kosher Chardonnay and Cabernet Sauvignon.

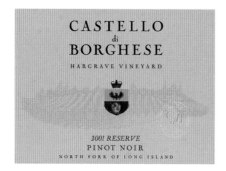

FRENCH AMERICAN VARIETIES

SOME NEW YORK AND EAST COAST WINEMAKERS have planted French American hybrid varieties, which combine European taste characteristics with American vine hardiness to withstand the cold winters in the Northeast. These varieties were originally developed by French viticulturists in the nineteenth century. Seyval Blanc and Vidal are the most prominent white wine varieties; Baco Noir and Chancellor are the most common reds.

What have been the trends in New York wines over the last twenty years?

The most significant developments are taking place on Long Island, which has experienced the fastest growth of new vineyards. In the last twenty years, its grape-growing acreage has increased from 100 acres to more than 3,000 acres, with more expansion expected in the future.

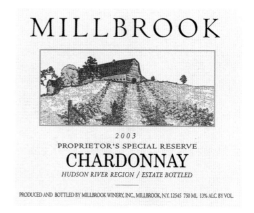

The predominant use of *Vitis vinifera* varieties allows Long Island wineries to compete more effectively in the world market, and Long Island's longer growing season offers greater potential for red grapes.

The Millbrook Winery in the Hudson Valley has shown that this region can produce world-class wines—not only white, but red, from such grapes as Pinot Noir and Cabernet Franc.

The wines of the Finger Lakes region continue to get better as the winemakers work with grapes that thrive in the cooler climate, including European varieties such as Riesling, Chardonnay, and Pinot Noir.

CALIFORNIA

NO WINEGROWING AREA IN THE WORLD has come so far so quickly as California. It seems ironic, because Americans historically have not been very interested in wine. But from the moment Americans first became "wine conscious," winemakers rose to the challenge. Twenty years ago we were asking if California wines were entitled to be compared to European wines. Now, California wines are available worldwide—shipments for export have increased dramatically over recent years to countries such as Japan, Germany, and England. California produces more than 90 percent of U.S. wine. If the state were a nation, it would be the fourth leading wine producer in the world!

AN INTRODUCTION TO CALIFORNIA WINES

What are the main viticultural areas of California?

The map at the beginning of the chapter should help familiarize you with the winemaking regions. It's easier to remember them if you divide them into four groups:

North Coast *(Best wines: Cabernet Sauvignon, Zinfandel, Sauvignon Blanc, Chardonnay, Merlot)*: Napa County, Sonoma County, Mendocino County, Lake County
North Central Coast *(Best wines: Syrah, Grenache, Viognier, Marsanne, Roussane)*: Monterey County, Santa Clara County, Livermore County
South Central Coast *(Best wines: Sauvignon Blanc, Chardonnay, Pinot Noir)*: San Luis Obispo County, Santa Barbara County
San Joaquin Valley *(Known for jug wines)*

Although you may be most familiar with the names Napa and Sonoma, only 12 percent of all California wine comes from these two regions combined. In fact, the bulk of California wine is from the San Joaquin Valley, where mostly "jug" wines are produced. This

CALIFORNIA WINES dominate American wine consumption, equaling 75% of all sales in the United States.

THERE ARE more than 60,000 wine labels registered in California.

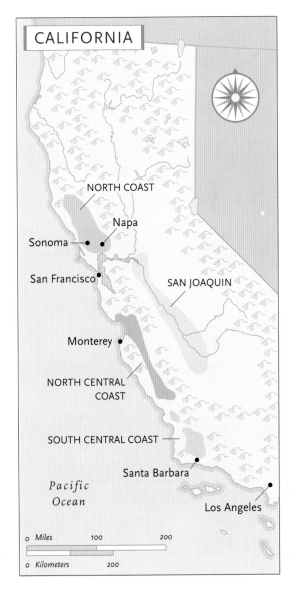

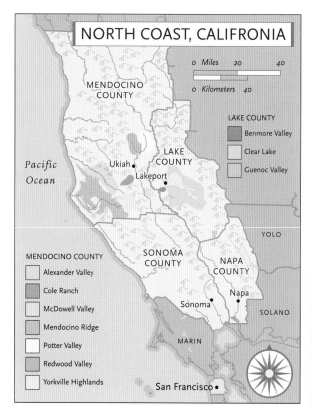

NORTH COAST, CALIFRONIA

MENDOCINO COUNTY

LAKE COUNTY

Benmore Valley

Clear Lake

Guenoc Valley

Pacific Ocean

Ukiah

LAKE COUNTY

Lakeport

YOLO

SONOMA COUNTY

NAPA COUNTY

Napa

Sonoma

SOLANO

MARIN

MENDOCINO COUNTY

Alexander Valley

Cole Ranch

McDowell Valley

Mendocino Ridge

Potter Valley

Redwood Valley

Yorkville Highlands

San Francisco

region accounts for 54 percent of the wine grapes planted. Maybe that doesn't seem too exciting—that the production of jug wine dominates California winemaking history—but Americans are not atypical in this respect. In France, for example, the AOC wines account for only 35 percent of all French wines, while the rest are everyday table wines.

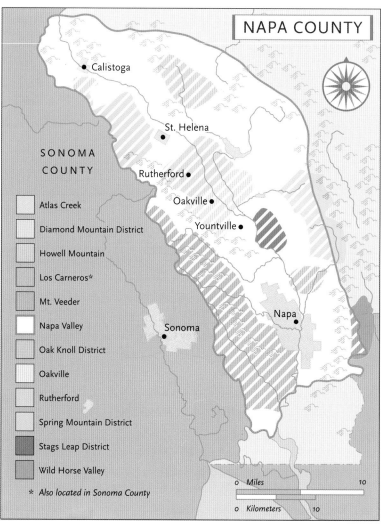

NAPA COUNTY

Calistoga

St. Helena

Rutherford

SONOMA COUNTY

Oakville

Yountville

Atlas Creek

Diamond Mountain District

Howell Mountain

Los Carneros*

Mt. Veeder

Napa Valley

Oak Knoll District

Oakville

Rutherford

Spring Mountain District

Stags Leap District

Wild Horse Valley

Napa

Sonoma

*   Also located in Sonoma County

IN 1930, THERE were 188,000 acres of vineyards in California. Today, there are more than 570,000 acres.

ACRES OF wine grapes planted in Napa:
 42,929
Number of wineries: 250

NAPA VALLEY represents less than 7% of California's wine production.

"There is more potential for style variation in California than Europe because of the greater generosity of the fruit."
—WARREN WINIARSKI, *winemaker/owner,*
Stag's Leap Wine Cellars, Napa Valley

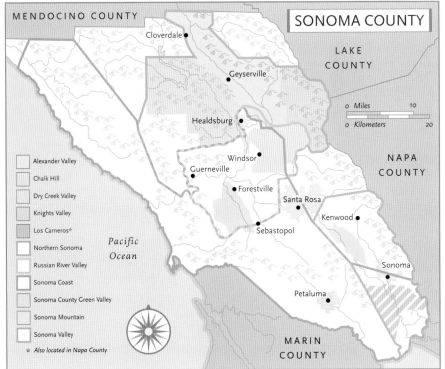

MENDOCINO COUNTY

SONOMA COUNTY

LAKE COUNTY

NAPA COUNTY

Cloverdale

Geyserville

Healdsburg

Windsor

Guerneville

Forestville

Santa Rosa

Kenwood

Sebastopol

Sonoma

Pacific Ocean

Petaluma

MARIN COUNTY

0 Miles   10
0 Kilometers 20

Alexander Valley
Chalk Hill
Dry Creek Valley
Knights Valley
Los Carneros*
Northern Sonoma
Russian River Valley
Sonoma Coast
Sonoma County Green Valley
Sonoma Mountain
Sonoma Valley
* Also located in Napa County

ACRES OF wine grapes planted in Sonoma: 55,877
Number of wineries: 190

LAST YEAR, more than 15 million people visited California wine-growing areas. Vineyards and wineries are the second most popular California tourist destinations after Disneyland!

BIGGER THAN HOLLYWOOD

Wine is California's most valuable finished agricultural product, with a $45 billion economic impact. The film industry: $30 billion.

When did California begin to make better-quality wines?

As early as the 1940s, Frank Schoonmaker, an importer and writer, and one of the first American wine experts, convinced some California winery owners to market their best wines using varietal labels.

Robert Mondavi may be one of the best examples of a winemaker who concentrated solely on varietal wine production. In 1966, Mondavi left his family's Charles Krug Winery and started the Robert Mondavi Winery. His role was important to the evolution of varietal labeling of California wines. He was among the first major winemakers to make the total switch that led to higher-quality winemaking.

ROBERT MONDAVI was a great promoter for the California wine industry. "He was able to prove to the public what the people within the industry already knew—that California could produce world-class wines," said Eric Wente.

A NOTE ON JUG WINES

The phrase "jug wine" refers to simple, uncomplicated, everyday drinking wine. You're probably familiar with these types of wine: They're sometimes labeled with a generic name, such as "Chablis" or "Burgundy." Inexpensive and well made, these wines were originally bottled in jugs, rather than in conventional wine bottles, hence the name "jug wine." They are very popular and account for the largest volume of California wine sold in the United States.

Ernest and Julio Gallo, who began their winery in 1933, are the major producers of jug wines in California. In fact, many people credit the Gallo brothers with converting American drinking habits from spirits to wine. Several other wineries also produce jug wines, among them Almaden, Paul Masson, and Taylor California Cellars.

In my opinion, the best-made jug wines in the world are from California. They maintain both consistency and quality from year to year.

EARLY CALIFORNIA winemakers sent their children to study oenology at Geisenheim (Germany) or Bordeaux (France). Today, many European winemakers send their children to the University of California at Davis and to Fresno State University.

THE UNIVERSITY of California at Davis graduated only five students from its oenology department in 1966. Today it has a waiting list of students from all over the world.

How did California become a world-class producer in just forty years?

There are many reasons for California's winemaking success, including:

Location—Napa and Sonoma counties, two of the major quality wine regions, are both less than a two-hour drive from San Francisco. The proximity of these regions to the city encourages both residents and tourists to visit the wineries in the two counties, most of which offer wine tastings and sell their wines in their own shops.

Weather—Abundant sunshine, warm daytime temperatures, cool evenings, and a long growing season all add up to good conditions for growing many grape varieties. California is certainly subject to sudden changes in weather, but a fickle climate is not a major worry.

The University of California at Davis and Fresno State University—Both schools have been the training grounds for many young California winemakers, and their curricula concentrate on the scientific study of wine, viticulture, and, most important, technology. Their research, focused on soil, different strains of yeast, hybridization, temperature-controlled fermentation, and other viticultural techniques, has revolutionized the wine industry worldwide.

FROM THE CORPORATE LADDER TO THE VINE

Some of the pioneers of the back-to-the-land movement:

"FARMER"	WINERY	PROFESSION
Robert Travers	Mayacamas	Investment banker
David Stare	Dry Creek	Civil engineer
Tom Jordan	Jordan	Geologist
Rodney Strong	Rodney Strong	Dancer/choreographer
James Barrett	Chateau Montelena	Attorney
Tom Burgess	Burgess	Air Force pilot
Jess Jackson	Kendall-Jackson	Attorney
Warren Winiarski	Stag's Leap	College professor
Brooks Firestone	Firestone	Take a guess!

Money and Marketing Strategy—This cannot be overemphasized. Marketing may not make the wine, but it certainly helps sell it. As more and more winemakers concentrated on making the best wine they could, American consumers responded with appreciation. They were willing to buy—and pay—more as quality improved. In order to keep up with consumer expectations, winemakers realized that they needed more research, development, and—most important—working capital. The wine industry turned to investors, both corporate and individual.

Since 1967, when the now-defunct National Distillers bought Almaden, multinational corporations have recognized the profit potential of large-scale winemaking and have aggressively entered the wine business. They've brought huge financial resources and expertise in advertising and promotion that have helped promote American wines domestically and internationally. Other early corporate participants included Pillsbury, Coca-Cola, and even Otsuka Pharmaceutical Company of Japan.

On the other side of the investor scale are the individual investor/growers drawn to the business by their love of wine and their desire to live the winemaking "lifestyle." These individuals were more focused on producing quality wines.

Both corporate and individual investors had, by the 1990s, helped California fine-tune its wine industry, which today produces not only delicious and reliable wines in great quantity but also truly outstanding wines, many with investment potential.

SO YOU WANT to buy a vineyard in California? Today, one acre in the Napa Valley costs between $100,000 to $200,000 unplanted, and it takes an additional $20,000 per acre to plant. This per-acre investment sees no return for three to five years. To this, add the cost of building the winery, buying the equipment, and hiring the winemaker.

RECORD PRICE

In 2002, Francis Ford Coppola, owner of Niebaum-Coppola Wine Estate, paid $350,000 an acre for vineyard land in Napa.

WHAT ARE the advantages of being a California winery owner?
1. You can wear all the latest styles from the L.L. Bean catalog.
2. You can bone up a lot on ecology and organic farming.
3. You can grow a beard, drive a pickup truck, and wear suspenders.

CREATIVE FINANCING

Overheard at a restaurant in Yountville, Napa: "How do you make a small fortune in the wine business?" "Start with a large fortune and buy a winery."

IN CALIFORNIA many winemakers move around from one winery to another, just as good chefs move from one restaurant to the next. This is not uncommon. They may choose to carry and use the same "recipe" from place to place, if it is particularly successful, and sometimes they will experiment and create new styles.

I'VE MENTIONED stainless-steel fermentation tanks so often, I'll give a definition, in case you need one. These tanks are temperature controlled, allowing winemakers to control the temperature at which the wine ferments. For example, a winemaker could ferment wines at a low temperature to retain fruitiness and delicacy, while preventing browning and oxidation.

AMBASSADOR ZELLERBACH, who created Hanzell Winery, was one of the first California winemakers to use small French oak aging barrels because he wanted to re-create a Burgundian style.

HOLLYWOOD AND VINE

What do the Smothers Brothers, Christina Crawford, Fess Parker, Wayne Rogers, and Francis Ford Coppola have in common? They all own vineyards in California.

What's meant by *style*? How are different styles of California wine actually created?

Style refers to the characteristics of the grapes and wine. It is the trademark of the individual winemaker—an "artist" who tries different techniques to explore the fullest potential of the grapes.

Most winemakers will tell you that 95 percent of winemaking is in the quality of the grapes they begin with. The other 5 percent can be traced to the "personal touch" of the winemaker. Here are just a few of the hundreds of decisions a winemaker must make when developing his or her style of wine:

- When should the grapes be harvested?

- Should the juice be fermented in stainless-steel tanks or oak barrels? How long should it be fermented? At what temperature?

- Should the wine be aged at all? How long? If so, should it be aged in oak? What kind of oak—American, French?

- What varieties of grape should be blended, and in what proportion?

- How long should the wine be aged in the bottle before it is sold?

The list goes on. Because there are so many variables in winemaking, producers can create many styles of wine from the same grape variety—so you can choose the style that suits your taste. With the relative freedom of winemaking in the United States, the "style" of California wines continues to be "diversity."

Why is California wine so confusing?

The renaissance of the California wine industry began only about forty years ago. Within that short period of time, some 1,400 new wineries have been established in California. Today, there are more than 1,600 wineries in California, most of them making more than one wine, and the price differences are reflected in the styles (you can get a Cabernet Sauvignon wine in any price range from Two Buck Chuck at $1.99 to Harlan Estate at more than $500 a bottle—so how do you choose?). The constant changes in the wine industry through experimentation keep California winemaking in a state of flux.

California Wineries selected by *Wine Spectator* for the 2004 California Wine Experience

Acadia	Dalla Valle	Iron Horse
Alban	Del Dotto	J Vineyards & Winery
Altamura	Diamond Creek	Jaffurs
Araujo	Dolce	Justin
Arrowood	Domaine Carneros	Keller
Artesa	Domaine Chandon	Kendall-Jackson
David Arthur	Dominus	Kathryn Kennedy
Au Bon Climat	The Donum Estate	Kenwood
Beaulieu	Duckhorn	Kistler
Benziger Family	DuMol	Charles Krug
Beringer	Dunn	Kunde
Bernardus	Dutton-Goldfield	Lagier Meredith
Bond	Merry Edwards	Lail
Brander	Etude	Landmark
David Bruce	Far Niente	Lang & Reed
Buehler	Gary Farrell	Laurel Glen
Burgess	Ferrari-Carano	Lewis
Byron	Fisher	Lokoya
Cakebread	Flora Springs	Loring
Caldwell	Flowers	Luna
Calera	Foley Estate	Markham
Cardinale	Foppiano	Marston Family
Carlisle	Franciscan Oakville	Matanzas Creek
Caymus	Freemark Abbey	Mendelson
Chalk Hill	Gallo of Sonoma	Mer Soleil
Chalone	Gemstone	Meridian
Chappellet	Geyser Peak	Merryvale
Chateau Montelena	Girard	Peter Michael
Chateau Potelle	Gloria Ferrer	Miner Family
Chateau St. Jean	Grgich Hills	Robert Mondavi
Chateau Souverain	Groth	Morgan
Chimney Rock	Hanna	Mueller
Clos du Bois	Hanzell	Mumm Cuvée Napa
Clos du Val	Harlan	Newton
B.R. Cohn	Hartwell	Neyers
Conn Creek	HdV	Nickel & Nickel
Constant	Heitz	Niebaum-Coppola
Cornerstone	Hess Collection	Novy
Robert Craig	Paul Hobbs	Opus One
Cuvaison	Hundred Acre	Pahlmeyer

Number of Bonded Wineries in California

Year	Wineries
1965	232
1970	240
1975	330
1980	508
1985	712
1990	807
1995	944
2000	1,210
2005	1,600+

Source: The Wine Institute

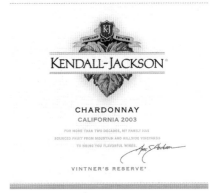

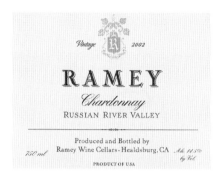

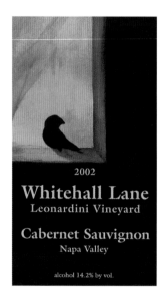

Paloma	Sanford	Testarossa
Patz & Hall	Saxum	Philip Togni
Peju Province	Schramsberg	Tor Wines
Joseph Phelps	Screaming Eagle	Marimar Torres
Pine Ridge	Sebastiani	Treana
Plumpjack	Seghesio	Trefethen
Pride Mountain	Selene	Trinchero
Provenance	Sequoia Grove	Truchard
Quintessa	Shafer	Verite
Qupe	Siduri	Villa Mt. Eden
Ramey	Silver Oak	Vine Cliff
Ravenswood	Silverado	Vision
Martin Ray	Simi	Vlader
Raymond	Snowden	Whitehall Lane
Renwood	Sonoma Cutrer	Williams Selyem
Reverie	Sonoma-Lobe	Ken Wright
Ridge	Spottswoode	
Rochioli	Stag's Leap Wine Cellars	
Roederer Estate	Stags' Leap Winery	
Rosenbloom	Steele	
Stephen Ross	Sterling	
Rudd	Stonestreet	
Rutherford Hill	Rodney Strong	
St. Clement	Tablas Creek	
St. Francis	Robert Talbott	
St. Supery	Talley	

What about the prices of California varietal wines?

You can't necessarily equate quality with price. Some excellent varietal wines that are produced in California are well within the budget of the average consumer. On the other hand, some varietals (primarily Chardonnay and Cabernet Sauvignon) may be quite expensive.

As in any market, it is mainly supply and demand that determines price. However, new wineries are affected by start-up costs, which sometimes are reflected in the price of the wine. Older, established wineries, which long ago amortized their investments, are able to keep their prices low when the supply/demand ratio calls for it. Remember, when you're buying California wine, price doesn't always reflect quality.

How do I choose a good California wine?

One of the reasons California produces such a wide variety of wine is that it has so many different climates. Some are as cool as Burgundy, Champagne, and the Rhein, while others are as warm as the Rhône Valley, Portugal, and the southern regions of Italy and Spain. If that's not diverse enough, these wine-growing areas have inner districts with "microclimates," or climates within climates. One of the microclimates (which are among the designated AVAs) in Sonoma County, for example, is the Russian River Valley.

To better understand this concept, let's take a close look at the Rudd label.

R U D D

Russian River Valley

BACIGALUPI VINEYARD
CHARDONNAY
2 0 0 1

PRODUCED & BOTTLED BY RUDD
OAKVILLE, CALIFORNIA
ALCOHOL 14.5% BY VOLUME
750 ML.
Product of U.S.A.

State:
California
County:
Sonoma
Viticultural Area (AVA):
Russian River Valley
Vineyard:
Bacigalupi
Winery:
Rudd

California labels tell you everything you need to know about the wine—and more. Here are some quick tips you can use when you scan the shelves at your favorite retailer. The label shown above will serve as an example.

The most important piece of information on the label is the producer's name. In this case, the producer is Rudd.

If the grape variety is on the label, a minimum of 75 percent of the wine must be derived from that grape variety. This label shows that the wine is made from the Chardonnay grape.

If the wine bears a vintage date, 95 percent of the grapes must have been harvested that year.

If the wine is designated "California," then 100 percent of the grapes must have been grown in California.

If the label designates a certain federally recognized viticultural area

CALIFORNIA WINE has no classification system that resembles the European equivalent.

THERE ARE 92 AVAs in California. Some of the best known are:

Napa Valley	Livermore Valley
Sonoma Valley	Paso Robles
Russian River Valley	Edna Valley
Alexander Valley	Fiddletown
Dry Creek Valley	Stag's Leap
Los Carneros	Chalk Hill
Anderson Valley	Howell Mountain
Santa Cruz Mountain	

FAMOUS INDIVIDUAL VINEYARDS OF CALIFORNIA

Bacigalupi
Bien Nacido
Dutton Ranch
Durell
Robert Young
Bancroft Ranch
Geyserville
Gravelly Meadow
Martha's Vineyard
McCrea
S.L.V.
To-Kalon
Beckstoffer
Monte Rosso

IF AN INDIVIDUAL vineyard is noted on the label, 95% of the grapes must be from the named vineyard, which must be located within an approved AVA.

THE LEGAL limits for the alcohol content of table wine are 7% to 13.9%, with a 1.5% allowance either way, so long as the allowance doesn't go beyond the legal limits. If the alcohol content of a table wine exceeds 14%, the label must show that. Sparkling wines may be 10% to 13.9%, with the 1.5% allowance.

"You are never going to stylize the California wines the same way that European wines have been stylized, because we have more freedom to experiment. I value my freedom to make the style of wine I want more than the security of the AOC laws. Laws discourage experimentation."

—LOUIS MARTINI

I'M SURE you'll recognize the names of some of the early European winemakers:
Finland
    Gustave Niebaum (Inglenook)—1879
France
    Paul Masson—1852
    Étienne Thée and Charles LeFranc
        (Almaden)—1852
    Pierre Mirassou—1854
    Georges de Latour (Beaulieu)—1900
Germany
    Beringer Brothers—1876
    Carl Wente—1883
Ireland
    James Concannon—1883
Italy
    Giuseppe and Pietro Simi—1876
    John Foppiano—1895
    Samuele Sebastiani—1904
    Louis Martini—1922
    Adolph Parducci—1932

(AVA), such as Russian River Valley (as on our sample label), then at least 85 percent of the grapes used to make that wine must have been grown in that location.

The alcohol content is given in percentages. Usually, the higher the percentage of alcohol, the "fuller" the wine will be.

"Produced and bottled by" means that at least 75 percent of the wine was fermented by the winery named on the label.

Some wineries tell you the exact varietal content of the wine, and/or the sugar content of the grapes when they were picked, and/or the amount of residual sugar (to let you know how sweet or dry the wine is).

How is California winemaking different from the European technique?

Many students ask me this, and I can only tell them I'm glad I learned all about the wines of France, Italy, Germany, Spain, and the rest of Europe before I tackled California. European winemaking has established traditions that have remained essentially unchanged for hundreds of years. These practices involve the ways grapes are grown and harvested, and in some cases include winemaking and aging procedures.

In California, there are few traditions, and winemakers are able to take full advantage of modern technology. Furthermore, there is freedom to experiment and create new products. Some of the experimenting the California winemakers do, such as combining different grape varieties to make new styles of wine, is prohibited by some European wine-control laws. Californians thus have opportunities to try many new ideas—opportunities sometimes forbidden to European winemakers.

Another way in which California winemaking is different from European is that many California wineries carry an entire line of wine. Many of the larger ones produce more than twenty different labels. In Bordeaux, most châteaus produce only one or two wines.

In addition to modern technology and experimentation, you can't ignore the fundamentals of wine growing: California's rainfall, weather patterns, and soils are very different from those of Europe. The greater abundance of sunshine in California can result in wines with a greater alcohol content, ranging on average from 13.5 percent to 14.5 percent, compared to 12 percent to 13 percent on average in Europe. This higher alcohol content changes the balance and taste of the wines.

EUROWINEMAKING IN CALIFORNIA

Many well-known and highly respected European winemakers have invested in California vineyards to make their own wine. There are more than forty-five California wineries owned by European, Canadian, or Japanese companies. For example:

- *One of the most influential joint ventures matched Baron Philippe de Rothschild, then the owner of Château Mouton-Rothschild in Bordeaux, and Robert Mondavi, of the Napa Valley, to produce a wine called Opus One.*
- *The owners of Château Pétrus in Bordeaux, the Moueix family, have vineyards in California. Their wine is a Bordeaux-style blend called Dominus.*
- *Moët & Chandon, which is part of Moët-Hennessy, owns Domaine Chandon in the Napa Valley. They also own the New York importing firm Schieffelin & Somerset Company, and Simi, a well-known winery in Sonoma.*

Other European wineries with operations in California:
- *Roederer has grapes planted in Mendocino County and produces Roederer Estate.*
- *Mumm produces a sparkling wine, called Mumm Cuvée Napa.*
- *Taittinger has developed its own sparkling wine called Domaine Carneros.*
- *The Spanish sparkling-wine house Codorniu owns a winery called Artesa; and Freixenet owns land in Sonoma County and produces a wine called Gloria Ferrer.*
- *The Torres family of Spain owns a winery called Marimar Torres Estate in Sonoma County.*
- *Frenchman Robert Skalli (Fortant de France) owns more than six thousand acres in Napa Valley and the winery St. Supery.*
- *Tuscan wine producer Piero Antinori owns Atlas Peak winery in Napa.*

What happened when phylloxera returned to the vineyards of California in the 1980s?

In the 1980s the plant louse phylloxera destroyed a good part of the vineyards of California, costing a billion dollars in new plantings. Now this may sound strange, but it proved that good can come from bad. So what's the good news?

This time, vineyard owners didn't have to wait to discover a solution; they already knew what they would have to do to replace the dead vines—by replanting with a different rootstock that they knew was resistant to phylloxera. So while the short-term effects were terribly expensive, the long-term effect should be better quality wine. Why is this?

THE TWO leading table wines produced in the United States in 2004:
1. Chardonnay
2. Sauvignon Blanc/Fumé Blanc

SOME 800 DIFFERENT California Chardonnays are available to the consumer.

THERE ARE more than 24 different varieties of white wine grapes grown in California.

IN THE 2003 vintage, Kistler Vineyards produced eight different Chardonnays!

ONE-THIRD of all grapes grown in Sonoma are Chardonnay.

WITH THE success of Italian Pinot Grigio, expect to see many more California wineries producing wines labeled as Pinot Grigio or Pinot Gris.

KEVIN ZRALY'S FAVORITE CHARDONNAYS

Acacia	Landmark
Arrowood	Marcassin
Beringer	Martinelli
Cakebread	Paul Hobbs
Chalk Hill	Peter Michael
Chateau Montelena	Phelps
Chateau St. Jean	Robert Mondavi
Dutton Goldfield	Rudd Estate
Ferrari-Carano	Saintsbury
Grgich Hills	Silverado
Kistler	Talbott
Kongsgaard	

In the early days of California grape growing, little thought was given to where a specific grape would grow best. Chardonnays were planted in climates that were much too warm, and Cabernet Sauvignons were planted in climates that were much too cold.

With the onset of phylloxera, winery owners were forced to rectify their errors, and, when replanting, they have matched the climate and soil with the best grape variety. Grape growers also have the opportunity to plant different grape clones. The biggest change is in the planting density of the vines themselves. Traditional spacing used by most wineries up until phylloxera was somewhere between 400 and 500 vines per acre. Today with the new replanting, it is not uncommon to have more than a thousand vines per acre.

The bottom line is that if you like California wines now, you'll love them more with time. The quality is already better and the costs are lower—making it a win-win situation for everyone.

THE WHITE WINES OF CALIFORNIA

What is the major white-grape variety grown in California?

The most important white wine grape grown in California is Chardonnay. This green-skinned (*Vitis vinifera*) grape is considered by many the finest white-grape variety in the world. It is responsible for all the great French white Burgundies, such as Meursault, Chablis, and Puligny-Montrachet. In California, it has been the most successful white grape, yielding a wine of tremendous character and magnificent flavor. The wines are often aged in small oak barrels, increasing their complexity. In the vineyard, yields are fairly low and the grapes command high prices. Chardonnay is always dry, and benefits from aging more than any other American white wine. Superior examples can keep and develop well in the bottle for five years or longer.

Why do some Chardonnays cost more than other varietals?

In addition to everything we've mentioned before, many wineries age these wines in wood—sometimes for more than a year. Oak barrels have doubled in price over the last five years, averaging six hundred dollars per barrel. Add to this the cost of the grapes and the length of time before the wine is actually sold, and you can see why the best of the California Chardonnays cost more than twenty-five dollars.

What makes one Chardonnay different from another?

Put it this way: There are many brands of ice cream on the market. They use similar ingredients, but there is only one Ben & Jerry's. The same is true for wine. Among the many things to consider: Is a wine aged in wood or stainless steel? If wood, what type of oak? Was it barrel fermentation? Did the wine undergo a malolactic fermentation? How long does it remain in the barrel (part of the style of the winemaker)? Where do the grapes come from?

MALOLACTIC FERMENTATION is a second fermentation that lowers tart malic acids and increases the softer lactic acids, making for a richer style wine. The result is what many wine-tasters refer to as a buttery bouquet.

CALIFORNIA CHARDONNAY BEST BETS

1997*   1999*   2000   2001*
2002*   2003*   2004

Note: * signifies exceptional vintage

What are the other major California white-wine grapes?

Sauvignon Blanc—Sometimes labeled Fumé Blanc. This is one of the grapes used in making the dry white wines of the Graves region of Bordeaux, and the white wines of Sancerre and Pouilly-Fumé in the Loire Valley of France, as well as New Zealand. California Sauvignon Blanc makes one of the best dry white wines in the world. It is sometimes aged in small oak barrels and occasionally blended with the Sémillon grape.

Chenin Blanc—This is one of the most widely planted grapes in the Loire Valley. In California, the grape yields a very attractive, soft, light-bodied wine. It is usually made very dry or semi-sweet; it is a perfect apéritif wine, simple and fruity.

Viognier—One of the major white grapes from the Rhône Valley in France, Viognier thrives in warmer and sunny climates, so it's a perfect grape for the weather conditions in certain areas of California. It has a distinct fragrant bouquet. Not as full-bodied as most Chardonnays, nor as light as most Sauvignon Blancs, it's an excellent food wine.

WHY IS SAUVIGNON BLANC often labeled as Fumé Blanc? Robert Mondavi realized that no one was buying Sauvignon Blanc, so he changed its name to Fumé Blanc. Strictly a marketing maneuver—it was still the same wine. Result: Sales took off. The only mistake Mondavi made was not trademarking the name, so now anyone can use it (and many producers do).

KEVIN ZRALY'S FAVORITE SAUVIGNON BLANCS

Mantanzas Creek	Caymus
Robert Mondavi	Mason
Simi	Phelps
Silverado	Chalk Hill
Ferrari-Carano	Chateau St. Jean

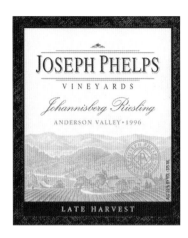

BOTRYTIS CINEREA is a mold that forms on the grapes, known also as "noble rot," which is necessary to make Sauternes and the rich German wines Beerenauslese and Trockenbeerenauslese.

Johannisberg Riesling—The true Riesling responsible for the best German wines of the Rhein and Mosel—and the Alsace wines of France—is also called White Riesling, or just Riesling. This grape produces white wine of distinctive varietal character in every style from bone-dry to very sweet dessert wines, which are often much better by themselves than with dessert. The smell of Riesling at its finest is always lively, fragrant, and both fruity and flowery.

In 1981, the California Wine Institute set industry-wide standard definitions for the terms "Late Harvest" and other similar designations that link wine style to picking time. The categories proposed with their associated grape-sugar levels at harvest generally follow the terms established by the German Wine Law of 1971 (see page 78).

Early Harvest: Equivalent to a German Kabinett, this term refers to wine made from grapes picked at a maximum of 200° Brix.

Regular or Normal: No specific label designation will be used to connote wines made from fruit of traditional maturity levels, 200° to 240° Brix.

Late Harvest: This term is equivalent to a German Auslese and requires a minimum sugar level of 240° Brix at harvest.

Select Late Harvest: Equivalent to a German Beerenauslese, the sugar-level minimum is 280° Brix.

Special Select Late Harvest: This, the highest maturity-level designation, requires that the grapes be picked at a minimum sugar content of 350° Brix, the same level necessary for a German Trockenbeerenauslese.

CALIFORNIA INGENUITY

Several wineries in California started to market their Late Harvest Riesling with German names such as Trockenbeerenauslese. The German government complained, and this practice was discontinued. One winemaker, though, began marketing his wine as TBA, the abbreviation for Trockenbeerenauslese. Again there was a complaint. This time the winemaker argued his case, saying that TBA was not an abbreviation for Trockenbeerenauslese, but for Totally Botrytis Affected.

Stay tuned for more.

What are the latest trends in the wines of California?

There has been a trend toward wineries specializing in particular grape varieties. Twenty years ago, I would have talked about which wineries in California were the best. Today, I'm more likely to talk about which winery or AVA makes the best Chardonnay; which winery makes the best Sauvignon Blanc; and the same would hold true for the reds, narrowing it down to who makes the best Cabernet Sauvignon, Pinot Noir, Merlot, or Zinfandel.

The era of great experimentation with winemaking techniques is slowly coming to an end, and now the winemakers are just making the finest possible wines they can from what they've learned in the 1980s and 1990s. I do expect to see some further experimentation to determine which grape varieties grow best in the various AVAs and microclimates. One of the biggest changes in the last twenty years is that wineries have also become more food-conscious in winemaking, adjusting their wine styles to go better with various kinds of food by lowering alcohol levels and increasing the acidity.

Chardonnay and Cabernet Sauvignon remain the two major grape varieties, but much more Syrah is being planted in California. Sauvignon Blanc (also called Fumé Blanc) wines have greatly improved. They're easier to consume young. Although they still don't have the cachet of a Chardonnay, I find them better matched with most foods. However, other white-grape varieties, such as Riesling and Chenin Blanc, aren't meeting with the same success, and they're harder to sell. Still, just to keep it interesting, some winemakers are planting more European varietals, including Italy's Sangiovese, and Grenache and Viognier from France.

Another significant development in California winemaking is the extent to which giant corporations have been buying up small, midsize, and even large wineries. The wine industry, like so many other businesses these days, has been subject to a great deal of consolidation as a result of mergers and acquisitions. See the list that follows for some notable examples of this trend.

FOR FURTHER READING

I recommend *The Oxford Companion to the Wines of North America* by Bruce Cass and Jancis Robinson; *The Wine Atlas of California* by James Halliday; *Making Sense of California Wine* and *New California Wine* by Matt Kramer; *California Wine* by James Laube; *American Vintage: The Rise of American Wine* by Paul Lukacs; and *The Wine Atlas of California and the Pacific Northwest* by Bob Thompson. Lovers of gossip will have fun reading *The Far Side of Eden* and *Napa: The Story of an American Eden* by James Conaway.

THE CRYSTAL BALL

Over the next ten years, look for China and Russia to become big importers of American wines.

THE 2004 HARVEST was one of the earliest ever, with some grapes being harvested at the beginning of August.

CONSTELLATION BRANDS, with its many acquisitions—including the Robert Mondavi Winery—edged past E. & J. Gallo Winery to be the biggest wine company in the world.

GALLO SOLD 75 million cases in 2003, accounting for nearly one out of every four bottles of American wine.

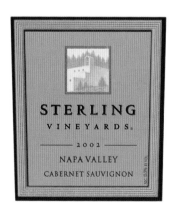

A WINERY BY ANY OTHER NAME

Here, listed by the parent company, is a selection of some well-known wineries and brands.

ALLIED DOMECQ PLC

Atlas Peak • Buena Vista • Callaway Coastal Vineyards • Clos du Bois • William Hill • Mumm Napa

BERINGER BLASS (FOSTER'S)

Beringer Vineyards • Carmenet • Chateau St. Jean • Chateau Souverian • Etude Wines • Meridian Vineyards • Stags' Leap Winery • St. Clement • Stone Cellars • Windsor

CONSTELLATION BRANDS, INC.

Batavia Wine Cellars • Canandaigua Winery (includes Richards, Arbor Mist, Taylor, J. Roget) • Columbia Winery • Covey Run Winery • Dunnewood Vineyards • Estancia Winery • Franciscan Vineyards • Mission Bell Winery (includes Almaden, Cook's Cribari, Inglenook, Paul Masson, Taylor California Cellars, Le Domaine) • Robert Mondavi Winery, Robert Mondavi Napa, Robert Mondavi Private Selection, Opus One, Woodbridge • Mount Veeder Winery • Quintessa • Ravenswood • Ste. Chapelle Winery • Simi Winery • Paul Thomas Winery • Turner Road Vintners (includes Talus, Nathanson Creek, Vendange, Heritage, La Terre)

DIAGEO

Beaulieu Vineyards • BV Coastal • Blossom Hill • The Monterey Vineyard • Painted Hills • Sterling Vineyards

E. & J. GALLO

Anapamu Cellars • Frei Brothers Reserve • Gallo of Sonoma • Indigo Hills • Louis M. Martini • MacMurray Ranch • Marcelina Vineyards • Mirassou Vineyards • Rancho Zabaco • Redwood Creek • Turning Leaf

THE WINE GROUP

Colony • Concannon • Corbett Canyon • Franzia • Glen Ellen • Lejon • M.G. Vallejo • Mogen David • Summit

Source: Wines & Vines 2004

WINE AND FOOD

MARGRIT BIEVER AND ROBERT MONDAVI: *With Chardonnay: oysters, lobster, a more complex fish with sauce beurre blanc, pheasant salad with truffles. With Sauvignon Blanc: traditional white meat or fish course, sautéed or grilled fish (as long as it isn't an oily fish).*

FRANCIS MAHONEY *(Carneros Creek Winery): With Chardonnay: fowl, ham, and seafood in sauces. With Sauvignon Blanc: fish, turkey, shellfish, and appetizers.*

DAVID STARE *(Dry Creek): With Chardonnay: fresh boiled Dungeness crab cooked in Zatarain's crab boil, a New Orleans–style boil. Serve this with melted butter and a large loaf of sourdough French bread. With Sauvignon Blanc, "I like fresh salmon cooked in almost any manner. Personally, I like to take a whole fresh salmon or salmon steaks and cook them over the barbecue in an aluminum foil pocket. Place the salmon, onion slices, lemon slices, copious quantities of fresh dill, salt, and pepper on aluminum foil and make a pocket. Cook over the barbecue until barely done. Place the salmon in the oven to keep it warm while you take the juices from the aluminum pocket, reduce the juices, strain and whisk in some plain yogurt. Enjoy!"*

WARREN WINIARSKI *(Stag's Leap Wine Cellars): With Chardonnay: seviche, shellfish, salmon with a light hollandaise sauce.*

JANET TREFETHEN: *With Chardonnay: barbecued whole salmon in a sorrel sauce. With White Riesling: sautéed bay scallops with julienne vegetables.*

RICHARD ARROWOOD: *With Chardonnay: Sonoma Coast Dungeness crab right from the crab pot, with fennel butter as a dipping sauce.*

BO BARRETT *(Chateau Montelena Winery): With Chardonnay: salmon, trout, or abalone, barbecued with olive oil and lemon leaf and slices.*

JACK CAKEBREAD: *"With my 2002 Cakebread Cellars Napa Valley Chardonnay: bruschetta with wild mushrooms, leek and mushroom–stuffed chicken breast, and halibut with caramelized endive and chanterelles."*

ED SBRAGIA *(Beringer Vineyards): With Chardonnay: lobster or salmon with lots of butter.*

RODNEY STRONG: *With Chardonnay: Dover sole.*

U.S. WINE exports have increased from $98 million in 1989 to $794 million in 2004. The top export markets are:
1. United Kingdom
2. Canada
3. Netherlands
4. Japan
5. Germany

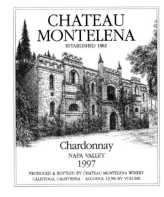

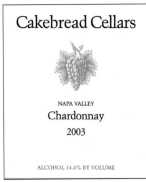

The White Wines of Germany

GRAPE VARIETIES • THE STYLE OF GERMAN WINES •

QUALITÄTSWEIN MIT PRÄDIKAT •

UNDERSTANDING GERMAN WINE LABELS • TRENDS

The Braune Kupp vineyard, a source of Riesling grapes, overlooks a bend in the Saar River in Germany's Mosel-Saar-Ruwer winemaking region.
(Charles O'Rear/Corbis)

About German Wines

THERE HAS been a 10% increase in the vineyards planted over the last ten years.

FRANCE PRODUCES 10 times as much wine as Germany.

IN GERMANY, 100,000 grape growers cultivate nearly 270,000 acres of vines, meaning the average holding per grower is 2.7 acres.

Before we begin our study of the white wines of Germany, tell me this: Have you memorized the 7 Grands Crus of Chablis, the 32 Grands Crus of the Côte d'Or, and the 250 different vineyards of the Napa Valley? I hope you have, so you can begin to memorize the more than 1,400 wine villages and 2,600-plus vineyards of Germany. No problem, right? What's four thousand simple little names?

Actually, if you were to have studied German wines before 1971, you would have had thirty thousand different names to remember. There used to be very small parcels of land owned by many different people; that's why so many names were involved.

In an effort to make German wines less confusing, the government stepped in and passed a law in 1971. The new ruling stated that a vineyard must encompass at least twelve and a half acres of land. This law cut the list of vineyard names considerably, but increased the number of owners.

Germany produces only 2 or 3 percent of the world's wines. (Beer, remember, is the national beverage.) And what wines it does produce depends largely on the weather. Why is this? Well, look at where the wines are geographically. Germany is the northernmost country in which vines can grow. And 80 percent of the

vineyards are located on hilly slopes. Germans can forget about mechanical harvesting.

The following chart should help give you a better idea of the hilly conditions vintners must contend with in order to grow grapes and produce German wines.

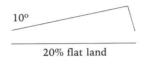
20% flat land

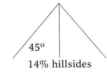
14% hillsides

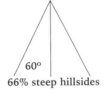
66% steep hillsides

What are the most important grape varieties?

Reisling—This is by far the most widely planted and the best grape variety produced in Germany. If you don't see the name "Riesling" on the label, then there's probably very little, if any, Riesling grape in the wine. And remember, if the label gives the grape variety, then there must be at least 85 percent of that grape in the wine, according to German law. Of the grapes planted in Germany, 23 percent are Riesling.

Silvaner—This is another grape variety that accounts for 7 percent of Germany's wines.

Müller-Thurgau—A cross between two grapes (Riesling and Chasselas).

What are the main winemaking regions of Germany?

There are thirteen winemaking regions. Do you have to commit them all to memory like the hundreds of other names I've mentioned in the book so far?

HOW COLD IS IT?

If you were to look at a map of the world, put your finger on Germany, and then follow the 50-degree north latitude westward across into North America, you'd be pointing to the island of Newfoundland, Canada.

ONE MECHANICAL harvester can do the work of 60 people.

GERMANY PRODUCES red wines, too, but only about 15%. Why? Red grapes simply don't grow as well as white ones in Germany's northerly climate.

WITH GERMAN WINES, 85 is the important number to remember:
- 85% of the wines Germany produces are white.
- If a wine label gives the grape variety—Riesling, for example—85% of the wine must be made from the Riesling grape.
- If a German wine shows a vintage on the label, 85% of the grapes used must be from that year. Top German wine producers use 100% of the varietal and the vintage on the label.

GRAPES IN GERMANY

Riesling: 23%
Müller-Thurgau: 21%
Silvaner: 7%

WITH THE reunification of Germany in 1989, there are now thirteen different regions that produce wine.

Absolutely not. Why should you worry about all thirteen when you only need to be familiar with four?

One of the reasons I emphasize these regions above the others is that in the United States you rarely see wine from the other German wine-growing regions. The other reason to look closely at these regions is that they produce the best German wines. They are

RHEINHESSEN

RHEINGAU

MOSEL-SAAR-RUWER

PFALZ
(UNTIL 1992 KNOWN
AS RHEINPFALZ)

What's the style of German wines?

A balance of sweetness with acidity and low alcohol. Remember the equation:

$$\text{Sugar} + \text{Yeast} = \text{Alcohol} + \text{Carbon Dioxide (CO}_2\text{)}$$

Where does the sugar come from? The sun! If you have a good year, and your vines are on a southerly slope, you'll get a lot of sun, and therefore the right sugar content to produce a good wine. In many years, however, the winemakers aren't so fortunate and they don't have enough sun to ripen the grapes. The result: higher acidity and lower alcohol. To compensate for this, some winemakers may add sugar to the must before fermentation to increase the amount of alcohol. As mentioned before, this process is called chaptalization. (Note: Chaptalization is not permitted for higher-quality German wines.)

The three basic styles of German wine are:

Trocken—dry
Halbtrocken—medium-dry
Fruity—semidry to very sweet

GIVEN GOOD weather, the longer the grapes remain on the vine, the sweeter they become—but the winemaker takes a risk when he does this because all could be lost in the event of bad weather.

FIFTY YEARS ago, most German wines were dry and very high in acidity. Even in the finer restaurants, you'd be offered a spoonful of sugar with a German wine to balance the acidity.

GERMAN WINES tend to be 8% to 10% alcohol, compared to an average 11% to 13% for French wine.

OF MOSEL wines, 80% are made from the Riesling grape, while 82% of Rheingau wines are made from Riesling.

A NOTE ON SÜSSRESERVE

A common misconception about German wine is that fermentation stops and the remaining residual sugar gives the wine its sweetness naturally. On the contrary, some wines are fermented dry. Many German winemakers hold back a certain percentage of unfermented grape juice from the same vineyards, the same varietal, and the same sweetness level. This Süssreserve contains all the natural sugar and it's added back to the wine after fermentation. The finest estates do not use the Süssreserve method, but rely on stopping the fermentation to achieve their style.

What are the different levels of German wine?

As a result of the German law of 1971, there are two main categories, Tafelwein and Qualitätswein.

Tafelwein—Literally, "table wine." The lowest designation given to a wine grown in Germany, it never carries the vineyard name. It is rarely seen in the United States.

Qualitätswein—Literally, "quality wine," of which there are two types.

1. *Qualitätswein bestimmter Anbaugebiete:* QbA indicates a quality wine that comes from one of the thirteen specified regions.
2. *Qualitätswein mit Prädikat:* This is quality wine with distinction—the good stuff. These wines may not be chaptalized: The winemaker is not permitted to add sugar. In ascending order of quality, price, and ripeness at harvest, here are the QmP levels:

Kabinett—Light, semidry wines made from normally ripened grapes. Cost: $10–$20.

Spätlese—Breaking up the word, *spät* means "late" and *lese* means "picking." Put them together and you have "late picking." That's exactly what this medium-style wine is made of—grapes that were picked after the normal harvest. The extra days of sun give the wine more body and a more intense flavor. Cost: $12–$30.

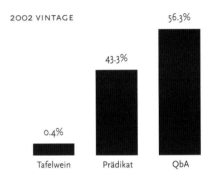

AS GERMAN winemakers say, "A hundred days of sun will make a good wine, but 120 days of sun will make a great wine."

JOSEF LEITZ

WEINGUT

1997

Rüdesheimer Berg Roseneck
Riesling Spätlese

Qualitätswein mit Prädikat
Erzeugerabfüllung
alc. 8,5% vol.   A. P. Nr. 24079 018 98   e 750 ml
Product of Germany

D-65385 RÜDESHEIM AM RHEIN
RHEINGAU

TODAY, MOST German wines, including
Beerenauslese and Trockenbeerenauslese,
are bottled in spring and early summer.
Many no longer receive additional cask
or tank maturation, because it has been
discovered that this extra barrel aging
destroys the fruit.

IN 1921, THE first Trockenbeerenauslese
was made in the Mosel region.

THE SPÄTLESE RIDER: THE FIRST LATE-HARVEST WINE

The story goes that at the vineyards of Schloss Johannisberg, the monks were not allowed to pick the grapes until the Abbot of Fulda gave his permission. During the harvest of 1775, the abbot was away attending a synod. That year the grapes were ripening early and some of them had started to rot on the vine. The monks, becoming concerned, dispatched a rider to ask the abbot's permission to pick the grapes. By the time the rider returned, the monks believed all was lost, but they went ahead with the harvest anyway. To their amazement, the wine was one of the best they had ever tasted. That was the beginning of Spätlese-style wines.

Auslese—Translated as "out picked," this means that the grapes are selectively picked out from particularly ripe bunches, which yields a medium to fuller style wine. You probably do the same thing in your own garden if you grow tomatoes: You pick out the especially ripe ones, leaving the others on the vine. Cost: $20–$45.

Beerenauslese—Breaking the word down, you get *beeren*, or "berries," *aus*, or "out," and *lese*, or "picking." Quite simply (and don't let the bigger names fool you), these are berries (grapes) that are picked out individually. These luscious grapes are used to create the rich dessert wines for which Germany is known. Beerenauslese is usually made only two or three times every ten years. It's not unheard of for a good Beerenauslese to cost up to $250.

Trockenbeerenauslese—A step above the Beerenauslese, but these grapes are dried (*trocken*), so they're more like raisins. These "raisinated" grapes produce the richest, sweetest, honeylike wine—and the most expensive.

WHAT IS *BOTRYTIS CINEREA*?

Botrytis cinerea, known as Edelfäule in German, is a mold that (under special conditions) attacks grapes, as was described in the section on Sauternes. I say "special" because this "noble rot" is instrumental in the production of Beerenauslese and Trockenbeerenauslese.

Noble rot occurs late in the growing season when the nights are cool and heavy with dew, the mornings have fog, and the days are warm. When noble rot attacks the grapes, they begin to shrivel and the water evaporates, leaving concentrated sugar. (Remember, 86 percent of wine is water.) Grapes affected by this mold may not look very appealing, but don't let looks deceive you: The proof is in the wine.

Eiswein—A very rare, sweet, concentrated wine made from frozen grapes left on the vine. They're pressed while still frozen. According to Germany's 1971 rules for winemaking, this wine must now be made from grapes that are at least ripe enough to make a Beerenauslese.

What's the difference between a $50 Beerenauslese and a $150 Beerenauslese (besides a hundred bucks)?

The major difference is the grapes. The $50 bottle is probably made from Müller-Thurgau grapes or Silvaner, while the $150 bottle is from Riesling. In addition, the region the wine comes from will, in part, determine its quality. Traditionally, the best Beerenauslese and Trockenbeerenauslese come from the Rhein or the Mosel.

Quality is higher in wine when:

1. The wine is produced from low yields.

2. The grapes come from great vineyards.

3. The wine is produced by great winemakers.

4. The grapes were grown in a great climate or are from a great vintage.

When I'm ordering a German wine in a restaurant or shopping at my local retailer, what should I look for?

The first thing I would make sure of is that it comes from one of the four major regions. These regions are the Mosel-Saar-Ruwer, Rheinhessen, Rheingau, and Pfalz, which, in my opinion, are the most important quality wine-producing regions in all of Germany.

Next, look to see if the wine is a Riesling. Anyone who studies and enjoys German wines finds that Riesling shows the best-tasting characteristics. Riesling on the label is a mark of quality.

Also, be aware of the vintage. It's important, especially with German wines, to know if the wine was made in a good year.

Finally, probably the most important consideration is to buy from a reputable grower or producer. A great source for that listing is the *Gault-Millau Guide to German Wine* by Henri Gault, Christian Millau, et al.

KEVIN ZRALY'S FAVORITE WINE PRODUCERS

Fritz Haag	Mosel
Egon Muller	Mosel
J.J. Prum	Mosel
Dr. Loosen	Mosel
Kesselstatt	Mosel
S.A. Prum	Mosel
Selbach-Oster	Mosel
Dr. H. Thanisch	Mosel
Robert Weil	Mosel
C. von Schubert	Mosel
Friedrich-Wilhelm-Gymnasium	Mosel
Dr. Pauly-Bergweiler	Mosel
Burklin Wolf	Pfalz
Muller-Catoir	Pfalz
Lingenfelder	Pfalz
Strub	Rheinhessen
Weil	Rheingau
Josef Leitz	Rheingau
Schloss Johannisberg	Rheingau

ONE QUICK way to tell the difference between a Rhein and a Mosel wine on sight is to look at the bottle. Rhein wine comes in a brown bottle, Mosel in a green bottle.

ALL QUALITÄTSWEIN and Qualitätswein mit Prädikat must pass a test by an official laboratory and tasting panel to be given an official number, prior to the wine's release to the trade.

WHOSE VINEYARD IS IT, ANYWAY?

Piesporter Goldtröpfchen—350 owners
Wehlener Sonnenuhr—250 owners
Brauneberger Juffer—180 owners

IMPRESS YOUR friends with this trivia:
A.P. Nr. 2 602 041 008 02
  2 = the government referral office or testing station
602 = location code of bottler
041 = bottler ID number
008 = bottle lot
  02 = the year the wine was tasted by the board

What's the difference between Rhein and Mosel wines?

Rhein wines generally have more body than do Mosels. Mosels are usually higher in acidity and lower in alcohol than are Rhein wines. Mosels show more autumn fruits like apples, pears, and quince, while Rhein wines show more summer fruits like apricots, peaches, and nectarines.

Some important villages to look for:

Rheingau: Eltville, Erbach, Rüdesheim, Rauenthal, Hochheim, Johannisberg

Mosel-Saar-Ruwer: Erden, Piesport, Bernkastel, Graach, Ürzig, Brauneberg, Wehlen

Rheinhessen: Oppenheim, Nackenheim, Nierstein, Pfalz, Deidesheim, Forst, Wachenheim, Ruppertsberg, Dürkheimer

Can you take the mystery out of reading German wine labels?

German wine labels give you plenty of information. For example, see the label on page 84.

Mosel-Saar-Ruwer is the region of the wine's origin. Note that the region is one of the big four we discussed earlier in this chapter.

2001 is the year the grapes were harvested.

Ürzig is the town and **Würzgarten** is the vineyard from which the grapes originate. The Germans add the suffix "er" to make *Ürziger,* just as a person from New York is called a New Yorker.

Auslese is the ripeness level, in this case from bunches of over-ripe grapes.

Riesling is the grape variety. Therefore, this wine is at least 85 percent Riesling.

Qualitätswein mit Prädikat is the quality level of the wine.

A.P. Nr. 2 602 041 008 02 is the official testing number—proof that the wine was tasted by a panel of tasters and passed the strict quality standards required by the government.

Gutsabfüllung means "estate-bottled."

What are the recent trends in the white wines of Germany?

As Americans' drinking tastes have shifted from generic wines to varietal wines, and so also toward drier wines, we've seen a decrease in the availability of German wines in the American market. German wines have also been hampered in the American market by the increase in their prices. Still, I feel the lighter-style Trocken (dry), Halbtrocken (medium-dry), German Kabinetts, and even Spätleses are wines that can be easily served as an apéritif, or with very light food and also grilled food, and in particular with spicy or Pacific Rim cuisines. If you haven't had a German wine in a long time, the 2001 and 2002 vintages show the greatness of what German white wines are all about.

And the great news is that those hard-to-read gothic script German wine labels have become more user-friendly—easier to read, with more modern designs.

BEST BETS FOR RECENT VINTAGES IN GERMANY

| 1996* | 1999 | 2001* | 2002* | 2003 |

Note: * signifies exceptional vintage

THE 2003 HARVEST was one of the earliest in decades.

PAST GREAT vintages of Beerenauslese and Trockenbeerenauslese: 1985, 1988, 1989, 1990.

MANY GERMAN winemakers consider 2001 to be the best vintage since 1976.

WINE AND FOOD

RAINER LINGENFELDER *(Weingut Lingenfelder Estate, Pfalz): With Riesling Spätlese Halbtrocken: "We have a tradition of cooking fresh water fish that come from a number of small creeks in the Palatinate forest, so my personal choice would be trout, either herbed with thyme, basil, parsley, and onion, and cooked in wine, or smoked with a bit of horseradish. We find it to be a very versatile wine, a very good match with a whole range of white meat. Pork is traditional in the Palatinate region, as are chicken and goose dishes."*

JOHANNES SELBACH *(Selbach-Oster, Mosel): "What kinds of food do we have with Riesling Spätlese? Anything we like! This may sound funny but there's a wide variety of food that goes very well with—and this is the key—a fruity, only moderately sweet, well-balanced Riesling Spätlese. Start with mild curries and sesame- or ginger-flavored not-too-spicy dishes. Or try either gravlax or smoked salmon. You can even have Riesling Spätlese with a green salad in a balsamic vinaigrette, preferably with a touch of raspberry, as long as the dressing is not too vinegary. Many people avoid pairing wine with a salad, but it works beautifully.*

"For haute cuisine, fresh duck or goose liver lightly sautéed in its own juice, or veal sweetbreads in a rich sauce. Also salads with fresh greens, fresh fruit, and fresh seafood marinated in lime or lemon juice or balsamic vinegar.

"With an old ripe Spätlese: roast venison, dishes with cream sauces, and any white-meat dish stuffed with or accompanied by fruit. It is also delicious with fresh fruit itself or as an apéritif."

With Riesling Spätlese Halbtrocken: "This is a food-friendly wine, but the first thing that comes to mind is fresh seafood and fresh fish. Also wonderful with salads with a mild vinaigrette, and with a course that's often difficult to match: cream soups. If we don't know exactly what to drink with a particular food, Spätlese Halbtrocken is usually the safe bet.

"It may be too obvious to say foie gras with Eiswein, but it is a classic."

SELBACH-OSTER

1997

ZELTINGER SCHLOSSBERG
RIESLING KABINETT

QUALITÄTSWEIN MIT PRÄDIKAT
GUTSABFÜLLUNG WEINGUT SELBACH-OSTER · D-54492 ZELTINGEN
L · A.P. NR. 2 606 319 019 98
Mosel · Saar · Ruwer
alc.8%vol · 750 ml e

Red Grapes of the World

CLASSES **F**OUR **THROUGH** **S**EVEN will delve into the great red wines of the world. Just as you studied the major white grape varieties before the classes on white wines, as you begin this journey you should understand the major red grape varieties and where in the world they produce the best wines.

In Class Four, I start with a list of what I consider to be the major red wine grapes, ranked from lightest to fullest-bodied style, along with the region or country in which the grape grows best. By looking at this chart, not only will you get an idea of the style of the wine, but also a feeling for gradations of weight, color, tannin, and ageability.

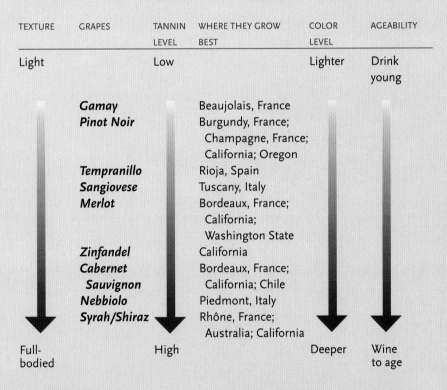

TEXTURE	GRAPES	TANNIN LEVEL	WHERE THEY GROW BEST	COLOR LEVEL	AGEABILITY
Light		Low		Lighter	Drink young
	Gamay		Beaujolais, France		
	Pinot Noir		Burgundy, France; Champagne, France; California; Oregon		
	Tempranillo		Rioja, Spain		
	Sangiovese		Tuscany, Italy		
	Merlot		Bordeaux, France; California; Washington State		
	Zinfandel		California		
	Cabernet Sauvignon		Bordeaux, France; California; Chile		
	Nebbiolo		Piedmont, Italy		
	Syrah/Shiraz		Rhône, France; Australia; California		
Full-bodied		High		Deeper	Wine to age

AT LAST count, about 40 different red-wine grapes were planted throughout the world. California alone grows 31 different red-wine grape varieties.

IN GENERAL, the lighter the color, the more perceived acidity.

ONCE YOU have become acquainted with these major red-wine grapes, you may wish to explore the following:

GRAPES	WHERE THEY GROW BEST
Barbera	Italy
Dolcetto	Italy
Cabernet Franc	Loire Valley and Bordeaux, France
Grenache	Rhône, France
Garnacha	Spain
Malbec	Bordeaux and Cahors, France; Argentina

To put this chart together is extremely challenging, given all the variables that go into making wine and the many different styles that can be produced. Remember, there are always exceptions to the rule, just as there are other countries and wine regions not listed here that produce world-class wine from some of the red grapes shown. You'll begin to see this for yourself if you do your homework and taste a lot of different wines. Good luck!

The Red Wines of Burgundy and the Rhône Valley

THE RED WINES OF BURGUNDY • WINE-PRODUCING AREAS • BEAUJOLAIS •

CÔTE CHÂLONNAISE • CÔTE D'ÔR • CÔTE DE BEAUNE •

CÔTE DE NUITS • RHÔNE VALLEY

A vineyard at Volnay, in Burgundy's Côte de Beaune, late autumn
(Charles O'Rear/Corbis)

The Red Wines of Burgundy

Now we're getting into a whole new experience in wines—the reds. Generally, my students and I become more intense and we concentrate more when we taste red wines.

2,000 YEARS OF EXPERIENCE

Burgundy's reputation for winemaking dates as far back as 51 B.C.

FRANCE

Paris ★

BURGUNDY

Atlantic
Ocean

CÔTES
DU RHÔNE

0 Miles 100 200

0 Kilometers 200

Mediterranean Sea

What's so different about red wines (beyond their color)?

We're beginning to see more components in the wines—more complexities. In the white wines, we were looking mainly for the acid/fruit balance, but now, in addition, we're looking for other characteristics, such as tannin.

WHAT'S TANNIN?

Tannin is what gives wine its longevity. It comes from the skins, the pits, and the stems of the grapes. Another source of tannin is wood, especially the French oak barrels in which some wines are aged or fermented.

A word used to describe the taste sensation of tannin is "astringent." Tannin is not a taste. It's a tactile sensation.

Tannin is also found in strong tea. And what can you add to the tea to make it less astringent? Milk—the fat and the proteins in milk soften the tannin. And so it is with a highly tannic wine. If you take another milk by-product, such as cheese, and have it with wine, it softens the tannin and makes the wine more appealing. Enjoy a beef entrée or one served with a cream sauce and a good bottle of red wine to experience it for yourself.

Why is Burgundy so difficult to understand?

Before we go any further, I must tell you that there are no shortcuts. Burgundy is one of the most difficult subjects in the study of wines. People get uptight about Burgundy. They say, "There's so much to know," and "It looks so hard." Yes, there are many vineyards and villages, and they're all important. But actually, there are only fifteen to twenty-five names with which you should familiarize yourself, if you'd like to know and speak about Burgundy wines intelligently. Not to worry. I'm going to help you decode all the mysteries of Burgundy: names, regions, and labels.

BLAME NAPOLEON

If you're having trouble understanding the wines of Burgundy, you're not alone. After the French Revolution in 1789, all the vineyards were sold off in small parcels. The Napoleonic Code also called for a law of equal inheritance for the children—continuing to fragment the vineyards even further.

LAND OF 1,000 NAMES

There are more than 1,000 names and over 110 appellations you must memorize to become a Burgundy wine expert.

What are the main red wine–producing areas of Burgundy?

Côte d'Or { Côte de Nuits   Beaujolais
           Côte de Beaune   Côte Châlonnaise

THE CÔTE D'OR is only 30 miles long and half a mile wide.

What major grape varieties are used in red Burgundy wines?

The two major grape varieties are Pinot Noir and Gamay. Under Appellation Contrôlée laws, all red Burgundies are made from the Pinot Noir grape, except Beaujolais, which is produced from the Gamay grape.

MANY OF the 10 crus of Beaujolais do not bear the name "Beaujolais" on the label—just the name of the village. Why, you ask? Because the producers of cru Beaujolais don't want to have their wines confused with basic Beaujolais.

IN AN average year, some 19 million cases of wine are produced in Burgundy. Twelve million cases of that are Beaujolais!

ONE-THIRD of the Beaujolais grapes are used to make Beaujolais Nouveau.

ALL GRAPES in the Beaujolais region are picked by hand.

BEAUJOLAIS

- Made from 100 percent Gamay grapes.

- This wine's style is typically light and fruity. It's meant to be consumed young. Beaujolais is the largest-selling Burgundy in the United States by far, probably because it's so easy to drink.

- Beaujolais can be chilled, and it's very affordable. Most bottles cost between eight and twenty dollars, although the price varies with the quality and the grade.

What are the quality levels of Beaujolais?

There are three different quality levels of Beaujolais:

Beaujolais: This basic Beaujolais accounts for the majority of all Beaujolais produced. (Cost: $)

Beaujolais-Villages: This comes from certain villages in Beaujolais. There are thirty-five villages that consistently produce better wines. Most Beaujolais-Villages is a blend of wines from these villages, and usually no particular village name is included on the label. (Cost: $$)

Cru: A cru is actually the name of a village that produces the highest quality of Beaujolais. (Cost: $$$$)

There are ten crus (villages):

BROUILLY	JULIÉNAS
CHÉNAS	MORGON
CHIROUBLES	MOULIN-À-VENT
CÔTE DE BROUILLY	RÉGNIÉ
FLEURIE	SAINT-AMOUR

What's Beaujolais Nouveau?

Beaujolais Nouveau is even lighter and fruitier in style than your basic Beaujolais and it is best drunk young. Isn't that true of all Beaujolais wines? Yes, but Nouveau is different. This "new" Beaujolais is picked, fermented, bottled, and available at your local retailer in a matter of weeks. (I don't know what you call that in your business, but I call it good cash flow in mine. It gives the winemaker a virtually instant return.)

There's another purpose behind Beaujolais Nouveau: Like a preview of a movie, it offers the wine-consuming public a sample of the quality of the vintage and style that the winemaker will produces in his regular Beaujolais for release the following spring.

Beaujolais Nouveau is meant to be consumed within six months of bottling. So if you're holding a 2000 Beaujolais Nouveau, now is the time to give it to your "friends."

How long should I keep a Beaujolais?

It depends on the level of quality and the vintage. Beaujolais and Beaujolais-Villages are meant to last between one and three years. Crus can last longer because they are more complex. I've tasted Beaujolais crus that were more than ten years old and still in excellent condition. This is the exception, though, not the rule.

Which shippers/producers should I look for when buying Beaujolais?

BOUCHARD   DROUHIN   DUBOEUF
JADOT   MOMMESSIN

BEST BETS FOR RECENT VINTAGES OF BEAUJOLAIS
2000   2002*   2003*

*Note: * signifies exceptional vintage*

BEAUJOLAIS NOUVEAU MADNESS

The exact date of release is the third Thursday in November, and Beaujolais Nouveau is introduced to the consumer amidst great hoopla. Restaurants and retailers all vie to be the first to offer the new Beaujolais to their customers.

"Beaujolais is one of the very few red wines that can be drunk as a white. Beaujolais is my daily drink. And sometimes I blend one-half water to the wine. It is the most refreshing drink in the world."

—DIDIER MOMMESSIN

TO CHILL OR NOT TO CHILL?

As a young student studying wines in Burgundy, I visited the Beaujolais region, excited and naive. In one of the villages, I stopped at a bistro and ordered a glass of Beaujolais. (A good choice on my part, don't you think?) The waiter brought the glass of Beaujolais and it was chilled, and I thought that these people had not read the right books! Every wine book I'd ever read always said you serve red wines at room temperature and white wines chilled.

Obviously, I learned from my experience that when it comes to Beaujolais Nouveau, Beaujolais, and Beaujolais-Villages, it's a good idea to give them a slight chill to bring out the fruit and liveliness (acidity) of the wines. That is why Beaujolais is my favorite red wine to have during the summer.

However, to my taste, the Beaujolais crus have more fruit and more tannin and are best served at room temperature.

WINE AND FOOD

Beaujolais goes well with almost anything—especially light, simple meals and cheeses—nothing overpowering. Generally, try to match your Beaujolais with light food, such as veal, fish, or fowl. Here's what some of the experts say:

GEORGES DUBOEUF: "A lot of dishes can be eaten with Beaujolais—what you choose depends on the appellation and vintage. With charcuteries and pâtés you can serve a young Beaujolais or Beaujolais-Villages. With grilled meat, more generous and fleshy wines, such as Juliénas and Morgon crus, can be served. With meats cooked in a sauce (for example, coq au vin), I would suggest a Moulin-à-Vent cru from a good vintage."

ANDRÉ GAGEY (Louis Jadot): "Beaujolais with simple meals, light cheeses, grilled meat—everything except sweets."

DIDIER MOMMESSIN: "Serve with an extremely strong cheese, such as Roquefort, especially when the wine is young and strong enough for it. Also with white meat and veal."

CÔTE CHALONNAISE

NOW WE'RE GETTING INTO classic Pinot Noir wines that offer tremendous value.

You should know three villages from this area:

Mercurey: (95 percent red)

Givry: (90 percent red)

Rully: (50 percent red)

Mercurey is the most important, producing wines of high quality. Because they are not well known in the United States, Mercurey wines are often a very good buy.

Which shippers/producers should I look for when buying wines from the Côte Châlonnaise?

MERCUREY	FAIVELEY
	DOMAINE DE SUREMAIN
	MICHEL JUILLOT
GIVRY	DOMAINE THENARD
	DOMAINE JABLOT
	LOUIS LATOUR
RULLY	ANTONIN RODET

CÔTE D'OR

NOW WE'RE GETTING TO the heart of Burgundy. The Côte d'Or (pronounced "coat door") means "golden slope." This region gets its name from the color of the foliage on the hillside, which in autumn is literally golden, as well as the income it brings to the winemakers. The area is very small and its best wines are among the priciest in the world. If you are looking for a $7.99 everyday bottle of wine, this is not the place.

What's the best way to understand the wines of the Côte d'Or?

First, you need to know that these wines are distinguished by quality levels—generic, Village, Premier Cru vineyards, and Grand Cru vineyards. Let's look at the quality levels with the double pyramid shown below. As you can see, not much Grand Cru wine is produced, but it is the highest quality and extremely expensive. Generic, on the other hand, is more readily available. Although much is produced, very few generic wines can be classified as outstanding.

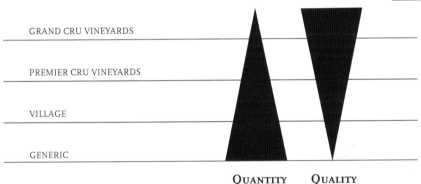

The Côte d'Or is divided into two regions:

Côte de Beaune: Red and white wines.

Côte de Nuits: The highest quality red Burgundy wines come from this region.

Another way to understand the wines of the Côte d'Or is to become familiar with the most important villages, Grand Cru vineyards, and some of the Premier Cru vineyards.

GENERIC WINES are labeled simply "Burgundy" or "Bourgogne." A higher level of generic wines will be labeled Côte de Beaune Villages or Côte de Nuits Villages, being a blend of different village wines.

THERE ARE 32 Grand Cru Vineyards:
- 8 white
- 24 red
- 24 from the Côte de Nuits
- 8 from the Côte de Beaune

GOOD VALUE VILLAGE WINES

Monthélie
Savigny les Beaune
Pernand-Vergelesses
Marsannay

THE IMPORTANCE OF SOIL TO BURGUNDY WINES

If you talk to any producers of Burgundy wines, they'll tell you the most important element in making their quality wines is the soil in which the grapes are grown. This, together with the slope of the land and the climatic conditions, determines whether the wine is a Village wine, a Premier Cru, or a Grand Cru. This concept of soil, slope, and climatic conditions in French is known as terroir.

During one of my trips to Burgundy, it rained for five straight days. On the sixth day I saw the workers at the bottom of the slopes with their pails and shovels, collecting the soil that had run down the hillside and returning the soil to the vineyard. This goes to show the importance of the soil to Burgundy wines.

Côte de Beaune—Red

BY FAR the largest red Grand Cru, in terms of production, is Corton, representing about 25% of all Grand Cru red wines.

THERE ARE more than 400 Premier Cru vineyards in Burgundy.

MOST IMPORTANT VILLAGES	MY FAVORITE PREMIER CRU VINEYARDS	GRAND CRU VINEYARDS
Aloxe-Corton	Fournières	Corton
	Chaillots	Corton Clos du Roi
		Corton Bressandes
		Corton Renardes
		Corton Maréchaude
Beaune	Grèves	None
	Fèves	
	Marconnets	
	Bressandes	
	Clos des Mouches	
Pommard	Épenots	None
	Rugiens	
Volnay	Caillerets	None
	Santenots	
	Clos des Chênes	
	Taillepieds	

1996

POMMARD
APPELLATION POMMARD CONTRÔLÉE

PRODUCED AND BOTTLED BY
BOUCHARD PÈRE & FILS
CHÂTEAU DE BEAUNE, CÔTE-D'OR, FRANCE
PRODUIT DE FRANCE · PRODUCT OF FRANCE
RED BURGUNDY WINE

Côte de Nuits—Red

Finally, we reach the Côte de Nuits. If you're going to spend any time studying your geography, do it now. The majority of Grand Cru vineyards are located in this area.

MOST IMPORTANT VILLAGES	MY FAVORITE PREMIER CRU VINEYARDS	GRAND CRU VINEYARDS
Gevrey-Chambertin	Clos St-Jacques Les Cazetiers Aux Combottes	Chambertin Chambertin Clos de Bèze Latricières-Chambertin Mazis-Chambertin Mazoyères-Chambertin Ruchottes-Chambertin Chapelle-Chambertin Charmes-Chambertin Griotte-Chambertin
Morey-St-Denis	Ruchots Les Genevrières Clos des Ormes	Clos des Lambrays Clos de Tart Clos St-Denis Clos de la Roche Bonnes Mares (partial)
Chambolle-Musigny	Les Amoureuses Charmes	Musigny Bonnes Mares (partial)
Vougeot		Clos de Vougeot
Flagey-Échézeaux		Échézeaux Grands-Échézeaux
Vosne-Romanée	Beaux-Monts	La Grande-Rue Malconsorts Romanée-Conti La Romanée La Tâche Richebourg Romanée-St-Vivant
Nuits-St-Georges	Les St-Georges Vaucrains Porets	None

CHAMBERTIN CLOS de Bèze was the favorite wine of Napoleon, who is reported to have said: "Nothing makes the future look so rosy as to contemplate it through a glass of Chambertin." Obviously, he ran out of Chambertin at Waterloo!

THE NEWEST GRAND CRU

La Grande-Rue, a vineyard tucked between the Grands Crus La Tâche and Romanée-Conti in Vosne-Romanée, was itself elevated to the Grand Cru level, bringing the number of Grands Crus in the Côte d'Or to 32.

HAS THIS ever happened to you? In a restaurant, you order a village wine—Gevrey Chambertin, for example—and by mistake the waiter brings you a Grand Cru Chambertin. What would you do?

Why are we bothering with all this geography? Must we learn the names of all the villages and vineyards?

I thought you'd never ask. First of all, the geography is important because it helps make you a smart buyer. If you're familiar with the most important villages and vineyards, you're more likely to make an educated purchase.

You really don't have to memorize all the villages and vineyards. I'll let you in on a little secret of how to choose a Burgundy wine and tell at a glance if it's a Village wine, a Premier Cru, or a Grand Cru—usually the label will tip you off in the manner illustrated here:

This is the method I use to teach Burgundy wine. Ask yourself the following:

Where is the wine from? France
What type of wine is it? Burgundy
Which region is it from? Côte d'Or
Which area? Côte de Nuits
Which village is the wine from?
Chambolle-Musigny
Does the label give more details?
Yes, it tells you that the wine is from a vineyard called Musigny, which is one of the thirty-two Grand Cru vineyards.

$
Village Only = Village wine

$$
Village + Vineyard
(Clos Saint-Jacques) = Premier Cru

$$$$
Vineyard Only
(Le Chambertin) = Grand Cru

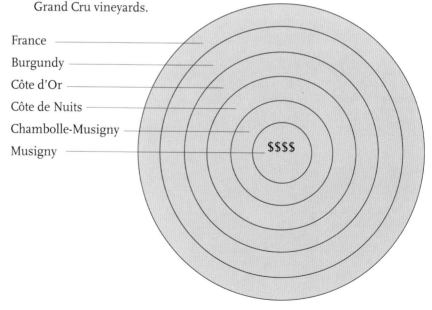

France
Burgundy
Côte d'Or
Côte de Nuits
Chambolle-Musigny
Musigny

$$$$

Has the style of Burgundy wines changed in the last twenty years?

There is a good deal of debate about this in the wine industry. I would have to answer, Yes, it has indeed changed. Winemakers used to make Burgundies to last longer. In fact, you couldn't drink a Burgundy for several years if you wanted to get the fullest flavor. It simply wasn't ready. Today the winemakers of Burgundy are complying with consumer demand for Burgundy they can drink earlier. In America, it seems no one has the patience to wait. A compromise had to be made, however, and that is in the body. Many wines are lighter in style and they can be consumed just a few years after the vintage.

Why are the well-known great Burgundies so expensive?

The answer is simple: supply and demand. The Burgundy growers and shippers of the Côte d'Or have a problem all business people would envy—not enough supply to meet the demand. It has been this way for years and it will continue, because Burgundy is a small region that produces a limited amount of wine. The Bordeaux wine region produces three times as much wine as Burgundy does.

BURGUNDY WINE HARVEST

(average number of cases over a five-year period for red and white)

Regional Appellations	2,136,674
Beaujolais	11,503,617
Côte Châlonnaise	357,539
Côte d'Or (Côte de Nuits)	511,594
Côte d'Or (Côte de Beaune)	1,391,168
Chablis	755,188
Mâconnais	2,136,674
Other Appellations	339,710
Total Burgundy Harvest	19,132,164 cases

BEST BETS FOR RECENT VINTAGES OF CÔTE D'OR

1996*   1997*   1999*   2000
         2002*   2003

*Note: * signifies exceptional vintage*

IN THE 1960s, Burgundy wines were fermented and vatted for up to three weeks. Today's Burgundy wines are usually fermented and vatted for six to twelve days.

SLEEPY HOLLOW

There is a village in Westchester County, New York, called Sleepy Hollow. It was originally called North Tarrytown, but the locals, trying to capitalize on "The Legend of Sleepy Hollow" for tourism, changed its name.

And so it is with some villages in Burgundy, as they have added the name of their most famous vineyard to the name of the village. For example, the village of Gevrey became Gevrey-Chambertin, and the village of Puligny became Puligny-Montrachet. Can you figure out the others?

IT'S THE LAW!

Beginning with the 1990 vintage, all Grand Cru Burgundies must include the words "Grand Cru" on the label.

IF YOU don't want to be disappointed by the Burgundy wine you select, make sure you know your vintages. Also, due to the delicacy of the Pinot Noir grape, red Burgundies require proper storage, so make sure you buy from a merchant who handles Burgundy wines with care.

ROBERT DROUHIN states that the 1999 vintage for red Burgundy "is one of the greatest vintages I've ever known."

HOW IMPORTANT is the producer? Clos Vougeot is the single largest Grand Cru vineyard in Burgundy, totaling 125 acres, with 70 different owners. Each owner makes his own winemaking decisions, such as when to pick the grapes, the style of fermentation, and how much oak aging. Obviously, all Clos Vougeot is not created equal.

Who are the most important shippers to look for when buying red Burgundy wine?

BOUCHARD PÈRE ET FILS   **LOUIS JADOT**
JOSEPH DROUHIN   **LOUIS LATOUR**
JAFFELIN   **LABOURÉ-ROI**

Although 80 percent of Burgundy wine is sold through shippers, some fine estate-bottled wines are available in limited quantities in the United States. Look for the following

DOMAINE CLERGET   **DOMAINE JEAN GRIVOT**
DOMAINE COMTE DE VOGÜE   **DOMAINE LEROY**
DOMAINE DANIEL RION   **DOMAINE LOUIS TRAPET**
DOMAINE DE LA ROMANÉE-CONTI   **DOMAINE MONGEARD-MUGNERET**
DOMAINE DUJAC   **DOMAINE PARENT**
DOMAINE GEORGES ROUMIER   **DOMAINE PIERRE DAMOY**
DOMAINE GROFFIER   **DOMAINE POUSSE D'OR**
DOMAINE HENRI GOUGES   **DOMAINE PRINCE DE MÉRODE**
DOMAINE HENRI LAMARCHE   **DOMAINE TOLLOT-BEAUT**
DOMAINE JAYER   **MAISON FAIVELEY**

FOR FURTHER READING

I recommend *Côte d'Or* by Clive Coates; *Burgundy* by Anthony Hanson; *Making Sense of Burgundy* by Matt Kramer; *The Great Domaines of Burgundy* by Remington Norman; and *Burgundy* by Robert M. Parker Jr.

WINE AND FOOD

To get the most flavor from both the wine and the food, some of Burgundy's famous winemakers offer these suggestions:

ROBERT DROUHIN: *"In my opinion, white wine is never a good accompaniment to red meat, but a light red Burgundy can match a fish course (not shellfish). Otherwise, for light red Burgundies, white meat—not too many spices; partridge, pheasant, and rabbit. For heavier-style wines, lamb and steak are good choices." Personally, Mr.*

Drouhin does not enjoy red Burgundies with cheese—especially goat cheese.

PIERRE HENRY GAGEY *(Louis Jadot): "With red Beaujolais wines, such as Moulin-á-Vent Château des Jacques, for example, a piece of pork like an andouillette from Fleury is beautiful. A Gamay, more fruity and fleshy than Pinot Noir, goes perfectly with this typical meal from our terroir. My favorite food combination with a red Burgundy wine is poulet de bresse*

demi d'oeil. The very thin flesh of this truffle-filled chicken and the elegance and delicacy from the great Pinot Noir, which come from the best terroir, go together beautifully."

LOUIS LATOUR: *"With Château Corton Grancey, filet of duck in a red wine sauce. Otherwise, Pinot Noir is good with roast chicken, venison, and beef. Mature wines are a perfect combination for our local cheeses, Chambertin and Citeaux."*

THE RED WINES OF THE RHÔNE VALLEY

As a former sommelier, I was often asked to recommend a big, robust red Burgundy wine to complement a rack of lamb or filet mignon. To the customers' surprise, I don't recommend a Burgundy at all. Their best bet is a Rhône wine, which is typically a bigger and fuller wine than one from Burgundy, and which usually has a higher alcoholic content. The reason is quite simple. It all goes back to location and geography.

Where's the Rhône Valley?

The Rhône Valley is in southeastern France, south of the Burgundy region, where the climate is hot and the conditions are sunny. The extra sun gives the grapes more sugar, which, as we have discussed, boosts the level of alcohol. The soil is full of rocks that retain the intense summer heat during both day and night.

Winemakers of the Rhône Valley are required by law to make sure their wines have a specified amount of alcohol. For example, the minimum alcoholic content required by the AOC is 10.5 percent for Côtes du Rhône and 12.5 percent for Châteauneuf-du-Pape.

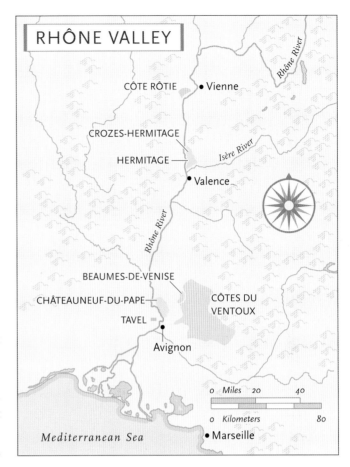

OF ALL the wines made in the Rhône Valley, 91% are red, 6% are rosé, and 3% are white.

SOME OF the oldest vineyards in France are in the Rhône Valley. Hermitage, for example, has been in existence for more than 2,000 years.

CÔTES DU RHÔNE wine can be produced from grapes grown in either or both the northern and southern Rhône regions.

What are the different quality levels of the Rhône Valley?

	% of Production
1. Côtes du Rhône ($)	58%
2. Côtes du Rhône Villages ($$)	8%
3. Côtes du Rhône Crus (specific regions) ($$$$)	10%
4. Other appellations	24%

MORE THAN 90% of all Côtes du Rhône wines come from the southern region.

TWO OTHER important red grapes in the Rhône Valley are:
  Cinsault
  Mourvèdre

THE 13 CRUS OF THE RHONE VALLEY

North
  Chateau-Grillet
  Condrieu
  Cornas
  Côte-Rotie
  Crozes-Hermitage
  Hermitage
  St-Joseph
  St-Peray
South
  Chateauneuf-du-Pape
  Gigondas
  Lirac
  Tavel
  Vacqueyras

What are the winemaking regions in the Rhône Valley?

The region is divided into two distinct areas: northern and southern Rhône. The most famous red wines that come from the northern region are:

HERMITAGE
CROZES-HERMITAGE
CÔTE RÔTIE

The most famous red wines from the southern region are **Châteauneuf-du-Pape** and **Gigondas**, one of the best French rosés is called **Tavel**.

Two distinct microclimates separate the north from the south. It is important for you to understand that these areas make distinctly different wines because of:

- Soil
- Location
- Different grape varieties used in making the wines of each area.

What are the main red-grape varieties used in the Rhône Valley?

The two major grape varieties in the Rhône Valley are:

GRENACHE
SYRAH

Which wines are made from these grapes?

The Côte Rôtie, Hermitage, and Crozes-Hermitage from the north are made primarily from the Syrah grape. These are the biggest and fullest wines from that region.

For Châteauneuf-du-Pape, as many as thirteen different grape varieties may be included in the blend. But the best producers use a greater percentage of Grenache and Syrah in the blend.

What's Tavel?

It's a rosé—an unusually dry rosé, which distinguishes it from most others. It's made primarily from the Grenache grape, although nine grape varieties can be used in the blend. When you come right down to it, Tavel is just like a red wine, with all the red wine components but less color. How do they make a rosé wine with red-wine characteristics but less color? It's all in the vatting process.

What's the difference between "short-vatted" and "long-vatted" wines?

When a wine is "short-vatted," the skins are allowed to ferment with the must (grape juice) for a short period of time—only long enough to impart that rosé color. It's just the opposite when a winemaker is producing red Rhône wines, such as Châteauneuf-du-Pape or Hermitage. The grape skins are allowed to ferment longer with the must, giving a rich, ruby color to the wine.

What's the difference between a $20 bottle of Châteauneuf-du-Pape and a $50 bottle of Châteauneuf-du-Pape?

A winemaker is permitted to use thirteen different grapes for his Châteauneuf-du-Pape recipe, as I mentioned earlier. It's only logical, then, that the winemaker who uses a lot of the best grapes (which is equivalent to cooking with the finest ingredients) will produce the best tasting—and the most expensive—wine.

For example, a twenty-dollar bottle of Châteauneuf-du-Pape may contain only 20 percent of top-quality grapes (Grenache, Mourvèdre, Syrah, and Cinsault) and 80 percent of lesser-quality grapes; a fifty-dollar bottle may contain 90 percent of the top-quality grapes and 10 percent of others.

BEST BETS FOR RED RHÔNE VALLEY WINES

North:	1995*	1996	1997*	1998*	1999*
	2000	2001	2003*	2004	
South:	1995*	1998*	1999	2000*	2001*
		2003*	2004		

Note: * signifies exceptional vintage

RHÔNE VALLEY vintages can be tricky: A good year in the north may be a bad year in the south, and vice versa.

OLDER GREAT VINTAGES

North: 1983, 1985, 1988, 1989, 1990, 1991
South: 1985, 1988, 1989, 1990

How do I buy a red Rhône wine?

You should first decide if you prefer a light Côtes du Rhône wine or a bigger, more flavorful one, such as an Hermitage. Then you must consider the vintage and the producer. Two of the oldest and best-known firms are M. Chapoutier and Paul Jaboulet Aîné. The wines of Guigal, Chave, Beaucastel, Domaine du Vieux Télégraphe, and Château Rayas are harder to find, but worth the search.

A SIMPLE Côtes du Rhône is similar to a Beaujolais—except the Côtes du Rhône has more body and alcohol. A Beaujolais, by AOC standards, must contain a minimum of 9% alcohol; a Côtes du Rhône, 10.5%.

TRIVIA QUESTION: What are the 13 grapes allowed in Châteauneuf-du-Pape?

Grenache	Vaccarèse
Syrah	Picardin
Mourvèdre	Cinsault
Picpoul	Clairette
Terret	Roussanne
Counoise	Bourboulenc
Muscardin	

THERE IS no official classification for Rhône Valley wines.

SUNSHINE QUOTIENT

	(hours per year)
Burgundy	2,000
Bordeaux	2,050
Chateauneuf-du-Pape	2,750

THE PAPAL coat of arms from medieval times appears on some Châteauneuf-du-Pape bottles. Only owners of vineyards are permitted to use this coat of arms on the label.

When should I drink my Rhône wine?

Tavel: Within two years.

Côtes du Rhône: Within three years.

Crozes-Hermitage: Within five years.

Châteauneuf-du-Pape: After five years, but higher-quality Châteauneuf-du-Pape is better at ten years.

Hermitage: Seven to eight years, but best at fifteen, in a great year.

RHÔNE VALLEY HARVEST

(average number of cases over a five-year period)

Côtes du Rhône regional appellation	18.8 million
Northern and southern Crus	2.6 million
Côtes du Rhône-Villages appellation	1.6 million
Total Rhône Valley harvest	23.0 million cases

THE RED RHÔNE VALLEY ROUNDUP

NORTHERN WINES	SOUTHERN WINES
Côte Rôtie	Châteauneuf-du-Pape
Hermitage	Tavel
Crozes-Hermitage	Côtes du Rhône
St. Joseph	Côtes du Rhône-Villages
Cornas	Côtes du Ventoux
	Gigondas

GRAPE	MAJOR GRAPES
Syrah	Grenache
	Syrah
	Cinsault
	Mourvèdre

WINE AND FOOD

JEAN PIERRE AND FRANÇOIS PERRIN *(Château de Beaucastel and La Vieille Ferme)*: *"The white wines of Château de Beaucastel can be drunk either very young—in the first three or four years—or should be kept for ten years or more. The combination of white meat with truffles and mushrooms is an exquisite possibility.*

"Red Rhône wines achieve their perfection from ten years and beyond, and are best when combined with game and other meats with a strong flavor.

"A good dinner could be wild mushroom soup and truffles with a white Beaucastel and stew of wild hare á la royale (with foie gras and truffles) served with a red Château de Beaucastel."

MICHEL CHAPOUTIER: *With a Côtes du Rhône wine, he recommends poultry, light meats, and cheese. Côte Rôtie goes well with white meats and small game. Châteauneuf-du-Pape complements the ripest of cheese, the richest venison, and the most lavish civet of wild boar. An Hermitage is suitable with beef, game, and any full-flavored cheese. Tavel rosé is excellent with white meat and poultry.*

FRÉDÉRIC JABOULET: *"My granddad drinks a bottle of Côtes du Rhône a day and he's in his eighties. It's good for youth. It goes with everything except old fish," he jokes.*

More specifically, *Mr. Jaboulet says, "Hermitage is good with wild boar and mushrooms. A Crozes Hermitage, particularly our Domaine de Thalabert, complements venison or roast rabbit in a cream sauce, but you have to be very careful with the sauce and the weight of the wine.*

"Beef ribs and rice go well with a Côtes du Rhône, as does a game bird like roast quail. Tavel, slightly chilled, is refreshing with a summer salad. Muscat de Beaumes-de-Venise, of course, is a beautiful match with foie gras."

HERMITAGE IS the best and the longest-lived of the Rhône wines. In a great vintage, Hermitage wines can last for fifty years.

U.S. IMPORTS of Rhône wines have risen over 200% in the last five years.

THE TWO most famous white wines of the Rhône Valley are called Condrieu and Château Grillet. Both are made from the grape variety called Viognier.

THERE IS a white Châteauneuf-du-Pape and a white Hermitage, but only a few thousand cases are produced each year.

CHÂTEAUNEUF-DU-PAPE means "new castle of the Pope," so named for the palace in the Rhône city of Avignon in which Pope Clément V (the first French pope) resided in the 14th century.

A GOOD VALUE is Côtes du Ventoux. One of the most widely available wines to look for in this category is La Vieille Ferme.

FOR THOSE who prefer sweet wines, try Beaumes-de-Venise, made from the Muscat grape.

The Red Wines of Bordeaux

APPELLATIONS • GRAPE VARIETIES • QUALITY LEVELS •

THE GREAT RED WINES OF BORDEAUX • MÉDOC • GRAVES •

POMEROL • ST-ÉMILION • CHOOSING A RED BORDEAUX

A cellar at Château Mouton-Rothschild
(Charles O'Rear/Corbis)

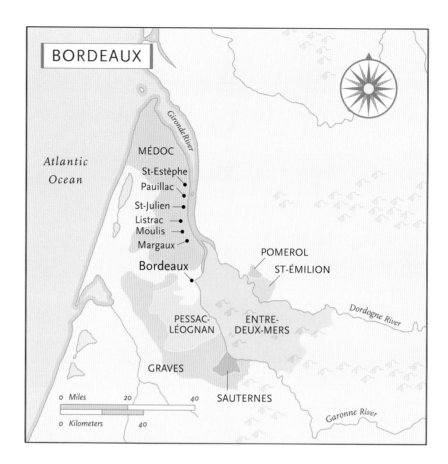

BORDEAUX

Atlantic Ocean

Gironde River

MÉDOC
St-Estèphe
Pauillac
St-Julien
Listrac
Moulis
Margaux

Bordeaux

POMEROL
ST-ÉMILION

PESSAC-LÉOGNAN

ENTRE-DEUX-MERS

Dordogne River

GRAVES

SAUTERNES

Garonne River

o Miles   20   40

o Kilometers   40

BORDEAUX IS much larger in acreage than Burgundy.

THE ENGLISH word *claret* refers to dry red wines from Bordeaux.

OF ALL the AOC wines of France, 25% come from the Bordeaux region.

IN DOLLAR value, the United States is the fourth largest importer of Bordeaux wines.

TODAY, 84% OF Bordeaux wine is red and 16% is white.

UNTIL 1970, BORDEAUX regularly produced more white wine than red.

The Red Wines of Bordeaux

T HIS PROVINCE OF FRANCE is rich with excitement and history, and the best part is that the wines speak for themselves. You'll find this region much easier to learn about than Burgundy. For one thing, the plots of land are bigger, and they're owned by fewer landholders. And, as Samuel Johnson once said, "He who aspires to be a serious wine drinker must drink claret."

Some fifty-seven wine regions in Bordeaux produce high-quality wine that enables them to carry the AOC designation on the label. Of these fifty-seven places, four stand out in my mind for red wine:

Médoc: 40,199 acres (produces only red wines)

Pomerol: 1,846 acres (produces only red wines)

Graves/Pessac-Léognan: 9,855 acres (produces both red and dry white wines)

St-Émilion: 23,384 acres (produces only red wines)

In the Médoc, there are seven important inner appellations you should be familiar with:

HAUT MÉDOC   ST-ESTÈPHE   PAUILLAC   ST-JULIEN

MARGAUX   MOULIS   LISTRAC

Which grape varieties are grown in Bordeaux?

The three major grapes are:

Merlot

Cabernet Sauvignon

Cabernet Franc

Unlike Burgundy, where the winemaker must use 100 percent Pinot Noir to make most red wines (100 percent Gamay for Beaujolais), in Bordeaux the red wines are almost always made from a blend of grapes.

What are the different quality levels of Bordeaux wine?

Bordeaux ($): This is the lowest level of AOC wine in Bordeaux—wines that are nice, inexpensive, and consistent "drinking" wines. These are sometimes known as "proprietary" wines—wines known by what you could almost call a brand name, such as Mouton-Cadet, rather than by the particular region or vineyard. These are usually the least expensive AOC wines in Bordeaux.

Bordeaux + Region ($$): Regional wines come from one of the fifty-seven different regions. Only grapes and wines made in those areas can be called by their regional names: Pauillac and St-Émilion, for example. These wines are more expensive than those labeled simply Bordeaux.

Bordeaux + Region + Château ($$–$$$$): Château wines are the products of individual vineyards. There are more than seven thousand châteaus in Bordeaux. As far back as 1855, Bordeaux officially classified the quality levels of some of its châteaus. Hundreds have been officially recognized for their quality. In the Médoc, for example, the sixty-one highest-level châteaus are called Grand Cru Classé. There are also 247 châteaus in the Médoc that are entitled to be called Cru Bourgeois, a step below Grand Cru Classé. Other areas, such as St-Émilion and Graves, have their own classification systems.

THE GRAVES region produces 60% red wine, 40% white wine.

IN 1987, A communal appellation was established to create a higher-level appellation in the northern Graves region. It's called Pessac-Léognan (for both reds and whites).

TAKE A LOOK at the map on page 108. As a general rule of thumb, red wines from the villages and regions on the left bank of the rivers primarily use the Cabernet Sauvignon grape and on the right bank they use Merlot.

IN ALL of Bordeaux, there are some 99,000 acres of Merlot, 62,000 acres of Cabernet Sauvignon, and 32,000 acres of Cabernet Franc.

TWO OTHER grapes that are sometimes used in the blending of Bordeaux wines are Petit Verdot and Malbec.

PROPRIETARY WINES you may be familiar with:

Lauretan	Mouton-Cadet
Maître d'Estournel	Baron Philippe
Lacour Pavillon	Michel Lynch

THE MAJOR shippers of regional wines from Bordeaux are:

Barton & Guestier (B & G)
Cordier
Dourthe Kressmann
Eschenauer
Sichel
Yvon Mau
Ets J-P Moueix
Baron Philippe de Rothschild
Borie-Manoux
Dulong

BORDEAUX (PROPRIETARY)	REGIONAL	CHÂTEAU

THE MÉDOC blend is 60% to 80% Cabernet Sauvignon, 25% to 40% Merlot, and 10% Cabernet Franc.

All three of these wines are owned by the same family, the Rothschilds, who also own Château Mouton-Rothschild.

IF YOU see a château on the label, French law dictates that a château really exists. What you see is what you get.

ACCORDING TO French law, a château is a house attached to a vineyard having a specific number of acres, as well as having winemaking and storage facilities on the property. A wine may not be called a château wine unless it meets these criteria. The terms *domaine*, *clos*, and *cru* are also used.

Here are the major Bordeaux classifications:

Médoc (Grands Crus Classés): 1855; sixty-one châteaus
Médoc (Crus Bourgeois): 1920, revised 1932, 1978, and 2003; 247 châteaus
Graves (Grands Crus Classés): 1959; sixteen châteaus
Pomerol: No official classification
St-Émilion: 1955, revised 1996; thirteen Premiers Grands Crus Classés and fifty-five Grands Crus Classés.

What is a château?

When most people think of a château, they picture a grandiose home filled with Persian rugs and valuable antiques and surrounded by rolling hills of vineyards. Well, I'm sorry to shatter your dreams, but most châteaus are not like that at all. Yes, a château could be a mansion on a large estate, but it could also be a modest home with a two-car garage.

Château wines are usually considered the best quality wines from Bordeaux. They are the most expensive wines; some examples of the best known of the Grand Cru Classé command the highest wine prices in the world!

Let's take a closer look at the châteaus. One fact I've learned from my years of teaching wine is that no one wants to memorize the names of thousands of châteaus, so I'll shorten the list by starting with the most important classification in Bordeaux.

THE GREAT RED WINES OF BORDEAUX

MÉDOC: GRAND CRU CLASSÉ, 1855; 61 CHÂTEAUS

When and how were the château wines classified?

One hundred fifty years ago in the Médoc region of Bordeaux, a wine classification was established. Brokers from the wine industry were asked by Napoleon III to select the best wines to represent France in the International Exposition of 1855. The top Médoc wines were ranked according to price, which at that time was directly related to quality. (After all, don't we class everything, from cars to restaurants?) The brokers agreed, provided the classification would never become official. Voilà! Refer to the chart on the opposite page for the Official Classification of 1855.

Is the 1855 classification still in use today?

Every wine person knows about the 1855 classification, but much has changed over the last 150 years. Some vineyards have doubled or tripled their production by buying up their neighbors' land, which is permitted by law. Obviously the chateaus have seen many changes of ownership. And, like all businesses, Bordeaux has seen good times and bad times.

A case in point was in the early 1970s, when Bordeaux wines were having a difficult time financially, even at the highest level. At Château Margaux, the well-known first-growth vineyard, the quality of the wine fell off from its traditional excellence for a while when the family that owned the château wasn't putting enough money and time into the vineyard. In 1977, Château Margaux was sold to a Greek-French family (named Mentzelopoulos) for $16 million, and since then the quality of the wine has risen even beyond its first-growth standards.

Château Gloria, in the commune of St-Julien, is an example of a vineyard that didn't exist at the time of the 1855 classification. The late mayor of St-Julien, Henri Martin, bought many parcels of second-growth vineyards. As a result, he produced top-quality wine that is not included in the 1855 classification.

It's also important to consider the techniques used to make wine today. They're a lot different from those used in 1855. Once again, the outcome is better wine. As you can see, some of the châteaus listed in the 1855 classification deserve a lesser ranking, while others deserve a better one.

That said, I believe, even on its 150th anniversary, in most cases it is still a very valid classification in terms of quality and price.

DON'T BE misled by the term *growth*. It might make the concept easier to understand if you substitute the word *classification*. Instead of saying a wine is first growth, you could say, "first classification."

"For a given vintage there is quite a consistent ratio between the prices of the different classes, which is of considerable help to the trade. So a fifth growth would always sell at about half the price of a second. The thirds and fourths would get prices halfway between the seconds and the fifths. The first growths are getting about 25% over the second growths."
—CH. COCKS, Bordeaux et Ses Vins, *1868*

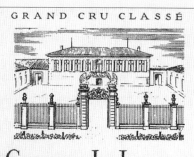

GRAND CRU CLASSÉ

CHATEAU LA LAGUNE
HAUT·MÉDOC
APPELLATION HAUT·MÉDOC CONTROLÉE
1995

SOCIÉTÉ CIVILE AGRICOLE DU CHATEAU LA LAGUNE
PROPRIÉTAIRE A LUDON (GIRONDE) FRANCE

PRODUCE OF FRANCE
MIS EN BOUTEILLE AU CHATEAU

GRAND VIN
DE
CHATEAU LATOUR
PREMIER GRAND CRU CLASSÉ
PAUILLAC
1993

12.5 % Vol.   750 ml

DÉPOSÉ   APPELLATION PAUILLAC CONTRÔLÉE
STE CIVILE DU VIGNOBLE DE CHATEAU LATOUR, PROPRIÉTAIRE A PAUILLAC (GIRONDE) LG 93

Château
Prieuré-Lichine
GRAND CRU CLASSÉ
1996

MARGAUX
APPELLATION MARGAUX CONTROLÉE
MIS EN BOUTEILLE AU CHATEAU
S.A. CHATEAU PRIEURÉ-LICHINE PROPRIÉTAIRE A CANTENAC · FRANCE
12.5% vol.   Cette bouteille porte le   N° Lr 249072   750 ml

1990
CHATEAU DUCRU-BEAUCAILLOU
GRAND CRU CLASSÉ DE MÉDOC EN 1855

SAINT·JULIEN

12.5% Vol.   750 ml
L.90.DB   APPELLATION SAINT-JULIEN CONTRÔLÉE
JEAN-EUGÈNE BORIE PROPRIÉTAIRE A SAINT-JULIEN-BEYCHEVELLE (GIRONDE)   PRODUCE OF FRANCE

MIS EN BOUTEILLE AU CHATEAU
CHATEAU MARGAUX
GRAND VIN

1995
PREMIER GRAND CRU CLASSÉ
MARGAUX
12.5%vol.   75 cl
APPELLATION MARGAUX CONTRÔLÉE
S.C.A. CHATEAU MARGAUX PROPRIÉTAIRE A MARGAUX · FRANCE

GRAND VIN

CHATEAU
LYNCH · BAGES
GRAND CRU CLASSÉ
PAUILLAC
1995   300cl
APPELLATION PAUILLAC CONTROLÉE
A. CAGES Propriétaire à PAUILLAC (Gironde)   13%

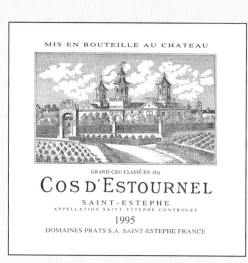

MIS EN BOUTEILLE AU CHATEAU

GRAND CRU CLASSÉ EN 1855
COS D'ESTOURNEL
SAINT·ESTEPHE
APPELLATION SAINT-ESTEPHE CONTROLEE
1995
DOMAINES PRATS S.A. SAINT-ESTEPHE FRANCE

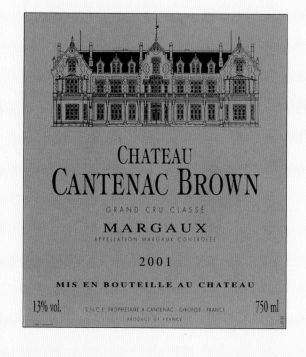

CHATEAU
CANTENAC BROWN
GRAND CRU CLASSÉ
MARGAUX
APPELLATION MARGAUX CONTROLÉE

2001
MIS EN BOUTEILLE AU CHATEAU

13% vol.   S.N.C.E. PROPRIÉTAIRE A CANTENAC · GIRONDE · FRANCE   750 ml
PRODUCE OF FRANCE

The Official (1855) Classification of the Great Red Wines of Bordeaux

THE MÉDOC

FIRST GROWTHS—PREMIERS CRUS (5)

Vineyard	AOC
Château Lafite-Rothschild	Pauillac
Château Latour	Pauillac
Château Margaux	Margaux
Château Haut-Brion	Pessac-Léognan (Graves)
Château Mouton-Rothschild	Pauillac

SECOND GROWTHS—DEUXIÈMES CRUS (14)

Vineyard	AOC
Château Rausan-Ségla	Margaux
Château Rausan Gassies	Margaux
Château Léoville-Las-Cases	St-Julien
Château Léoville-Poyferré	St-Julien
Château Léoville-Barton	St-Julien
Château Durfort-Vivens	Margaux
Château Lascombes	Margaux
Château Gruaud-Larose	St-Julien
Château Brane-Cantenac	Margaux
Château Pichon-Longueville-Baron	Pauillac
Château Pichon-Longueville-Lalande	Pauillac
Château Ducru-Beaucaillou	St-Julien
Château Cos d'Estournel	St-Estèphe
Château Montrose	St-Estèphe

THIRD GROWTHS—TROISIÈMES CRUS (14)

Vineyard	AOC
Château Giscours	Margaux
Château Kirwan	Margaux
Château d'Issan	Margaux
Château Lagrange	St-Julien
Château Langoa-Barton	St-Julien
Château Malescot-St-Exupéry	Margaux
Château Cantenac-Brown	Margaux
Château Palmer	Margaux
Château La Lagune	Haut-Médoc
Château Desmirail	Margaux
Château Calon-Ségur	St-Estèphe
Château Ferrière	Margaux
Château d'Alesme (formerly Marquis d'Alesme)	Margaux
Château Boyd-Cantenac	Margaux

FOURTH GROWTHS—QUATRIÈMES CRUS (10)

Vineyard	AOC
Château St-Pierre	St-Julien
Château Branaire-Ducru	St-Julien
Château Talbot	St-Julien
Château Duhart-Milon-Rothschild	Pauillac
Château Pouget	Margaux
Château La Tour-Carnet	Haut-Médoc
Château Lafon-Rochet	St-Estèphe
Château Beychevelle	St-Julien
Château Prieuré-Lichine	Margaux
Château Marquis de Terme	Margaux

FIFTH GROWTHS—CINQUIÈMES CRUS (18)

Vineyard	AOC
Château Pontet-Canet	Pauillac
Château Batailley	Pauillac
Château Grand-Puy-Lacoste	Pauillac
Château Grand-Puy-Ducasse	Pauillac
Château Haut-Batailley	Pauillac
Château Lynch-Bages	Pauillac
Château Lynch-Moussas	Pauillac
Château Dauzac	Haut-Médoc
Château d'Armailhac (called Château Mouton-Baron-Philippe from 1956 to 1988)	Pauillac
Château du Tertre	Margaux
Château Haut-Bages-Libéral	Pauillac
Château Pédesclaux	Pauillac
Château Belgrave	Haut-Médoc
Château Camensac	Haut-Médoc
Château Cos Labory	St-Estèphe
Château Clerc-Milon-Rothschild	Pauillac
Château Croizet Bages	Pauillac
Château Cantemerle	Haut-Médoc

ON THE 1945 Mouton-Rothschild bottle there is a big V that stands for "victory" and the end of World War II. Since 1924, Philippe de Rothschild asked a different artist to design his labels, a tradition continued by the Baroness Philippine, his daughter. Some of the most famous artists in the world have agreed to have their work grace the Mouton label, including:

Jean Cocteau—1947
Salvador Dalí—1958
Henry Moore—1964
Joan Miró—1969
Marc Chagall—1970
Pablo Picasso—1973
Robert Motherwell—1974
Andy Warhol—1975
John Huston—1982
Saul Steinberg—1983
Keith Haring—1988
Francis Bacon—1990
Setsuko—1991
Antoni Tàpies—1995
Gu Gan—1996

"The classified growths are divided in five classes and the price difference from one class to another is about 12 percent." —WILLIAM FRANK, Traité Sur Les Vins du Médoc, *1855*

HAVE THERE EVER BEEN ANY CHANGES IN THE 1855 CLASSIFICATION?

Yes, but only once, in 1973. Château Mouton-Rothschild was elevated from a second-growth to a first-growth vineyard. There's a little story behind that.

EXCEPTION TO THE RULE . . .

In 1920, when the Baron Philippe de Rothschild took over the family vineyard, he couldn't accept the fact that back in 1855 his château had been rated a second growth. He thought it should have been classed a first growth from the beginning—and he fought to get to the top for some fifty years. While the baron's wine was classified as a second growth, his motto was:

First, I cannot be.
Second, I do not deign to be.
Mouton, I am.

When his wine was elevated to a first growth in 1973, Rothschild replaced the motto with a new one:

First, I am.
Second, I was.
But Mouton does not change.

PABLO PICASSO, 1973

Is there an easier way to understand the 1855 classification?

I've always found the 1855 classification to be a little cumbersome, so one day I sat down and drew up my own chart. I separated the classification into growths (first, second, third, etc.) and then I listed the communes (Pauillac, Margaux, St-Julien, etc.) and set down the number of distinctive vineyards in each one. My chart shows which communes of Bordeaux have the most first growths—all the way down to fifth growths. It also shows which commune corners the market on all growths. Since I was inspired to figure this out during baseball's World Series, I call my chart a box score of the 1855 classification.

KEVIN ZRALY'S BOX SCORE OF THE 1855 CLASSIFICATION

Commune	1st	2nd	3rd	4th	5th	Total
Margaux	1	5	10	3	2	21
Pauillac	3	2	0	1	12	18
St-Julien	0	5	2	4	0	11
St-Estèphe	0	2	1	1	1	5
Haut-Médoc	0	0	1	1	3	5
Graves	1	0	0	0	0	1
Total Châteaus	5	14	14	10	18	61

A quick glance at my box score gives you some instant facts that may guide you when you want to buy a Bordeaux wine from Médoc.

Tallying the score, Pauillac has three of the five first growths. Margaux practically clean-sweeps the third growths. In fact, Margaux is the overall winner, because it has the greatest number of classed vineyards in all of Médoc. Margaux is also the only area to have a château rated in each category. St-Julien has no first or fifth growths, but is very strong in the second and fourth.

CRU BOURGEOIS:
1920, REVISED 1932, 1978, AND 2003; 247 CHÂTEAUS

What does *Cru Bourgeois* mean?

The Crus Bourgeois of the Médoc are châteaus that were originally classified in 1920, and not in the 1855 classification. In 1932 there were 444 properties listed, but by 1962 there were only 94 members. Today there are 247. The latest classification of Crus Bourgeois of the Médoc and Haut-Médoc was in 2003. Because of the high quality of the 1995, 1996, 2000, 2003, and 2004 vintages, some of the best values in wine today are in the Cru Bourgeois classification.

The following is a partial list of Crus Bourgeois to look for:

CHÂTEAU D'ANGLUDET	CHÂTEAU PATACHE D'AUX
CHÂTEAU LES ORMES-DE-PEZ*	CHÂTEAU LA CARDONNE
CHÂTEAU LES ORMES-SORBET	CHÂTEAU POUJEAUX*
CHÂTEAU PHÉLAN-SÉGUR*	CHÂTEAU SIRAN*
CHÂTEAU COUFRAN	CHÂTEAU DE PEZ*
CHÂTEAU CHASSE-SPLEEN*	CHÂTEAU PONTENSAC*
CHÂTEAU MEYNEY	CHÂTEAU GLORIA
CHÂTEAU SOCIANDO-MALLET	CHÂTEAU PIBRAN
CHÂTEAU FOURCAS-HOSTEN	CHÂTEAU MONBRISON
CHÂTEAU LAROSE-TRINTAUDON	CHÂTEAU VIEUX ROBIN
CHÂTEAU GREYSAC	CHÂTEAU LABÉGORCE-ZÉDÉ*
CHÂTEAU MARBUZET	CHÂTEAU DE LAMARQUE
CHÂTEAU HAUT-MARBUZET*	

= Crus exceptionnels

LAROSE-TRINTAUDON is the largest vineyard in the Médoc area, making nearly 100,000 cases of wine per year.

BEGINNING WITH the 2003 vintage, the Cru Bourgeois classification has now been divided into three levels. It will be reviewed every ten years.

Crus exceptionnels	9
Crus superieurs	87
Cru bourgeois	151
	247

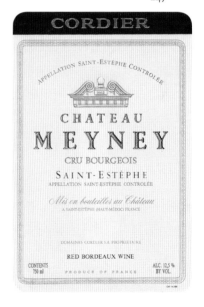

GRAVES (PESSAC-LÉOGNAN): 1959

The most famous château—we have already seen it in the 1855 classification—is Château Haut-Brion. Other good red Graves classified in 1959 as Grands Crus Classés are:

CHÂTEAU BOUSCAUT
CHÂTEAU HAUT-BAILLY
CHÂTEAU CARBONNIEUX
DOMAINE DE CHEVALIER
CHÂTEAU DE FIEUZAL
CHÂTEAU OLIVIER
CHÂTEAU MALARTIC-LAGRAVIÈRE
CHÂTEAU LA TOUR-MARTILLAC
CHÂTEAU SMITH-HAUT-LAFITTE
CHÂTEAU PAPE-CLÉMENT
CHÂTEAU LA MISSION-HAUT-BRION
CHÂTEAU LA TOUR-HAUT-BRION

THE RED wines of Pomerol tend to be softer, fruitier, and ready to be drunk sooner than the Médoc wines.

THE MAJOR grape used to produce wine in the Pomerol region is Merlot. Very little Cabernet Sauvignon is used in these wines.

IT TAKES Château Pétrus one year to make as much wine as Gallo makes in six minutes.

THE VINEYARD at Château Pétrus makes one of the most expensive wines of Bordeaux. It's planted with 95% Merlot.

POMEROL: NO OFFICIAL CLASSIFICATION

This is the smallest of the top red-wine districts in Bordeaux. Pomerol produces only 15 percent as much wine as St-Émilion; as a result, Pomerol wines are relatively scarce. And if you do find them, they'll be expensive. Although no official classification exists, here's a list of some of the finest Pomerols on the market:

CHÂTEAU PÉTRUS
CHÂTEAU LE PIN
CHÂTEAU LA CONSEILLANTE
CHÂTEAU BEAUREGARD
CHÂTEAU PETIT-VILLAGE
CHÂTEAU NÉNIN
CHÂTEAU TROTANOY
CHÂTEAU LATOUR-À-POMEROL
CHÂTEAU L'ÉVANGILE
CHÂTEAU BOURGNEUF
VIEUX CHÂTEAU-CERTAN
CHÂTEAU CLINET
CHÂTEAU LA POINTE
CHÂTEAU L'EGLISE CLINET
CHÂTEAU LAFLEUR
CHÂTEAU PLINCE

CHÂTEAU LA FLEUR-PÉTRUS
CHÂTEAU GAZIN

ST-ÉMILION: 1955, REVISED 1996; THIRTEEN PREMIERS GRANDS CRUS CLASSÉS, FIFTY-FIVE CHÂTEAUS GRANDS CRUS CLASSÉS

This area produces about two-thirds as much wine as the entire Médoc, and it's one of the most beautiful villages in France (in my opinion). The wines of St-Émilion were finally classified officially in 1955, one century after the Médoc classification. There are thirteen first growths comparable to the cru classé wines of the Médoc.

THE THIRTEEN FIRST GROWTHS OF ST-ÉMILION (PREMIERS GRANDS CRUS CLASSÉS)

Château Ausone
Château Cheval Blanc
Château L'Angélus
Château Beau-Séjour-Bécot
Château Beauséjour-
    Duffau-Lagarosse
Château Belair

Château Figeac
Château Canon
Château Magdelaine
Château La Gaffelière
Château Trottevieille
Château Pavie
Clos Fourtet

Important Grands Crus Classés and other St-Émilion wines available in the United States:

Château Canon-La Gaffelière
Château La Tour-Figeac
Château Trimoulet
Château Dassault
Château Monbousquet
Clos des Jacobins
Château Tertre Roteboeuf

Château Troplong Mondot
Château Trotanoy
Château Faugères
Château Pavie Marquin
Château Haut-Corbin
Château Grand-Mayne

THERE ARE 55 St-Émilion châteaus entitled to the Grand Cru Classé designation.

GRAPE VARIETIES OF ST-ÉMILION

Merlot	70%
Cabernet Franc	25%
Cabernet Sauvignon	5%

SOME OTHER appellations to look for in Bordeaux red wines:
    Fronsac
    Côtes de Blaye
    Côtes de Bourg

THE 1999 VINTAGE was the largest harvest ever in Bordeaux.

ABOUT VINTAGES, Alexis Lichine, a noted wine expert, said: "Great vintages take time to mature. Lesser wines mature faster than the greater ones. . . . Patience is needed for great vintages, hence the usefulness and enjoyment of lesser vintages." He summed up: "Often vintages which have a poorer rating—if young—will give a greater enjoyment than a better-rated vintage—if young."

DRINK YOUR lighter vintages such as 1997 and 1999 Bordeaux while you wait patiently for your great vintages such as 2000 to mature.

THE EARLIEST harvest since 1893 was 2003.

THE 2003 VINTAGE suffered summer heat waves, fierce storms, and hail, reducing production to the lowest since 1991.

Now that you know all the greatest red wines of Bordeaux, let me take you a step further and show you some of the best vintages.

BORDEAUX VINTAGES

"LEFT BANK"
MÉDOC/ST-JULIEN/MARGAUX/
PAUILLAC/ST-ESTÈPHE/GRAVES

GOOD VINTAGES	GREAT VINTAGES	OLDER GREAT VINTAGES
1994	1990*	1982*
1997	1995	1985
1998	1996	1986
1999	2000*	1989
2001	2003	
2002	2004	

"RIGHT BANK"
ST-ÉMILION/POMEROL

GOOD VINTAGES	GREAT VINTAGES	OLDER GREAT VINTAGES
1995	1990	1982
1996	1998*	1989
1997	2000*	
1999	2001	
2002	2004	
2003		

*Note: * signifies an exceptional year*

How do I buy—and drink—a red Bordeaux?

One of the biggest misconceptions about Bordeaux wines is that they are all very expensive. In reality, there are more than seven thousand châteaus at all different price ranges.

First and foremost, ask yourself if you want to drink the wine now, or if you want to age it. A great château in a great vintage needs a *minimum* of ten years to age. Going down a level, a Cru Bourgeois or a second label in a great vintage needs a minimum of five years to age. A regional wine may be consumed within two or three years of the vintage year, while a wine labeled simply Appellation Bordeaux Contrôlée is ready to drink as soon as it's released.

The next step is to be sure the vintage is correct for what you want. If you're looking for a wine you want to age, in order to be able to age it you must look for a great vintage. If you want a wine that's ready to drink now and you want a greater château, you should choose a lesser vintage. If you want a wine that's ready to drink now and you want a great vintage, you should look for a lesser château.

Another consideration in buying the red wines of Bordeaux is to remember that Bordeaux wines are a blend. Ask yourself if you're looking for a Merlot-style Bordeaux, such as St-Émilion or Pomerol, or if you're looking for a Cabernet style, such as Médoc or Graves, remembering that the Merlot is more accessible and easier to drink when young.

What separates a $20 red Bordeaux from a $200 red Bordeaux?

- The place the grapes are grown
- The age of the vines (usually the older the vine, the better the wine)
- The yield of the vine (lower yield means higher quality)
- The winemaking technique (for example, how long the wine is aged in wood)
- The vintage

ON DRINKING THE WINES OF BORDEAUX

"The French drink their Bordeaux wines too young, afraid that the Socialist government will take them away.

"The English drink their Bordeaux wines very old, because they like to take their friends down to their wine cellars with the cobwebs and dust to show off their old bottles.

"And the Americans drink their Bordeaux wines exactly when they are ready to be drunk, because they don't know any better."

—AUTHOR UNKNOWN

HAD YOU dined at the Four Seasons restaurant in New York when it first opened in 1959, you could have had a 1918 Château Lafite-Rothschild for $18, or a 1934 Château Latour for $16. Or if those wines were a bit beyond your budget, you could have had a 1945 Château Cos d'Estournel for $9.50.

A BORDEAUX FOR VALENTINE'S DAY:

At one time the Marquis de Ségur owned Château Lafite, Château Latour, and Château Calon-Ségur. He said, "I make my wines at Lafite and Latour, but my heart is at Calon." Hence the label.

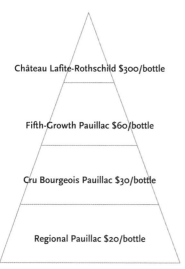

Château Lafite-Rothschild $300/bottle

Fifth-Growth Pauillac $60/bottle

Cru Bourgeois Pauillac $30/bottle

Regional Pauillac $20/bottle

Is it necessary to pay a tremendous sum of money to get a great-tasting red Bordeaux wine?

It's nice if you have it to spend, but sometimes you don't. The best way to get the most for your money is to use what I call the reverse pyramid method. For example: Let's say you like Château Lafite-Rothschild, which is at the top of the pyramid at left ($$$$), but you can't afford it. What do you do? Look at the region. It's from Pauillac. You have a choice: You can go back to the 1855 classification and look for a fifth-growth wine from Pauillac that gives a flavor for the region at a lesser price ($$$), though not necessarily one-fifth the price of a first growth. Still too pricey? Drop a level farther on the inverted pyramid and go for a Cru Bourgeois from Pauillac ($$). Your other option is to buy a regional wine labeled "Pauillac" ($).

I didn't memorize the seven thousand châteaus myself. When I go to my neighborhood retailer, I find a château I've never heard of. If it's from Pauillac, from a good vintage, and it's twenty to twenty-five dollars, I buy it. My chances are good. Everything in wine is hedging your bets.

Another way to avoid skyrocketing Bordeaux châteaus prices is to take the time to look for their second-label wines. These wines are from the youngest parts of the vineyard and are lighter in style and quicker to mature but are usually half the price of the château wine.

Château	Second Label
Château Lafite-Rothschild	Carruades de Lafite Rothschild
Château Latour	Les Forts de Latour
Château Haut-Brion	Bahans du Château Haut-Brion
Château Margaux	Pavillon Rouge du Château Margaux
Château Mouton-Rothschild	Petit Mouton
Château Léoville-Barton	La Réserve de Leoville Barton
Château Léoville-Las-Cases	Clos du Marquis
Château Pichon Lalande	Réserve de la Comtesse
Château Pichon Longueville	Les Tourelles de Pichon
Château Palmer	Réserve du Général
Château Lynch-Bages	Château Haut Bages-Averous

FOR FURTHER READING

I recommend *Grands Vins* by Clive Coates, M.W.; *The Bordeaux Atlas and Encyclopedia of Chateaux* by Hubrecht Duijker and Michael Broadbent; and *Bordeaux* by Robert M. Parker Jr.

WINE AND FOOD

DENISE LURTON-MOULLE (*Château La Louvière, Château Bonnet*): *With Château La Louvière Rouge: roast leg of lamb or grilled duck breast.*

JEAN-MICHEL CAZES (*Château Lynch-Bages, Château Haut-Bages-Averous, Château Les Ormes-de-Pez*): *"For Bordeaux red, simple and classic is best! Red meat, such as beef and particularly lamb, as we love it in Pauillac. If you can grill the meat on vine cuttings, you are in heaven."*

JACQUES AND FIONA THIENPONT (*Château Le Pin*): *Sunday lunches at Le Pin include lots of local oysters with chilled white Bordeaux followed by thick entrecôte steaks on the barbecue with shallots and a selection of the family's Pomerols, Margaux, or Côtes de France red Bordeaux.*

ANTONY PERRIN (*Château Carbonnieux*): *With red Bordeaux: magret de canard (duck breast) with wild mushrooms, or pintade aux raisins (Guinea hen with grapes).*

CHRISTIAN MOUEIX (*Château Pétrus*): *With red Bordeaux, especially Pomerol wine: lamb is a must.*

SINCE 1882, WHEN the venerable French company Guerlain first produced a lip balm containing Bordeaux wine, nursing mothers have used it as a salve for chapped nipples. "It's a wonderfully soothing emollient, and red wine's tannic acid has healing properties," says Elisabeth Sirot, *attaché de presse* at Guerlain's Paris office. "Frenchwomen have always known this secret." Sirot used it when nursing all four of her children (she learned the tip from her own mother). How sensual—especially considering the American alternative is petroleum jelly.

WHILE NAPOLEON BONAPARTE preferred the Burgundy Chambertin, the late president Richard Nixon's favorite wine was Château Margaux. Nixon always had a bottle of his favorite vintage waiting at his table from the cellar of the famous "21" Club in New York.

MIS EN BOUTEILLE AU CHATEAU

CHATEAU LES ORMES DE PEZ

SAINT-ESTÈPHE

1995

13.0%Vol   APPELLATION SAINT-ESTÈPHE CONTRÔLÉE   750ml

A. CAZES, PROPRIETAIRE A SAINT ESTEPHE (FRANCE)

PRODUCE OF FRANCE

The Red Wines of California

RED VS. WHITE • MAJOR RED GRAPES OF CALIFORNIA •

RED-GRAPE BOOM • MERITAGE • STYLES • TRENDS

A Cabernet Sauvignon vineyard in Napa Valley
(Jim Sugar/Corbis)

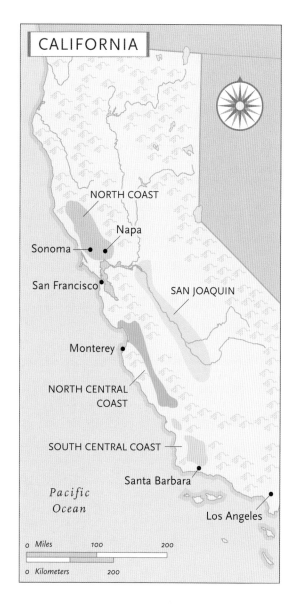

CALIFORNIA

NORTH COAST

Napa

Sonoma

San Francisco

SAN JOAQUIN

Monterey

NORTH CENTRAL COAST

SOUTH CENTRAL COAST

Santa Barbara

Pacific Ocean

Los Angeles

Miles 100 200

Kilometers 200

ACREAGE IN CALIFORNIA

Currently there are 288,262 acres in red grapes and 201,317 in white grapes planted in California.

More About California Wines

SINCE WE'VE ALREADY COVERED THE history and geography of California in Class Two, it might be a good idea to go back and review the main viticultural areas of California wine country on page 67, before you continue with the red wines of California. Then, consider the following question that inevitably comes up in my class at the Windows on the World Wine School.

Are Americans drinking more white wine or red?

The chart below shows you the trend of wine consumption in the United States over the last thirty years. When I first began studying wines in 1970, people were more interested in red wine than white. From the mid-1970s, when I started teaching, into the mid-1990s, my students showed a definite preference for white wine. Fortunately for me (since I am a red wine drinker), the pendulum is surely swinging back to more red wine drinkers.

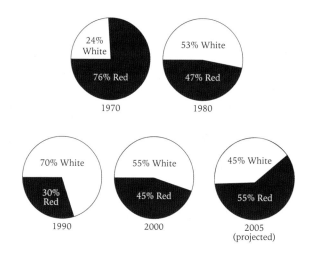

1970 — 24% White / 76% Red
1980 — 53% White / 47% Red
1990 — 70% White / 30% Red
2000 — 55% White / 45% Red
2005 (projected) — 45% White / 55% Red

RED VS. WHITE—CONSUMPTION IN THE UNITED STATES

Why this change?

Looking back at the American obsession with health and fitness in the 1970s and 1980s, many people switched from meat and potatoes to fish and vegetables—a lighter diet that called more for white wine than red. "Chardonnay" became the new buzzword that replaced the call for "a glass of white wine." Bars that never used to stock wine—nothing decent, anyway—began to carry an assortment of fine wines by the glass, with Chardonnay, by far, the best-selling wine. Today, steak is back and the new buzzwords are Cabernet Sauvignon and Merlot.

Another major reason for the dramatic upturn in red wine consumption is the power of the media.

THE FRENCH PARADOX

In the early 1990s, the TV series *60 Minutes* twice aired a report on a phenomenon known as the French Paradox—the fact that the French have a lower rate of heart disease than Americans, despite a diet that's higher in fat. Since the one thing the American diet lacks, in comparison to the French diet, is red wine, some researchers were looking for a link between the consumption of red wine and a decreased rate of heart disease. Not surprisingly, in the year following this report, Americans increased their purchases of red wines by 39 percent.

Finally, perhaps the most important reason that red wine consumption has increased in the United States is that California is producing a much better quality red wine than ever before. One of the reasons for improved quality is the replanting of vines over the last twenty years due to the phylloxera problem. Some analysts thought the replanting would be financially devastating to the California wine industry, but in reality it may have been a blessing in disguise, especially with regard to quality.

The opportunity to replant allowed vineyard owners to increase their red grape production. It enabled California grape growers to utilize the knowledge they have gained over the years with regard to soil, climate, microclimate, trellising, and other viticultural practices.

Bottom line: California reds are already some of the greatest in the world, with more and better to come.

TOP THREE red grapes planted in California:
1. Cabernet Sauvignon
2. Zinfandel
3. Merlot

THERE ARE more than 30 red wine grape varieties planted in California.

CALIFORNIA TOTALS IN 2004

Varietal	Acreage
Chardonnay	95,000
Cabernet	76,000
Merlot	52,000

ACCORDING TO the U.S. Dietary Guidelines:
5 oz. wine = 100 calories
12 oz. beer = 150 calories
1.5 oz. distilled spirits = 100 calories

FROM 1991 TO 2004, sales of red wine in the United States grew by more than 125%.

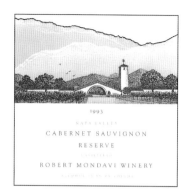

"RESERVE" ON the label has no legal meaning. In other words, there is no law that defines it. Some wineries, such as Beaulieu Vineyards and Robert Mondavi Winery, still mark some of their wines Reserve. BV's Reserve is from a particular vineyard. Mondavi's Reserve is made from a special blend of grapes, presumably their best. Others include Cask wines, Special Selections, or Proprietor's Reserve. The California Wine Institute has proposed a definition of Reserve to meet the requirement by some export markets.

THERE ARE more than 1,000 different California Cabernet Sauvignons available to the consumer.

MOST CABERNET Sauvignons are blended with other grapes, primarily Merlot. To use the grape variety on the label, the winemaker must use at least 75% Cabernet Sauvignon.

THE 1997 VINTAGE was the largest Cabernet Sauvignon harvest ever.

OLDER CABERNET vintages to look for: 1985, 1986, 1987, 1990, and 1991.

CABERNET SAUVIGNON aromas:
Blackberry   Black cherry
Cassis   Eucalyptus

What are the major red grapes in California?

Cabernet Sauvignon: Considered the most successful red grape in California, it yields some of the greatest red wines in the world. Cabernet Sauvignon is the predominant variety used in the finest red Bordeaux wines, such as Château Lafite-Rothschild and Château Latour. Almost all California Cabernets are dry, and depending upon the producer and vintage, they range in style from light and ready to drink, to extremely full-bodied and long-lived. California Cabernet has become the benchmark for some of the best California wines.

My favorite California Cabernet Sauvignons are:

Arrowood	Joseph Phelps
Beaulieu Private Reserve	La Jota
Beringer Private Reserve	Laurel Glen
Cakebread	Mondavi Reserve
Caymus Special Selection	Opus One
Chateau Montelena	Paul Hobbs
Chateau St. Jean, Cinq Cepages	Pine Ridge
Dalla Valle	Pride Mountain
Diamond Creek	Ridge Monte Bello
Duckhorn	Shafer Hillside Select
Dunn Howell Mountain	Silver Oak
Gallo of Sonoma Estate	Spottswood
Groth Reserve	Staglin
Heitz	Stag's Leap Cask
Hess Collection	Whitehall Lane
Jordan	

BEST BETS FOR CABERNET SAUVIGNON

1994*	1995*	1996*	1997*	1999*	2000
	2001*	2002*	2003*	2004	

*Note: * signifies exceptional vintage*

Pinot Noir: Known as the "headache" grape because of its fragile quality, Pinot Noir is temperamental, high-maintenance, expensive, and difficult to grow and make into wine. The great grape of the Burgundy region of France—responsible for such famous wines as Pommard, Nuits-St-Georges, and Gevrey-Chambertin—is also one of the principal grapes in French Champagne. In California, many years of experimentation in finding the right location to plant the Pinot Noir and to perfect the fermentation techniques have elevated some of the Pinot Noirs to the status of great wines. Pinot Noir is usually less tannic than Cabernet and matures more quickly, generally in two to five years. Because of the extra expense involved in growing this grape, the best examples of Pinot Noirs from California may cost more than other varietals.

My favorite California Pinot Noirs are:

Acacia	Marcassin
Artesa	Merry Edwards
Au Bon Climat	Morgan
Calera	Paul Hobbs
Carneros Creek	Robert Mondavi
Cline	Ramey
Dehlinger	J. Rochioli
Etude	Saintsbury
Flowers	Sanford
Gary Farrell	Williams Selyem

BEST BETS FOR PINOT NOIR

1999   2000   2001*   2002*   2003*

*Note: * signifies exceptional vintage*

Napa really is red wine country, with 27,000-plus acres in red grapes versus 11,000 acres in whites. Leading the red grapes is Cabernet Sauvignon, with 14,000 acres, while Chardonnay is king of the whites, with 9,000 acres.
Source: MKF

ONE AUTHOR, trying to sum up the difference between a Pinot Noir and a Cabernet Sauvignon, said, "Pinot is James Joyce, while Cabernet is Dickens. Both sell well, but one is easier to understand."

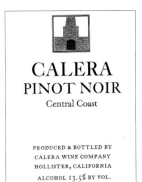

COMMON PINOT NOIR aromas:
Red berries	Red cherry
Leather	Tobacco (older)

SOUTHERN CALIFORNIA—especially the Santa Barbara area, as the characters in *Sideways* could tell you—has become one of the prime locations for Pinot Noir production, with plantings up by more than 200% in the past decade. In fact, Pinot Noir sales overall have increased at least 20% since the film came out.

THE CARNEROS district is one of the better places to grow Pinot Noir because of its cooler climate.

76% ZINFANDEL, 18% CARIGNANE, 6% PETITE SIRAH
SONOMA COUNTY   14.6% ALCOHOL BY VOLUME
PRODUCED & BOTTLED BY RIDGE VINEYARDS, INC.
17100 MONTE BELLO ROAD, BOX 1810, CUPERTINO, CA 95015

RECENT DNA studies have concluded that Zinfandel is the same grape as the Primitivo in Italy.

ONE OF the hottest wines today in terms of popularity is white Zinfandel, which at 35 million cases sold in 2003 far outsells red Zinfandel, and is also the largest-selling varietal wine in the United States.

SOME ZINFANDELS have more than 16% alcohol.

WHICH TURLEY WAS IT?

In the 2002 vintage, Turley winery made 18 different Zinfandels.

MERLOT MADNESS

There were only two acres of Merlot planted in all of California in 1960. Today there are more than 50,000!

COMMON MERLOT aromas:
Blackberry
Cassis
Cherry
Chocolate
Coffee
Oak

Zinfandel: The surprise grape of California, Zinfandel was used to make "generic" or "jug" wines in the early years of California winemaking. Over the past fifteen years, however, it has developed into one of the best red varietal grapes. The only problem in choosing a Zinfandel wine is that so many different styles are made. Depending on the producer, the wines can range from a big, rich, ripe, high-alcohol, spicy, smoky, concentrated, intensely flavored style with substantial tannin, to a very light, fruity wine. And let's not forget white Zinfandel!

My favorite Zinfandels are

Carlisle	J. Rochioli
Cline	Rosenblum
Dry Creek Winery	Roshambo
Fife	Seghesio
Merry Edwards	Signorello
Rafanelli	St. Francis
Ravenswood	Turley
Ridge	

BEST BETS FOR ZINFANDEL

| 1994* | 1995* | 1997* | 1999* |
| 2001 | 2002* | 2003* | 2004 |

*Note: * signifies exceptional vintage*

Merlot: For many years Merlot was thought of as a grape only to be blended with Cabernet Sauvignon, because Merlot's tannins are softer and its texture is more supple. Merlot has now achieved its own identity as a superpremium varietal. Of red-grape varietals in California, Merlot saw the fastest rate of new plantings over the last twenty years. It produces a soft, round wine that generally does not need the same aging as a Cabernet Sauvignon. It is a top seller at restaurants, where its early maturation and compatibility with food make it a frequent choice by consumers.

My favorite Merlots are:

Beringer Howell Mountain	Newton
Chimney Rock	Phelps
Clos du Bois	Pine Ridge
Duckhorn	Pride
Franciscan	Provenance
Havens	St. Francis
Lewis Cellars	Shafer
Markham	Whitehall Lane
Matanzas Creek	

BEST BETS FOR MERLOT

1994* 1997* 1999* 2001*
2002* 2003* 2004

*Note: * signifies exceptional vintage*

Syrah: The up-and-coming red grape in California is definitely Syrah. I don't why it's taken so long, since Syrah has always been one of the major grapes of the Rhône Valley in France, making some of the best and most long-lived wines in the world. Further, the sales of Australian Syrah (which they call Shiraz) have been phenomenal in the United States. Americans like the spicy, robust flavor of this grape. It's a perfect grape for California because it thrives in sunny, warm weather.

My favorite Syrahs are:

Cakebread	Ojai
Clos du Bois	Phelps
Edmunds St. John	Qupe
Fess Parker	Wild Horse
Geyser Park	Zaca Mesa

BEST BETS FOR SYRAH

2002* 2003*

*Note: * signifies exceptional vintage*

SOME EXAMPLES of Meritage wines of California:

Cinq Cepages (Chateau St. Jean)
Dominus (Christian Moueix)
Insignia (Phelps Vineyards)
Magnificat (Franciscan)
Rubicon (Niebaum Coppola Estate)
Opus One (Mondavi/Rothschild)
Cain Five

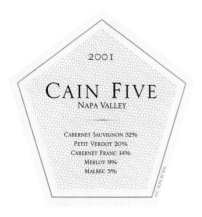

RED-GRAPE BOOM

LOOK AT THE CHART BELOW to see how many acres of the major red grapes were planted in California in 1970, and how those numbers have increased. Rapid expansion has been the characteristic of the California wine industry!

TOTAL BEARING ACREAGE OF RED-WINE GRAPES PLANTED

GRAPE-BY-GRAPE COMPARISON

GRAPE	1970	1980	1990	2004
Cabernet Sauvignon	3,200	21,800	24,100	75,994
Merlot	100	2,600	4,000	52,190
Zinfandel	19,200	27,700	28,000	50,381
Pinot Noir	2,100	9,200	8,600	23,879
Syrah			400	16,054

What are Meritage wines?

Meritage (which rhymes with "heritage") is the name for red and white wines made in America from a blend of the classic Bordeaux wine-grape varieties. This category was created because many winemakers felt stifled by the required minimum amount (75 percent) of a grape that must go into a bottle for it to be named for that variety. Some winemakers knew they could make a better wine with a blend of, say, 60 percent of the major grape and 40 percent of secondary grapes. This blending of grapes allows producers of Meritage wines the same freedom that Bordeaux winemakers have in making their wines.

For red wine, the varieties include Cabernet Sauvignon, Merlot, Cabernet Franc, Petit Verdot, and Malbec. For white wine, the varieties include Sauvignon Blanc and Sémillon.

When I buy a Cabernet, Zinfandel, Merlot, Pinot Noir, Syrah, or Meritage wine, how do I know which style I'm getting? Is the style of the wine indicated on the label?

Unless you just happen to be familiar with a particular vineyard's wine, you're stuck with trial-and-error tastings. You're one step ahead, though, just by knowing that you'll find drastically different styles from the same grape variety.

With some 1,600 wineries in California and more than half of them producing red wines, it is virtually impossible to keep up with the ever-changing

OPUS ONE

Amidst grand hoopla in the wine world, Robert Mondavi and the late Baron Philippe de Rothschild released Opus One. "It isn't Mouton and it isn't Mondavi," said Robert Mondavi. Opus One is a Bordeaux-style blend made from Cabernet Sauvignon, Merlot, and Cabernet Franc grapes grown in Napa Valley. It was originally produced at the Robert Mondavi Winery in Napa Valley, but is now produced across Highway 29 in its own spectacular winery.

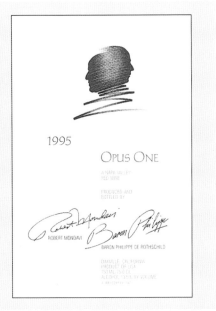

TROPHY HUNTING

Wine collectors started a frenzy by buying Cabernet Sauvignon from small California wineries at extraordinary prices. These "cult" wineries produce very little wine—with hefty price tags.

Araujo	4,000 cases
Dalla Valle	2,500 cases
Harlan Estate	1,800 cases
Bryant Family	1,000 cases
Screaming Eagle	500 cases
Colgin Cellars	400 cases
Grace Family	48 cases

styles that are being produced. One of the recent improvements in labeling is that more wineries are adding important information to the back label indicating when the wine is ready to drink, if it should be aged, and many even offer food suggestions.

To avoid any unpleasant surprises, I can't emphasize enough the importance of an educated wine retailer. One of the strongest recommendations I give—especially to a new wine drinker—is to find the right retailer, one who understands wine and your taste.

Do California red wines age?

Absolutely, especially from the best wineries that produce Cabernet Sauvignon and Zinfandel. I have been fortunate to taste some early examples of Cabernet Sauvignon going back to the 1930s, 1940s, and 1950s, which for the most part were drinking well—some of them were outstanding—proving to me the longevity of certain Cabernets. Cabernet Sauvignons and Zinfandels from the best wineries in great vintages will need a minimum of five years before you drink them, and they will get better over the next ten years. That's at least fifteen years of great enjoyment.

ONE OF THE most memorable tastings I have ever attended in my career was for the fiftieth anniversary of Beaulieu's Private Reserve wine. Over a two-day period, we tasted every vintage from 1936 to 1986 with winemaker André Tchelistcheff. I think everyone who attended the tasting was amazed and awed by how well many of these vintages aged.

However, one of the things I have noticed in the last ten years, not only tasting as many California wines as I have, but also tasting so many European wines, is that California wines seem to be more accessible when young, as opposed to, say, a Bordeaux. I believe this is one of the reasons California wines sell so well in retail stores and in restaurants.

What have been the trends in the red wines of California over the last fifteen years?

To best answer that question, we should go back even further to see where the trends have been going for the last thirty or so years. The 1960s were a decade of expansion and development. The 1970s were a decade of growth, especially in terms of the number of wineries that were established in California and the corporations and individuals that became involved. The 1980s and 1990s were the decades of experimentation, in grape growing as well as in winemaking and marketing techniques.

Over the past ten years, I have seen the winemakers finally get a chance to step back and fine-tune their wine. Today, they are producing wines that have tremendous structure, finesse, and elegance that many lacked in the early years of the California winemaking renaissance. They are also making wines that can give pleasure when young, and also great wines that I hope I will be around to share with my grandchildren. The benchmark for quality has increased to such a level that the best wineries have gotten better, but more important to the consumer, even the everyday wines (under ten dollars) are better than ever before.

Though California winemakers have settled down, they have not given up experimentation altogether, if you consider the many new grape varieties coming out of California these days. I expect to see more wines made with grapes such as the Mourvèdre, Grenache, Sangiovese, and especially Syrah continuing the trend toward diversity in California red wines.

Red wines are no longer the sole domain of Napa and Sonoma. Many world-class reds are being produced in the Central Coast regions of California such as Monterey and Santa Barbara, San Luis Obispo, and Santa Clara.

FOR FURTHER READING

I recommend *The Wine Atlas of California* by James Halliday; *Making Sense of California Wine* and *New California Wine* by Matt Kramer; *Wine Spectator's California Wine* by James Laube; and *The Wine Atlas of California and the Pacific Northwest* by Bob Thompson.

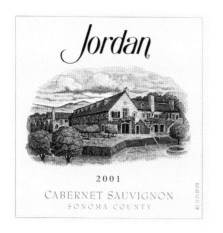

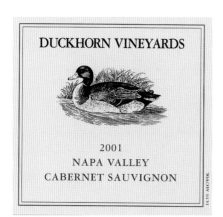

WINE AND FOOD

MARGRIT BIEVER AND ROBERT MONDAVI: *With Cabernet Sauvignon: lamb, or wild game such as grouse and caribou. With Pinot Noir: pork loin, milder game such as domestic pheasant, coq au vin.*

TOM JORDAN: *"Roast lamb is wonderful with the flavor and complexity of Cabernet Sauvignon. The wine also pairs nicely with sliced breast of duck, and grilled squab with wild mushrooms. For a cheese course with mature Cabernet, milder cheeses such as young goat cheeses, St. André and Taleggio, are best so the subtle flavors of the wine can be enjoyed."*

MARGARET AND DAN DUCKHORN: *"With a young Merlot, we recommend lamb shanks with crispy polenta, or grilled duck with wild rice in Port sauce. One of our favorites is barbecued leg of lamb with a mild, spicy fruit-based sauce. With older Merlots at the end of the meal, we like to serve Cambazzola cheese and warm walnuts."*

JANET TREFETHEN: *With Cabernet Sauvignon: prime cut of well-aged grilled beef; also—believe it or not—with chocolate and chocolate-chip cookies. With Pinot Noir: roasted quail stuffed with peeled kiwi fruit in a Madeira sauce. Also with pork tenderloin in a fruity sauce.*

PAUL DRAPER *(Ridge Vineyards): With Zinfandel: a well-made risotto of Petaluma duck. With aged Cabernet Sauvignon: Moroccan lamb with figs.*

WARREN WINIARSKI *(Stag's Leap Wine Cellars): With Cabernet Sauvignon: lamb or veal with a light sauce.*

JOSH JENSEN *(Calera Wine Co.): "Pinot Noir is so versatile, but I like it best with fowl of all sorts—chicken, turkey, duck, pheasant, and quail, preferably roasted or mesquite grilled. It's also great with fish such as salmon, tuna, and snapper."*

RICHARD ARROWOOD: *With Cabernet Sauvignon: suggests Sonoma County spring lamb or lamb chops prepared in a rosemary herb sauce.*

DAVID STARE *(Dry Creek Vineyard): "My favorite food combination with Zinfandel is marinated, butterflied leg of lamb. Have the butcher butterfly the leg, then place it in a plastic bag. Pour in half a bottle of Dry Creek Zinfandel, a cup of olive oil, six mashed garlic cloves, salt and pepper to taste. Marinate for several hours or overnight in the refrigerator. Barbecue until medium rare. While the lamb is cooking, take the marinade, reduce it, and whisk in several pats of butter for thickness. Yummy!"*

BO BARRETT *(Chateau Montelena Winery): With Cabernet Sauvignon: a good rib eye, barbecued with a teriyaki-soy-ginger-sesame marinade; venison or even roast beef prepared with olive oil and tapenade with rosemary, or even lamb. But when it comes to a good Cabernet Sauvignon, Bo is happy to enjoy a glass with "nothing at all—just a good book."*

PATRICK CAMPBELL *(owner/winemaker, Laurel Glen Vineyard): "With Cabernet Sauvignon, try a rich risotto topped with wild mushrooms."*

JACK CAKEBREAD: *"I enjoy my 1994 Cakebread Cellars Napa Valley Cabernet Sauvignon with farm-raised salmon with a crispy potato crust or an herb-crusted Napa Valley rack of lamb, with mashed potatoes and a red-wine sauce."*

ED SBRAGIA *(winemaker, Beringer Vineyards): "I like my Cabernet Sauvignon with rack of lamb, beef, or rare duck."*

TOM MACKEY *(winemaker, St. Francis Merlot): With St. Francis Merlot Sonoma County: Dungeness crab cakes, rack of lamb, pork roast, or tortellini. With St. Francis Merlot Reserve: hearty minestrone or lentil soup, venison, or filet mignon, or even a Caesar salad.*

Wines of the World: Italy, Spain, Australia, Chile, and Argentina

❧

ITALY • DOC • TUSCANY • PIEDMONT • VENETO • TRENDS • SPAIN • RIOJA •

AUSTRALIA • HOW TO READ AN AUSTRALIAN LABEL • CHILE • ARGENTINA

Vineyards in the Barolo wine area of Piedmont, Italy
(John Heseltine/Corbis)

The Red Wines of Italy

ITALY PRODUCES 50% white wines and 50% red.

ITALY IS THE WORLD'S LARGEST producer of wine. It has been producing wine for more than three thousand years, and the vines grow everywhere. As one retailer of fine Italian wine once told me, "There is no country. Italy is one vast vineyard from north to south."

Italian wines are good for any occasion—from quaffing to serious tasting. Some of my favorite wines are Italian. In fact, 25 percent of my personal wine cellar is stocked with them.

There are more than two thousand different wine labels, if you care to memorize them, twenty regions, and ninety-six provinces. But don't worry. If you want to know the basics of Italian wines, concentrate on the three regions listed below, and you'll be well on your way to having Italy in the palm of your hand.

TUSCANY

PIEDMONT

VENETO

What are the major red-grape varieties in Italy?

There are hundreds of indigenous grapes planted throughout Italy. In Tuscany, the major red-grape variety is Sangiovese, and in Piedmont it is Nebbiolo.

How are Italian wines controlled?

The Denominazione di Origine Controllata (abbreviated DOC), the Italian equivalent of the French AOC, controls the production and labeling of the wine. Italy's DOC laws went into effect in 1963.

In 1980 the Italian wine board took quality control even one step beyond the regular DOC, when they added the higher-ranking DOCG. The G stands for *Garantita*, meaning that, through tasting-control boards, they absolutely guarantee the stylistic authenticity of a wine.

As of 2004, the wines from Piedmont and Tuscany that qualified for the DOCG were:

TUSCANY	PIEDMONT
Vernaccia di San Gimignano	Moscato d'Asti/Asti
Chianti	Gattinara
Chianti Classico	Barbaresco
Vino Nobile di Montepulciano	Barolo
Carmignano Rosso	Brachetto d'Acqui
Brunello di Montalcino	Ghemme
	Gavi
	Roero

Eight of the Italian DOCG wines are from Piedmont and six are from Tuscany. That tells you why these are two of the regions you should study.

DOC LAWS

The DOC governs:

1. *The geographical limits of each region*
2. *The grape varieties that can be used*
3. *The percentage of each grape used*
4. *The maximum amount of wine that can be produced per acre*
5. *The minimum alcohol content of the wine*
6. *The aging requirements, such as how long a wine should spend in wood or bottle, for certain wines*

MANY WINE producers in Italy are now making wines from Cabernet Sauvignon, Merlot, and Chardonnay.

TOP THREE REGIONS IN PRODUCTION OF ITALIAN WINES

1.	Veneto	17.7%
2.	Piedmont	17.1%
3.	Tuscany	10.7%

MY ITALIAN-WINE friends sometimes refer to Veneto as Tri-Veneto, which includes Trentino, Alto-Aldige, and Friuli. Some of the best white wines of Italy come from these regions.

AT PRESENT, there are 25 wines that are entitled to the DOCG designation.

DOCG WINES from regions other than Tuscany and Piedmont include Taurasi, Greco di Tufo, and Fiano di Avellino from Campania; Albana di Romagna from Emilia-Romagna; Torgiano Rosso Riserva and Montefalco Sagrantino di Montefalco from Umbria; Franciacorta and Valtellina Superiore from Lombardy; Recioto di Soave and Bardolino from Veneto; and Vermentino de Gallura from Sardinia.

THERE ARE more than 300 DOC wines accounting for 20% of Italy's total wine production.

OF ALL Italian DOC wines, 60% are red.

THE BIGGEST difference between the AOC of France and the DOC of Italy is that the DOC has aging requirements.

ONLY ONE-FIFTH of all Chianti is Chianti Classico Riserva.

THAT'S TRADITION!

The name "Chianti" was first recorded in A.D. 700. Brolio, a major producer of Chianti, has been in business since 1141. Thirty-two generations of this family have tended to the vineyards and made the wine.

SUPER TUSCAN

As in California, some winemakers in Italy wanted to experiment with grape varieties and blends beyond what was permitted by the DOC regulations, so they decided to produce their own styles of wine. In Tuscany, these wines have become known as the "Super Tuscans." Among the better known of these proprietary Italian wines are Sassicaia, Tignanello, Ornellaia, Cabreo Il Borgo, Solaia, Summus, and Excelsus.

TUSCANY—THE HOME OF CHIANTI

Why did Chianti have such a bad image until recently?

One reason was the little straw-covered flasks (*fiaschi*) that the wine was bottled in—nice until restaurants hung the bottles from the ceiling next to the bar, along with the sausage and the provolone. So Chianti developed an image as a cheap little red wine to be bought for five dollars a jug.

My own feeling is that Chianti Classico Riserva is one of the best values in Italian wine today.

What are the different levels of Chianti?

Chianti ($)—The first level.

Chianti Classico ($$)—From the inner historic district of Chianti.

Chianti Classico Riserva ($$$$)—From a Classico area, and must be aged for a minimum of two years, three months

How should I buy Chianti?

First of all, find the style of Chianti you like best. There is a considerable variation in Chianti styles. Second, always buy from a shipper or producer whom you know—one with a good, reliable reputation. Some quality Chianti producers are:

ANTINORI	**FRESCOBALDI**
BADIA A COLTIBUONO	**MELINI**
BROLIO	**MONSANTO**
CASTELLO BANFI	**NOZZOLE**
CASTELLO DI AMA	**RICASOLI**
FONTODI	**RUFFINO**

Which grapes are used in Chianti?

According to updated DOCG requirements, winemakers are required to use at least 80 percent Sangiovese to produce Chianti. The DOCG also encourages the use of other grapes by allowing an unprecedented 20 percent nontraditional grapes (Cabernet Sauvignon, Merlot, Syrah, etc.). These changes, along with better winemaking techniques and better vineyard development, have all contributed greatly to improving Chianti's image over the last twenty years. A separate DOCG has been established for Chianti Classico, and producers of this wine may now use 100 percent Sangiovese.

Which other high-quality wines come from Tuscany?

Three of the greatest Italian red wines are Brunello di Montalcino, Vino Nobile di Montepulciano, and Carmignano. If you purchase the Brunello, keep in mind that it probably needs more aging (five to ten years) before it reaches peak drinkability. There are more than 150 producers of Brunello. My favorite producers of Brunello are: Biondi-Santi, Barbi, Altesino, Il Poggione, Col d'Orcia, Castello Banfi, and Caparzo. Those of Vino Nobile are: Avignonesi, Boscarelli, Fassati, and Poggio alla Sala. For Carmignano, look for Villa Capezzana, Poggiolo, and Artimino.

BEST BETS FOR TUSCANY

1997*   1999*   2000   2001*   2003   2004*

*Note: * signifies exceptional vintage*

PIEDMONT—THE BIG REDS

SOME OF THE FINEST RED WINES are produced in Piedmont. Two of the best DOCG wines to come from this region in northwest Italy are Barolo and Barbaresco.

The major grapes of Piedmont:

DOLCETTO
BARBERA
NEBBIOLO

Barolo and Barbaresco, the "heavyweight" wines from Piedmont, are made from the Nebbiolo variety. These wines have the fullest style and a high alcohol content. Be careful when you try to match young vintages of these wines with your dinner; they may overpower the food.

My favorite producers of Piedmont wines are: Antonio Vallana, Fontanafredda, Gaja, Pio Cesare, Prunotto, Renato Ratti, Ceretto, G. Conterno,

BRUNELLO DI MONTALCINO, because of its limited supply, is sometimes very expensive. For one of the best values in Tuscan red wine, look for Rosso di Montalcino.

BRUNELLO
DI MONTALCINO
DENOMINAZIONE DI ORIGINE CONTROLLATA E GARANTITA
RED WINE · PRODUCT OF ITALY
1991
COL D'ORCIA
BOTTLED BY TENUTA COL D'ORCIA S.P.A. · MONTALCINO · ITALIA
750 ML   ALC. 13.5% BY VOL.

BRUNELLO IS CHANGING

Beginning with the 1995 vintage, Brunellos are required to be aged in oak for a minimum of two years instead of the previous three. Result? A fruitier, more accessible wine.

SOME TUSCAN winemakers are saying that the 1997 vintage is the best since 1947.

MORE THAN 50% of the vineyards in Piedmont are Barbera.

MORE THAN 90% of the Piedmont grapes are planted on hillsides.

BOTH THE 2002 and 2003 vintages in Italy were well below normal production levels, and the 2002 vintage is the smallest harvest in ten years.

OLDER GREAT vintages of Piedmont: 1982, 1985, 1988, 1989

THE PIEDMONT region had six great vintages in a row: 1996–2001.

THE 2002 VINTAGE in Piedmont lost most of its grapes to a September hailstorm.

PIEDMONT'S PRODUCTION:

65% red
18% spumante (sparkling white)
17% white

THE PRODUCTION of Barolo and Barbaresco at 11 million bottles a year is only equivalent to that of a medium-size California winery!

IT IS SAID that when you begin drinking the red wines of Piedmont, you start with the lighter-style Barbera and Dolcetto, move on to the fuller-bodied Barbaresco, until finally you can fully appreciate a Barolo. As the late vintner Renato Ratti said, "Barolo is the wine of arrival."

IN ONE of the biggest changes in the DOCG regulations, the wines of Barolo now have to be aged in wood for only one year, and the minimum alcohol has been changed to 12.5%. Before 1999, Barolo had a mandatory two years of wood aging and 13% minimum alcohol.

ANOTHER GREAT Piedmont wine is called Gattinara. Look for the Antoniolo Reservas.

A. Conterno, M. Chiarlo, B. Giacosa, Marchesi di Gresy, Marchesi di Barolo, Vietti, Marcarini, Sandrone, Conterno Fintino, and Produttori d'Barbaresco.

BEST BETS FOR PIEDMONT

1990*   1996*   1997*   1998*
1999*   2000*   2001*   2003   2004*

*Note: * signifies exceptional vintage*

BAROLO VS. BARBARESCO

BAROLO (MORE THAN 8 MILLION BOTTLES)	BARBARESCO (NEARLY 3 MILLION BOTTLES)
Nebbiolo grape	Nebbiolo grape
Minimum 12.5% alcohol	Minimum 12.5% alcohol
More complex flavor, more body	Lighter; sometimes less body than Barolo, but fine and elegant
Must be aged at least three years (one in wood)	Requires two years of aging (one in wood)
"Riserva" = five years of aging	"Riserva" = four years of aging

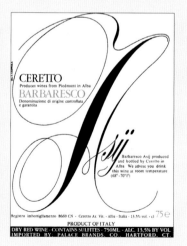

VENETO—THE HOME OF AMARONE

THIS IS ONE OF ITALY's largest wine-producing regions. Even if you don't recognize the name immediately, I'm sure you've had Veronese wines at one time or another, like Valpolicella, Bardolino, and Soave. All three are very consistent, easy to drink, and ready to be consumed whenever you buy them. They don't fit into the category of a Brunello di Montalcino or a Barolo, but they're very good table wines and they're within everyone's budget. The best and most improved of the three is Valpolicella. Look for Valpolicella Superiore made by the *ripasso* method.

Easy-to-find Veneto producers are Bolla, Folonari, and Santa Sofia. Harder to find and higher-priced but worth it come from Allegrini, Anselmi, and Quintarelli.

THE NAME "Amarone" derives from *amar* meaning "bitter" and *one* (pronounced "oh-nay"), meaning "big."

THE TOP five wines imported to the United States from Italy are:
1. Riunite
2. Casarsa
3. Bolla
4. Cavit
5. Ecco Domani

The above wines equal 43% of all imported table wine in the United States.

What's Amarone?

Amarone is a type of Valpolicella wine made by a special process in the Veneto region. Only the ripest grapes from the top of each bunch are used. After picking, they're left to "raisinate" (dry and shrivel) on straw mats. Does this sound familiar to you? It should, because this is similar to the process used to make German Trockenbeerenauslese and French Sauternes. One difference is that with Amarone, the winemaker ferments most of the sugar, bringing the alcohol content to 14 to 16 percent.

My favorite producers of Amarone are Masi, Bertani, Allegrini, Quintarelli, and Tommasi.

CLASSICO: All the vineyards are grown in the historical part of the region.

SUPERIORE: Higher levels of alcohol and longer aging.

BEST BETS FOR AMARONE
1990* 1993 1995* 1997* 1998 1999 2000* 2001

*Note: * signifies exceptional vintage*

FOR A NEW experience with Italian whites, try Gavi from Piedmont, and wines from the Friuli region.

PINOT GRIGIO is a white grape variety that is also found in Alsace, France, where it is called Pinot Gris. It is also having success in Oregon and California.

Is PINOT GRIGIO HOT?

In 1970, Italy produced only 11,000 cases of Pinot Grigio, and by 2003, Pinot Grigio was the number one imported Italian varietal in the United States.

AN INTERESTING trend in Italy: Bottled water and beer consumption are both increasing, while wine consumption is decreasing.

HAVE PIEDMONT wines changed over the last ten years? Many have. The wines of the past were more tannic and difficult to appreciate when young, while many of the present-day wines are easier to drink.

HOW ITALIAN WINES ARE NAMED

Winemaking regions have different ways of naming their wines. In California, you look for the grape variety on the label. In Bordeaux, most often you will see the name of a château. But in Italy, there are three different ways that wine is named—by grape variety, village or district, or simply a proprietary name. See the examples below

GRAPE VARIETY	VILLAGE OR DISTRICT	PROPRIETARY
Barbera	Chianti	Tignanello
Nebbiolo	Barolo	Sassicaia
Sangiovese	Montalcino	Summus

What have been the trends in the red wines of Italy over the last two decades?

Going back a little further, we can see that as recently as twenty-five years ago most Italian wine was made to be consumed in Italy, and not for the export market. As one wine producer commented, "They didn't drink the wine, they ate the wine." To the Italians, wine was an everyday thing like salt and pepper on their table to enhance the taste of the food.

But over the last twenty years, winemaking has become more of a business, and the Italian winemakers' philosophy has changed considerably from making casual-drinking wines to much better-made wines that are also much more marketable around the world. They've accomplished this by using modern technology, modern vinification procedures, and updated vineyard management as a basis for experimentation.

Another area of major experimentation is with nontraditional grape varieties such as Cabernet Sauvignon and Merlot. One of the newest trends is single-vineyard labeling. As a result, the biggest news in the whole wine industry is the change in Italian wines over the last twenty years. When I talk about experimentation, you must remember that this isn't California we're talking about, but Italy, with thousands of years of traditions that are being changed. In Italy, the producers have had to unlearn and relearn winemaking techniques in order to make better wines.

The prices of Italian wines have also increased tremendously over the last ten years, which may be good news for the Italian wine producers (in that it enhances the image of their wines), but it isn't such good news for consumers. Some of the wines from Italy have become among the most expensive in the world. That's not to say they're not worth it, but the pricing situation isn't the same as it was twenty years ago.

Beyond the best-known regions of Tuscany, Piedmont, and Veneto, many of the other twenty regions in Italy—especially Friuli and Trentino in the north and places like Umbria, Campania, Basilicata, Apulia, and Sicily in the south—are producing better and better wines, many of them made with indigenous grapes (Vermentino, Fiano, Negramora, etc.).

ITALIAN WHITES

I AM OFTEN ASKED WHY I don't teach a class on Italian white wines. The answer is quite simple. Take a look at the most popular white wines: Soave, Frascati, and Pinot Grigio, among others. Most of them retail for less than fifteen dollars. The Italians traditionally do not put the same effort into making their white wines that they do with their reds—in terms of style or complexity—and they are the first to admit it.

Plantings of international white varieties such as Chardonnay and Sauvignon Blanc, along with some of the better indigenous grapes, have recently elevated the quality of Italian white wines.

FOR FURTHER READING

I recommend *The Pocket Guide to Italian Wines* and *Wine Atlas of Italy* by Burton Anderson; *Vino Italiano* by Joseph Bastianich and David Lynch; *Italian Wine* by Victor Hazan; and *Italian Wines for Dummies* by Mary Ewing Mulligan and Ed McCarthy;.

WINE AND FOOD

In Italy, the wine is made to go with the food. No meal is served without wine. Take it from the experts.

The following food-and-wine suggestions are based on what some of the Italian wine producers enjoy having with their wine. You don't have to take their word for it. Get yourself a bottle of wine, a tasty dish, and mangia!

AMBROGIO FOLONARI (*Ruffino*): *"Chianti with prosciutto, chicken, pasta, and of course pizza."* When it comes to a Chianti Classico Riserva, Dr. Folonari says, *"Pair it with a hearty prime-rib dinner or a steak."*

EZIO RIVELLA (*Castello Banfi*): *"A Chianti is good with all meat dishes, but I save the Brunello for 'stronger' dishes, such as steak, wild boar, pheasant, and other game, as well as Pecorino Toscano cheese."*

Continued . . .

IN THE last 10 years, Italians have become more weight- and health-conscious, so they're changing their eating habits. As a result, the leisurely four-hour lunch and siesta is a thing of the past. Yes, all good things must come to an end.

THREE REASONS to visit Piedmont in the fall: the harvest, the food, and the white truffles.

"Piedmontese wines show better with food than in a tasting." —ANGELO GAJA

"When you're having Italian wines, you must not taste the wine alone. You must have them with food."
—GIUSEPPE COLLA OF PRUNOTTO

IN ITALY, vineyards aren't classified as they are in Bordeaux and Burgundy. There are neither Grands Crus nor Premiers Crus.

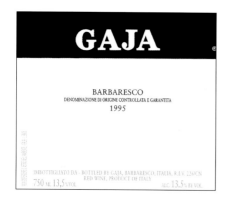

GIUSEPPE COLLA of Prunotto offers his "Best Bets" in the form of advice. His general rule: In a good vintage, set a Barbaresco aside for a minimum of four years before drinking. In the same situation, put away a Barolo for six years. However, in a great vintage year, lay down a Barbaresco for six years and a Barolo for eight years. As they say, "Patience is a virtue"—especially with wine.

ANGELO GAJA: *"Barbaresco with meat and veal, and also with mature cheeses that are 'not too strong,' such as Emmenthaler and Fontina."* Mr. Gaja advises against Parmesan and goat cheese when you have a Barbaresco. And if you're having a Barolo, Mr. Gaja's favorite is roast lamb.

GIUSEPPE COLLA (Prunotto): *"I enjoy light-style Dolcetto with all first courses and all white meat—chicken and veal especially."* He prefers not to have Dolcetto with fish. *"The wine doesn't stand up well to spicy sauce, but it's great with tomato sauce and pasta."*

RENATO RATTI: *Mr. Ratti once told me that both Barbera and Dolcetto are good with chicken and lighter foods. However, Barolo and Barbaresco need to be served with heavier dishes to match their own body. Mr. Ratti also suggests: a roast in its natural sauce or, better yet,* brasato al Barolo—braised in Barolo; meat cooked with wine; pheasant, duck, wild rabbit; and cheeses. For a special dish, try risotto al Barolo (rice cooked with Barolo wine). And when serving wine with dessert, Mr. Ratti recommends *"strawberries or peaches with Dolcetto wine."* The dryness in the wine, contrasted with the natural sweetness of the fruit, makes for a taste sensation!

LORENZA DE'MEDICI (Badia a Coltibuono): Since Tuscan cooking is very simple, she recommends *"an assortment of simple foods."* She prefers herbs to heavy sauces. With young Chianti, she suggests *"roast chicken, squab, or pasta with meat sauce."* To complement an older Chianti, she recommends a wide pasta with braised meat in Chianti, pheasant or other game, wild boar, or roast beef.

PIERO ANTINORI: *"I enjoy Chianti with the grilled foods for which Tuscany is famous, especially its bistecca alla Fiorentina (steak)."* He suggests poultry and even hamburgers as other tasty possibilities. With Chianti Classico Riserva, Mr. Antinori enjoys having the best of the vintages with wild boar and fine aged Parmesan cheese. *"The wine is a perfect match for roast beef, roast turkey, lamb, or veal."*

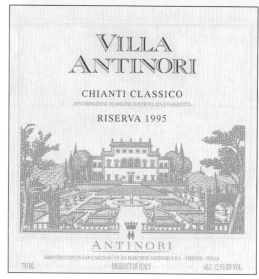

THE WINES OF SPAIN

THE MAIN WINEMAKING REGIONS IN Spain are:

LA RIOJA   CATALUÑA (PENEDÉS AND PRIORATO)

RIBERA DEL DUERO   THE SHERRY DISTRICT

We'll put aside the region of Sherry for now, since you'll become a Sherry expert in the next chapter. Let's start with Rioja, which is located in northern Spain, very near the French border.

In fact, it's less than a five-hour (200-mile) drive to Bordeaux from Rioja, so it's no coincidence that Rioja wines often have a Bordeaux style. Back in the 1800s, many Bordeaux wine producers brought their expertise to this region.

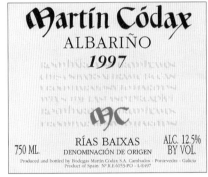

OTHER WINE-PRODUCING AREAS OF SPAIN

Rias Baixas

Toro

Jumilla

ALSO, LOOK for the great rosés of the Navarra region.

MARQUÉS DE CÁCERES is owned by a Spaniard, who also owns Château Camensac, a fifth-growth Bordeaux.

THE NEW RIOJA

A new style of wine is emerging in Rioja. It is a contemporary wine that is bigger and more concentrated. Wineries of this style include Allende, Remelluri, Palacios, Remondo, and Remirez de Ganuza.

VIÑOS DE PAGOS means that the wine comes from a single estate.

GRENACHE IS the French spelling of Garnacha, a Spanish grape, which was brought to France from Spain during the time of the popes of Avignon, some of whom were Spanish.

THE VIURA is the most used grape in white Rioja.

IN RIOJA, 80% of the grapes are red.

ALTHOUGH THERE are nearly 800 different wineries in Spain, about 80% of their production comes from a handful of companies.

Why would a Frenchman leave his château in Bordeaux to go to a Spanish bodega in Rioja?

I'm glad you asked. It so happens that Frenchmen did travel from Bordeaux to Rioja at one point in history. Do you remember phylloxera? (See "Prelude to Wine.") It's a plant louse that at one time killed nearly all the European vines and almost wiped out the Bordeaux wine industry.

Phylloxera started in the north and moved south. It first destroyed all the vines in Bordeaux, and some of the Bordeaux vineyard owners decided to establish vineyards and wineries in the Rioja district. It was a logical place for them to go because of the similar climate and growing conditions. The influence of the Bordelaise is sometimes apparent even in today's Rioja wines.

Which grapes are used in Rioja wines?

The major grapes used in Rioja wine are:

TEMPRANILLO

GARNACHA

These grapes are blended with others to give Rioja wines their distinctive taste. On some labels you will see the word *cosecha*, which in Spanish means "harvest" or "vintage."

SPAIN'S WINE RENAISSANCE

Spain is the world's third largest producer of wine, behind France and Italy. Spain has more land dedicated to vines than any other country: 4.5 million acres!

Spain is also a country with a rich winemaking tradition. Many types of wine are produced: Cava (Méthode Champenoise sparkling wines) are produced in the Penedés region not far from Barcelona. Red wines and rosés are produced throughout the entire country. Fortified wines are produced mainly in the south. The best-known region for such wines is Jerez (Sherry), as you will see in Class Eight.

A twentieth-century renaissance extends nationwide to Spain's wine industry, where tremendous investments have been made throughout the country in viticulture and winemaking equipment. In Rioja alone, the number of wineries has increased from 42 to 210 since 1982.

Why are Rioja wines so easy to understand?

All you need to know when buying a Rioja wine is the style (level) and the reputation of the Rioja winemaker/shipper. The grape varieties are not found on the wine labels, and there's no classification to be memorized. The three major levels of Rioja wines are:

Crianza ($)—Released after two years of aging, with a minimum of one year in oak barrels.

Reserva ($$)—Released after three years of aging, with a minimum of one year in oak barrels.

Gran Reserva ($$$$)—Released after five to seven years of aging, with a minimum of two years in oak barrels.

THREE NEW CATEGORIES OF AGE FOR SPANISH WINES

Noble	12 months in barrel
Anejo	24 months in barrel
Viejo	36 months in barrel

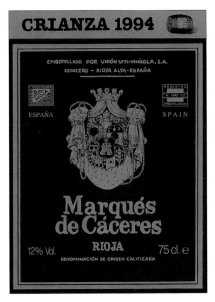

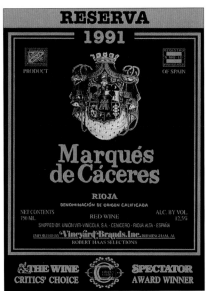

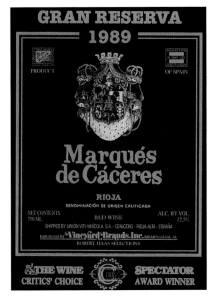

How would I know which Rioja wine to buy in the store?

You mean besides going with your preferred style and the reputation of the winemaker/shipper? You may also be familiar with a Rioja wine by its

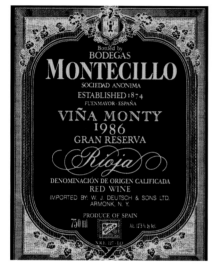

MARQUÉS DE MURRIETA was the first commercial bodega in Rioja, established in 1850.

SOME OF the top Rioja winemakers are saying that the 1994 and 2001 vintages are the best they have ever tasted.

RIBERA DEL DUERO wines are made from the Tinto Fino grape, a close cousin of Rioja's Tempranillo. The laws also allow the use of Cabernet Sauvignon, Malbec, Merlot, and small amounts of a white grape called Albillo.

proprietary name. The following are some bodegas to look for, along with some of their better-known proprietary names:

ALLENDE

BODEGAS BRETON

BODEGAS LAN

BODEGAS MONTECILLO—VIÑA CUMBRERO, VIÑA MONTY

BODEGAS MUGA—MUGA RESERVA, PRADO ENEA, TORREMUGA

BODEGAS REMIREZ DE GANUZIA

BODEGAS RIOJANAS—MONTE REAL, VIÑA ALBINA

C.U.N.E.—IMPERIAL, VIÑA REAL

CONTINO

LA RIOJA ALTA—VIÑA ALBERDI, VIÑA ARDANZA

LOPEZ-HEREDIA

MARQUÉS DE CÁCERES

MARQUÉS DE MURRIETA

MARQUÉS DE RISCAL

MARTÍNEZ BUJANDA—CONDE DE VALDEMAR

PALACIOS REMONDO

REMELLURI

BEST BETS FOR RIOJA

1994* 1995* 1996 1999
2000 2001* 2003

Note: * signifies exceptional vintage

The two other famous winegrowing regions in Spain are Penedés (outside Barcelona) and the Ribera del Duero (between Madrid and Rioja). The most famous wine of the Penedés region is the sparkling wine called *cava*, of which the two best-known names in the United States are Codorniu and Freixenet. These are two of the biggest producers of bottle-fermented sparkling wine in the world, and one of the best features of these wines is their reasonable price. The Penedés region is also known for high-quality table wine. The major producer of this region (and synonymous with the quality of the area) is the Torres family. Their famous wine, Gran Coronas

Black Label, is made with 100 percent Cabernet Sauvignon, and is rare and expensive, though the Torres family produces a full range of fine Spanish wines in all price categories.

The Ribera del Duero has been around since the 1800s (though it was officially delimited in 1982), but is now becoming quite prominent in the United States. Some of the most expensive Spanish wines are from Ribera del Duero, such as Vega Sicilia. Other wines from that region, which are less expensive and more readily available, are Pesquera, Viña Mayor, Pago de los Capellanes, Bodegas Emilio Moro, Dominio de Pingus, Abadia Retverta, and Alejandro Fernández.

PRIORATO

This area just south of Barcelona near the Mediterranean produces some of the fullest-bodied wines of Spain, primarily from the Garnacha grape. Look for the wines of Alvaro Palacios and Mas Igneus.

BEST BETS FOR RIBERA DEL DUERO

1995   1996*   1999   2001*   2004

*Note: * signifies exceptional vintage*

Have Spanish wines changed in style over the last twenty years?

Yes, without a doubt. As has been the case in countries like Chile and Italy, modern technology and new viticultural procedures have made for much better wines, many of which merit long-term aging. Hand selection of grapes, smaller barrels for fermentation, and using more French oak rather than the traditional American oak are all new changes in the wines of Spain.

There is also an increase in experimentation with Cabernet Sauvignon and single-vineyard bottlings.

BEST BETS FOR PENEDÉS AND PRIORATO

1998   2000   2001*

*Note: * signifies exceptional vintage*

FOR FURTHER READING:

I recommend *The Wines of Rioja* by Hubrecht Duijker; *The New Spain* by John Radford; and *The New and Classical Wines of Spain* by Jeremy Watson.

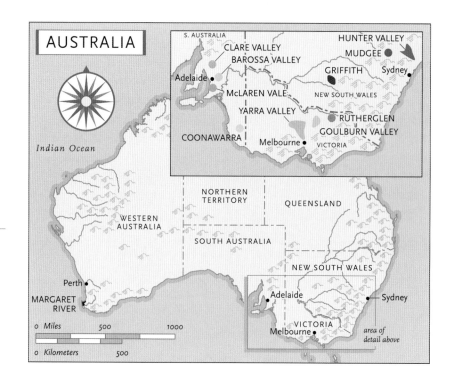

AUSTRALIA IS now the second largest importer of wine to the United States. (Italy is the first).

AMERICANS LIKE YELLOW TAIL

The number one imported wine in the United States is Yellow Tail. Sales rocketed from 200,000 cases in 2001 to 8 million cases in 2004.

TWENTY COMPANIES produce more than 90% of Australian wines.

THE AUSTRALIAN wine industry began in 1788 with the planting of Australia's first grapevines.

AUSTRALIAN WINE EXPORTS TO THE UNITED STATES (IN CASES)

1990	578,000
2004	20,000,000

THE WINES OF AUSTRALIA

THERE ARE ABOUT FORTY DISTINCT winegrowing regions in Australia, with more than eighty districts and subdistricts. Do you need to know them all? Probably not, but you should be familiar with the best districts in four of Australia's six states:

NEW SOUTH WALES (N.S.W.)—Griffith, Hunter Valley, Mudgee

SOUTH AUSTRALIA (S.A.)—Barossa Valley, McLaren Vale, Coonawarra, Clare Valley

VICTORIA (VIC.)—Yarra Valley, Goulburn Valley, Rutherglen

WESTERN AUSTRALIA (W.A.)—Margaret River, Pemberton

The wine industry is by no means new to Australia. In fact, many of Australia's leading wine companies were established more than 175 years ago. Lindemans, Penfolds, Orlando, Henschke, and Seppelt are just a few of the companies that were founded during the nineteenth century. They are now among Australia's largest, or most prestigious, companies, and they continue to produce excellent wines.

Which grape varieties are grown in Australia?

Major red-grape varieties are:

Shiraz: Called Syrah in the Rhône Valley of France and in California, it can produce spicy, robust, long-lived, and full-bodied wines. It is the most widely planted red grape in Australia at 61,775 acres (representing one-quarter of Australia's wine country).

Cabernet Sauvignon: As in Bordeaux and California, Australia's Cabernet Sauvignon grapes produce some of the best wines in the country. Always dry, Cabernet yields wines that range in style from medium to extremely full-bodied, depending on the producer and the region. It is often blended with Shiraz.

Pinot Noir: The great grape of Burgundy. In many cooler districts of Victoria, South Australia, and Western Australia, it is beginning to show signs of reaching quality levels similar to those of its famous brethren.

Merlot: A relative newcomer to Australia, but it is quickly gaining on Pinot Noir in terms of production.

The main white-grape varieties are:

Chardonnay: As in Burgundy and California, Australia's Chardonnay makes dry, full-flavored wines, as well as providing a base for sparkling wines.

Sémillon: In France, this grape is blended with Sauvignon Blanc to make white Bordeaux. In Australia it makes medium-style dry wines, is often blended with Chardonnay, and the best can benefit from aging. The Sémillon grape has been planted for more than 200 years in Australia.

Riesling: A variety also grown in Germany; Alsace; France; Washington; and New York State, this grape ranges in style from dry to sweet.

Sauvignon Blanc: Over the past few years, this grape has shown the largest increase in Australia's white wine production.

What kinds of wine are produced in Australia?

Australia produces many different kinds of table wine, ranging from light, fruit-driven whites made from blends of grapes from different areas to vineyard-specific, barrel-aged reds from vines more than a hundred years old. It is not unusual to find Shiraz on original—not grafted—rootstock, because many Australian wine regions were not affected by phylloxera or other diseases.

Among the most interesting winemaking practices of Australia are the white blends made from Chardonnay and Sémillon and the red blends made of Cabernet and Shiraz. Many of these represent high quality at reasonable prices, and they are also very enjoyable everyday wines.

SOME OF the wine regions in Australia specialize in certain grapes. For example Coonawarra is noted for its excellent Cabernet Sauvignon, Barossa for Shiraz, and the Hunter Valley for the white wines made from Sémillon.

IN THE 1830s, Cabernet Sauvignon vine cuttings from Château Haut-Brion in Bordeaux were planted near Melbourne. In 1832, James Busby brought back Shiraz cuttings from the Chapoutier vineyards in the Rhône Valley, which he planted in the Hunter Valley.

AUSSIE REDS ON THE MOVE

Only a few years ago, 65% of Australian wine grapes were white varieties. Today, white wines account for 53% and the reds contribute the remaining 47% to the harvest.

UP UNTIL the 1960s, Australian wine was primarily sweet wine and portlike products. The Australians have graduated (with honors, I might add) to producing excellent dry table wines, but many of the best producers still pride themselves on luscious "stickies," the Australian term for dessert wine.

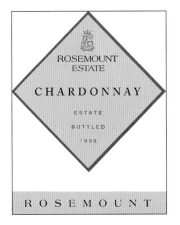

PRODUCED FROM ORGANICALLY GROWN GRAPES

EST 1844

Penfolds

CLARE VALLEY
CABERNET SAUVIGNON · SHIRAZ · PETIT VERDOT
VINTAGE 1997

Organically grown grapes from Penfolds Clare Valley Vineyard in South Australia
have been vintaged to produce this full bodied red wine in the Penfolds tradition.
Blending Cabernet Sauvignon, Shiraz and Petit Verdot the winemakers have produced
a wine with ripe berry characters, subtle oak and an appealing lingering finish.

750 ml   13.0% alc./vol.

PRODUCED BY PENFOLDS WINES, PENFOLD ROAD, MAGILL, SOUTH AUSTRALIA, AUSTRALIA 5072
RED WINE   PRODUCT OF AUSTRALIA   VIN ROUGE   PRODUIT D'AUSTRALIE
61% CABERNET SAUVIGNON · 31% SHIRAZ · 8% PETIT VERDOT

OUT OF the 150 different Australian wineries distributed in the United States, here is my list of the top wineries: Hardy's, Lindemans, Orlando, Clarendon Hills, Michelton, Yalumba, Tahbilk, Rothbury, Penfolds, Petaluma, Rosemount, Wolf Blass, Henschke, Mountadam, D'Arenberg, Peter Lehmann, Leeuwin, Leasingham.

THE VINTAGE in Australia occurs in the first half of the year. The grapes are harvested from February to May. For any given vintage, Australia will have its wines approximately six months before Europe or America.

BIN NUMBERS are often found on Australian labels. These numbers were originally intended to indicate where the wines were stored in the cellar. Today they are used to denote the style or blend of a producer's wine.

How are wines labeled?

Effective with the 1990 vintage, the Australian wine industry's Label Integrity Program (LIP) took effect. Although it does not govern as many aspects as France's AOC laws, the LIP does regulate and oversee vintage, varietal, and geographical indication claims. In order to conform to LIP and other regulations set by the Australian Food Standards' Code, Australian wine labels, such as the one at left, give a great deal of information.

One of the most important pieces of information is the producer's name. In this case, the producer is Penfolds. If a single grape variety is printed on the label, the wine must be made from at least 85 percent of that variety. In a blend listing the varieties, as above, the percentages of each must be shown. (Note that the first grape listed is always the larger percentage.) If the label specifies a particular wine-growing district (for example, Clare Valley), at least 85 percent of the wine must originate there. If a vintage is given, 95 percent of the wine must be of that vintage.

What about vintages?

Australian winegrowing regions extend across three thousand miles with many diverse climatic and microclimatic conditions. As in California, there are not the extreme highs and lows that one may find in European vineyards, which is why I sometimes refer to them as "hassle-free" vintages. Case in point: Over the past ten years, Australia has had a string of good-to-great vintages. As for value, the Australian dollar in 2004 was worth about seventy-five cents American, so Australian wines remain an excellent buy.

BEST BETS FOR AUSTRALIA

1998*	1999	2000	2001**	2002*	2003*

Note: * signifies exceptional vintage

** 2001 was an extraordinarily good year for Shiraz

FOR FURTHER READING

I recommend *The Wine Atlas of Australia & New Zealand* and *The Wine Companion 2003* by James Halliday.

THE WINES OF CHILE

Why is Chile the hottest wine-growing region in the world?

First and foremost is the quality of the wines for the price. In my opinion, the best value in red wines of the world comes from Chile. These are definitely the best South American wines today.

I did not include the wines of Chile in the first edition of this book, in 1985, but I followed the country's progress from the sidelines while tremendous expansion was taking place with plantings of international grape varieties. Since my most recent visit to wine country there, tasting the fruit of their labor, I am absolutely convinced that the Chileans are producing world-class wines, especially the reds.

Why did it take so long for Chile to produce world-class wines?

Chile has been making wine for more than 450 years, since the first grapes were planted in Chile in 1551 and the first wine was produced in 1555. Things really started getting interesting in the mid-1800s when French varietals such as Cabernet Sauvignon and Merlot were imported into Chile.

But all this progress came to a grinding halt in 1938 when the government of Chile decreed that no new vineyards could be planted. This law lasted until 1974. The renaissance of the modern wine industry of Chile really only began in the early 1980s, when the new technology of stainless-steel fermentors and the old technology of French oak barrels were combined to produce higher-quality wines.

CHILE IS the fourth largest exporter of wine to the United States.

THE COUNTRY of Chile runs almost 2,600 miles north to south but only 60 miles wide at its broadest point.

THE NUMBER one Chilean wine imported into the United States is Concha y Toro It is also one of the oldest wineries, started in 1883.

EXPORTS TO THE UNITED STATES

In 1996, Chile exported 100,000 cases of wine to the United States. Since then, Chilean wine exports have increased to more than 5 million cases.

IN 1995 THERE were only 12 wineries in Chile. Today there are more than 70.

WHICH GRAPE IS IT?

It was recently discovered that 40% of the Merlot planted in Chile is not really Merlot, but another grape called Carmenere.

IN 1985 THERE were only 30 acres of Chardonnay planted in Chile. In 2002 there were more than 15,000.

CABERNET SAUVIGNON accounts for 37% of the total acreage of premium grapes planted in Chile.

THE 1997 and 2003 vintages were two of the best ever produced in Chile.

What's happening in Chile today?

It's exciting. Going to Chile today is like going to California twenty-five years ago. And like California and Australia, there's no tradition of technique. Chile is a work in progress.

The Chilean winemakers have a lot going for them: The climate in Chile is somewhere between California and Bordeaux, and the Andes are spectacular. No matter where you are in the country, those majestic, snowcapped mountains always catch your eye.

What are the major winemaking regions in Chile?

There are twelve different regions for wine production in Chile. The seven most important are:

ACONCAGUA VALLEY	MAIPO VALLEY
CASABLANCA VALLEY	MAULE
COLCHAGUA VALLEY	RAPEL VALLEY
CURICÓ VALLEY	

What are the major grapes grown in Chile?

The main white varieties are:

SAUVIGNON BLANC
CHARDONNAY
MUSCAT

The main red varieties are:

CABERNET SAUVIGNON
MERLOT (CARMENERE)
PAÍS (MISSION GRAPE)

PRE-PHYLLOXERA

To this day, Chile can still boast about having pre-phylloxera wines. As you may recall, the phylloxera louse destroyed all the vineyards in France in the 1870s and the Chileans brought over their vine cuttings prior to this infestation. To this day, the phylloxera bug has not been a problem in Chile.

How do I buy the wines of Chile?

Almost all Chilean wines are dry, and there are no official classifications. Most of the wineries in Chile produce wines of different quality levels and price points, and label their wines by grape variety. The wine laws are very much like those in California. For example, if the grape variety is named on the label, the wine must contain a minimum of 85 percent of that grape. The best Chilean wineries also have their own special names for their highest-quality wines.

The best way to buy Chilean wines is from the top producers. The following is a list of my favorite wineries. In parentheses are names of the best wines:

> CALITERRA (RESERVE)
> CARMEN (VIDURE CABERNET RESERVE)
> CASA LAPOSTOLLE (CUVÉE ALEXANDRE, CLOS APALTA)
> CONCHA Y TORO (DON MELCHOR, ALMAVIVA)
> COUSIÑO MACUL (FINIS TERRAE, ANTIGUAS RESERVAS)
> DOMAINE PAUL BRUNO
> VIÑA ERRAZÚRIZ (DON MAXIMIANO)
> LOS VASCOS (RESERVA DE FAMILIA)
> VIÑA MONTES (ALPHA M)
> SANTA RITA (CASA REAL)
> SEÑA
> UNDURRAGA (RESERVE)
> VERAMONTE (PRIMUS)
> VINA SANTA CAROLINA

Will Chilean wines age?

On my most recent visit to Chile, I was lucky enough to taste the 1969, 1965, and 1960 vintages of Cousiño Macul Antiguas Cabernet Sauvignon, which were just coming into their prime.

BEST BETS FOR CHILE: RED VINTAGES

| 1997* | 1999* | 2001* | 2002 | 2003* |

Note: * signifies exceptional vintage

THE TOP FIVE CHILEAN WINE BRANDS IN THE UNITED STATES

1. Concha y Toro
2. Walnut Crest
3. San Pedro
4. Santa Rita
5. Santa Carolina

Source: Impact Databank

WINE REGIONS AND THEIR SPECIALTIES

Region	Specialty
Casablanca	Chardonnay, Sauvignon Blanc
Maipo	Cabernet Sauvignon
Rapel	Merlot

KEVIN ZRALY'S CHOICE

The Best of Chile
Almaviva
Montes (Alpha M)
Seña
Le Dix de Los Vascos
Errazúriz (Don Maximiano)
Cousiño-Macul (Antiguas Reservas)

THE SEVEN LARGEST WINERIES IN CHILE

Winery	Date Founded
Concha y Toro	1883
San Pedro	1865
Santa Rita	1880
Santa Carolina	1875
Errazúriz	1870
Undurraga	1885
Viña Canepa	1930

CHILE IS a melting pot of Germans, French, Spanish, Italians, and Swiss.

ARGENTINA HAS been producing wine for more than 400 years. The first grapes in Argentina were planted in 1554.

THE FRENCH CONNECTION
(FRENCH INVESTMENT IN CHILE)

FRENCH INVESTOR	CHILEAN WINERY
Grand Marnier	Casa Lapostolle
Domaines Lafite Rothschild	Los Vascos
Bruno Prats & Paul Pontalier	Aquitania/Paul Bruno
William Fèvre	Fèvre
Château Larose-Trintaudon	Casas del Toqui
Baron Philippe de Rothschild	Concha y Toro
	(Viña Almaviva Puente Alto)

OTHER FOREIGN INVESTORS IN CHILE INCLUDE:

Quintessa, California	Veramonte
Torres Winery, Spain	Miguel Torres Winery
Kendall-Jackson	Viña Calina

THE WINES OF ARGENTINA

What's happening in Argentina?

Great things are happening in Argentina's wine industry! A growing number of wineries have changed their philosophy and now concentrate on producing higher-quality wines rather than manufacturing large quantities.

Until recently, Argentina was more interested in producing inexpensive bulk wine. Now its winemakers are beginning to understand the worldwide demand for quality wine. Still, today 90 percent of Argentina's wine is consumed in Argentina, which is the problem.

As it was in Spain and Italy twenty years ago (and Chile fifteen years ago), wineries were confronted with the dilemma of whether to produce wine for the domestic market—wine that was sometimes bland and oxidized—or try to make better wine for the export market. Today a new, higher style of Argentinian wine is emerging.

Why has it taken so long for Argentina to become a player in the wine world?

Any wine region must have capital to produce great wine. In fact, more investment has been poured into Argentina's wine industry in the last ten years than in the previous fifty!

Who's investing in Argentina?

From California, Jess Jackson (Kendall-Jackson); from Bordeaux, the Lurton family, and also the owners of Château Cheval Blanc, who have created a wine called Cheval des Andes; and the Domaines Barons de Rothschild (Lafite).

Even wineries from Chile, such as Concha y Toro and Santa Rita, are investing their money and expertise in Argentina.

Why is Argentina easier to understand than Chile?

Think red. Think Mendoza. Think Malbec. The best wines of Argentina are red. The major region is Mendoza, which produces 75 percent of all wines coming from Argentina. Malbec is the best-quality grape planted in Mendoza. Other red grapes produced are Cabernet Sauvignon and Merlot. In the future, look for Syrah. Argentina is also producing world-class Chardonnay.

How do I buy wine from Argentina?

As with Chile, buy from the best producers. There are more than 100 wineries in Argentina. Here is a list of some of the best:

ACHAVEL-FERRER	J&F LURTON	NORTON
BIANCHI	LA RURAL	PAUL HOBBS
BODEGAS ESMERALDA	LOPEZ	SALENTEIN
CATENA ZAPATA	LUCA	TIKA
ETCHART	LUIS BOSCA	TRAPICHE
FINCA FLICHMAN	MARIPOSA	WEINERT

BEST BETS FOR ARGENTINA

1997*   1999*   2000   2002*   2003*

*Note: * signifies exceptional vintage*

ARGENTINA IS the largest producer of wines in South America. It's the fifth largest wine producer in the world. Argentina is also the sixth largest consumer of wines in the world.

OF THE 500,000 acres of vineyards planted in Argentina, 350,000 acres are in Mendoza.

WHEN IT comes to quality, 5% of the wines of Argentina were considered quality in 1973. Today, 25% are considered quality wines.

ALL ARGENTINEAN varietal wines are 100% of the grape named.

WITH 300 days of sunshine and only eight inches of rain annually, the Argentineans have set up an elaborate network of canals and dams to irrigate their vineyards.

Champagne, Sherry, and Port

CHAMPAGNE • MÉTHODE CHAMPENOISE • STYLES OF CHAMPAGNE •

OPENING CHAMPAGNE • CHAMPAGNE GLASSES •

SPARKLING WINE • SHERRY • PORT

*Barrels of Port await shipping at the Dow & Co. warehouse
in Oporto, Portugal
(Charles O'Rear/Corbis)*

Champagne and Fortified Wines

THE CHAMPAGNE region covers about 85,000 acres, or 2.5% of French vineyards. Production is about 280 million bottles a year, which represents about 10% of world production of sparkling wines.

Now we're beginning our last class—the last chapter on the wine itself. This is where the course ends—on a happy note, I might add. What better way to celebrate than with Champagne?

Why do I group Champagne, Sherry, and Port together? Because as diverse as these wines are, the way the consumer will buy them is through the reputation and reliability of the shipper. Since these are all blended wines, the shipper is responsible for all phases of the production—you concern yourself with the house style. In Champagne, for example, Moët & Chandon is a well-known house; in Port, the house of Sandeman; and in Sherry, the house of Pedro Domecq.

CHAMPAGNE

What's Champagne?

We all know that Champagne is a sparkling bubbly that everyone drinks on New Year's Eve. It's more than that. Champagne is a region in France—the country's northernmost winemaking region, to be exact—and it's an hour and a half northeast of Paris.

Why do I stress its northern location? Because this affects the taste of the wines. In the Champagne region, the grapes are picked with higher acidity than in most other regions, which is one

CHAMPAGNE · SHERRY · PORT

Paris

CHAMPAGNE

FRANCE

Atlantic Ocean

Oporto

DOURO

Madrid

PORTUGAL

SPAIN

Mediterranean Sea

Lisbon

0 Miles 100 200 300

0 Kilometers 300

SHERRY DISTRICT

of the reasons for Champagne's distinct taste. The Champagne region is divided into four main areas:

VALLEY OF THE MARNE

MOUNTAIN OF REIMS

CÔTE DES BLANCS

CÔTE DES BAR

Three grapes can be used to produce Champagne:

Pinot Noir: Accounts for 37 percent of all grapes planted
Pinot Meunier: Accounts for 37 percent of all grapes planted
Chardonnay: Accounts for 26 percent of all grapes planted

In France, only sparkling wines that come from the region of Champagne may be called "Champagne." Some American producers have borrowed the name *Champagne* to put on the label of their sparkling wines. These cannot and should not be compared with Champagne from France.

What are the three major types of Champagne?

Non-vintage/multiple vintage: A blend of two or more harvests
Vintage: From a single vintage
"Prestige" cuvée: From a single vintage with longer aging requirements

Why is there such a tremendous price difference between non-vintage and "prestige" cuvée Champagnes?

"Prestige" Champagnes usually meet the following requirements to be designated as such:

- Made from the best grapes of the highest-rated villages.

- Made from the first pressing of the grapes.

- Spent more time aging in the bottle than non-vintage Champagnes.

- Made only in vintage years.

- Made in small quantity, and the demand is high. Price is dictated largely by supply and demand.

THE NERVOUS SYSTEM OF WINE

Acidity in Champagne not only gives freshness to the wines, but it is also important to their longevity, and it stimulates the palate before lunch or dinner.

THE BALANCE of the fruit and acidity, together with the bubbles (CO_2), are what make good Champagne.

A TYPICAL Champagne is a blend of 60% to 70% Pinot grapes and 30% to 40% Chardonnay.

NON-VINTAGE Champagne is more typical of the house style than vintage Champagne.

VINTAGE CHAMPAGNE must contain 100% of that vintage year's harvest.

MORE THAN 80% of the Champagnes produced are not vintage dated. This means they are blends of several years' wines.

THE 2004 HARVEST in Champagne was the largest ever.

SHIPPERS DON'T always agree on the quality of the wines produced in any given vintage, so the years for vintage Champagnes vary from shipper to shipper. Historically, each house usually declares a vintage three years out of each decade.

TWO METHODS of making rosé Champagne: 1) add red wine to the blend; 2) leave the red grape skins in contact with the must for a short period of time.

WINE PRESSES are placed throughout the vineyards so the winemaker can press the grapes immediately without extracting any of their color.

MOST CHAMPAGNES are fermented in stainless steel.

CLASSIC CHAMPAGNES (non-vintage) must be aged for a minimum of 15 months in the bottle after bottling. Vintage Champagnes must be aged for a minimum of three years after bottling.

DOM PÉRIGNON Champagne is aged six to eight years before it is put on the market.

Is every year a vintage year?

No, but more recently, 1995*, 1996*, 1999, 2000, and 2002* were. Note: These were vintage years for most Champagne houses. "Vintage" in Champagne is different from other wine regions, because each house makes its own determination on whether or not to declare a vintage year.

Note: * signifies exceptional vintage

How is Champagne made?

Champagne is made by a process called *Méthode Champenoise*. When a similar method is used outside La Champagne, it is called *Méthode Traditionnelle* or Classic Method or *Método Tradicional*, etc. The use of the expression *Méthode Champenoise* is not allowed in the European Union outside of Champagne.

MÉTHODE CHAMPENOISE

Harvest—The normal harvest usually takes place in late September or early October.

Pressing the Grapes—Only two pressings of the grapes are permitted. Prestige cuvée Champagnes are usually made exclusively from the first pressing. The second pressing, called the *taille*, is generally blended with the cuvée to make vintage and non-vintage Champagnes.

Fermentation—All Champagnes undergo a first fermentation when the grape juice is converted into wine. Remember the formula: Sugar + Yeast = Alcohol + CO_2. The carbon dioxide dissipates. The first fermentation takes two to three weeks and produces still wines.

Blending—The most important step in Champagne production is the blending of the still wines. Each of these still wines is made from a single grape variety from a single village of origin. The winemaker has to make many decisions here. Three of the most important ones are:

1. Which grapes to blend—how much Chardonnay, Pinot Noir, and Pinot Meunier?
2. From which vineyards should the grapes come?
3. Which years or vintages should be blended? Should the blend be made only from the wines of the harvest, or should several vintages be blended together?

Liqueur de Tirage—After the blending process, the winemaker adds *Liqueur de Tirage* (a blend of sugar and yeast) which will begin the wine's second fermentation. At this point, the wine is placed in its permanent bottle with a temporary bottle cap.

Second Fermentation—During this fermentation, the carbon dioxide stays in the bottle. This is where the bubbles come from. The second fermentation also leaves natural sediments in the bottle. Now the problems begin. How do you get rid of the sediments without losing the carbon dioxide? Go on to the next steps.

Aging—The amount of time the wine spends aging on its sediments is one of the most important factors in determining the quality of the wine.

Riddling—The wine bottles are now placed in A-frame racks, necks down. The *remueur*, or riddler, goes through the racks of Champagne bottles and gives each bottle a slight turn while gradually tipping the bottle farther downward. After six to eight weeks, the bottle stands almost completely upside down, with the sediments resting in the neck of the bottle.

Dégorgement—The top of the bottle is dipped into a brine solution to freeze it, and then the temporary bottle cap is removed and out fly the frozen sediments, propelled by the carbon dioxide.

Dosage—A combination of wine and cane sugar is added to the bottle after *dégorgement*. At this point, the winemaker can determine whether he wants a sweeter or a drier Champagne.

Recorking—The wine is recorked with real cork instead of a bottle cap.

DOSAGE

The dosage determines whether the wine will be dry, sweet, or any style in between. The following shows you the guidelines the winemaker uses when he adds the dosage.

Brut: *Dry*
Extra dry: *Semidry*
Sec: *Semisweet*
Demi-sec: *Sweet*

COMMON CHAMPAGNE aromas:

Apple	Yeast (bread dough)
Toast	Hazelnuts/walnuts
Citrus	

WOMEN AND CHAMPAGNE

Women, particularly ones attached to royal courts, deserve much of the credit for Champagne's international fame. Madame de Pompadour said that Champagne was the only drink that left a woman still beautiful after drinking it. Madame de Parabère once said that Champagne was the only wine to give brilliance to the eyes without flushing the face.

IT IS RUMORED that Marilyn Monroe once took a bath in 350 bottles of Champagne. Her biographer George Barris said that she drank and breathed Champagne "as if it were oxygen."

WHEN A London reporter asked Madame Lilly Bollinger when she drank Champagne, Madame Bollinger replied: "I drink it when I'm happy and when I'm sad. Sometimes I drink it when I'm alone. When I have company I consider it obligatory. I trifle with it if I'm not hungry and drink it when I am. Otherwise I never touch it—unless I'm thirsty."

UNTIL AROUND 1850, all Champagne was sweet.

OCCASIONALLY A Champagne will be labeled "extra brut," which is drier still than brut.

BRUT AND extra-dry are the wines to serve as apéritifs, or throughout the meal. Sec and demi-sec are the wines to serve with desserts and wedding cake!

BLANC DE BLANCS Champagne is made from 100% Chardonnay.

BLANC DE NOIR Champagne is made from 100% Pinot Noir.

THERE ARE more than 100 Champagne houses in France and about 40 Champagnes available in the United States.

What accounts for the different styles of Champagne?

Going back to the three grapes we talked about that are used to make Champagne, the general rule is: The more white grapes in the blend, the lighter the style of the Champagne. And more red grapes in the blend, the fuller the style of the Champagne.

Also, some producers ferment their wines in wood. Bollinger ferments some, and Krug ferments all their wines this way. This gives the Champagne fuller body and bouquet than those fermented in stainless steel.

How do I buy a good Champagne?

First, determine the style you prefer, whether full-bodied or light-bodied, a dry brut or a sweet demi-sec. Then make sure you buy your Champagne from a reliable shipper/producer. Each producer takes pride in its distinctive house style, and strives for a consistent blend, year after year. The following are some brands in national distribution to look for. While it is difficult to be precise, the designations generally conform to the style of the houses.

LIGHT, DELICATE

A. Charbaut et Fils
Jacquesson
Lanson

LIGHT TO MEDIUM

Billecart-Salmon
Deutz
Nicolas Feuillatte
Laurent-Perrier
G.H. Mumm
Perrier-Jouët
Pommery
Ruinart Père & Fils
Taittinger

MEDIUM

Charles Heidsieck
Moët & Chandon
Piper-Heidsieck
Pol Roger

MEDIUM TO FULL

Henriot
Louis Roederer

FULL, RICH

Bollinger
A. Gratien
Krug
Veuve Clicquot

When is Champagne ready to drink?

As soon as you buy it. Champagne is something you can drink right away. Non-vintage Champagnes are meant to be drunk within two to three years, and vintage and prestige cuvée Champagnes can be kept longer, about ten to fifteen years. So if you're still saving that Dom Pérignon that you received for your tenth wedding anniversary fifteen years ago, don't wait any longer. Open it!

What's the correct way to open a bottle of Champagne?

Before we sip Champagne in class, I always take a few moments to show everyone how to open a bottle of Champagne properly. I do this for a good reason. Opening a bottle of Champagne can be dangerous, and I'm not kidding. If you know the pounds per square inch that are under pressure in the bottle, you know what I'm talking about.

OPENING CHAMPAGNE CORRECTLY

1. It is especially important that the bottle be well chilled before you open it.

2. Cut the foil around the top of the bottle.

3. Place your hand on top of the cork, never removing your hand until the cork is pulled out completely. (I know this may seem a bit awkward, but it's very important.)

4. Undo the wire. At this point, it's probably safer to leave the wire on.

5. Carefully put a cloth napkin over the top of the cork; if the cork pops, it will go safely into the napkin.

6. Remove the cork gently, slowly turning the bottle in one direction and the cork in another. The idea behind opening a bottle is to ease the cork out gently rather than cracking the bottle open with a loud pop and letting it foam. That may be a lot of fun, but it does nothing for the Champagne. When you pop off the cork, you allow the carbon dioxide to escape. That carbon dioxide is what gives Champagne its sparkle. If you open a bottle of Champagne in the way I've just described, it can be opened hours before your guests arrive with no loss of carbon dioxide.

1. Moët & Chandon
2. Veuve Clicquot
3. Perrier-Jouët
4. Mumm
5. Taittinger

CHAMPAGNE HOUSES market about two-thirds of Champagne's wines, but they own less than 10% of the vineyards.

"It's not a Burgundy; it's not a Bordeaux; it's a white wine; it's a sparkling wine that should be kept no longer than two to three years. It should be consumed young."
—CLAUDE TAITTINGER

THE PRESSURE in a bottle of Champagne is close to 90 pounds per square inch (or "six atmospheres," or roughly three times the pressure in your automobile tire).

CHAMPAGNE IS put into heavy bottles to hold the pressurized wine. This is another reason why Champagne is more expensive than ordinary wine.

IN 1999, a record 327 million bottles of Champagne were sold.

Which glasses should Champagne be served in?

AS BEAUTIFUL as Helen was, the resulting glass was admittedly wide and shallow.

No matter which Champagne you decide to serve, you should serve it in the proper glass. There's a little story behind the Champagne glass, dating back to Greek mythology. The first *coupe* was said to be molded from the breast of Helen of Troy. The Greeks believed that wine drinking was a sensual experience, and it was only fitting that the most beautiful woman take part in shaping the chalice.

Centuries later, Marie Antoinette, Queen of France, decided it was time to create a new Champagne glass. She had coupes molded to her own breasts, which changed the shape of the glass entirely, since Marie Antoinette was, shall we say, a bit more well-endowed than Helen of Troy.

The glasses shown to the left are the ones commonly used today—the flute and the tulip-shaped glass. Champagne does not lose its bubbles as quickly

TO EVALUATE Champagne, look at the bubbles. The better wines have smaller bubbles and more of them. Also, with a good Champagne, the bubbles last longer. Bubbles are an integral part of the wines of Champagne. They create texture and mouth feel.

HOW MANY bubbles are in a bottle of Champagne? According to scientist Bill Lembeck, 49 million per bottle!

CHAMPAGNE BOTTLE SIZES

Magnum	2 bottles
Jeroboam	4 bottles
Rehoboam	6 bottles
Methuselah	8 bottles
Salmanazar	12 bottles
Balthazar	16 bottles
Nebuchadnezzar	20 bottles

WINE AND FOOD

Champagne is one of the most versatile wines that you can drink with a number of foods, from apéritif to dessert. Here are some Champagne-and-food combinations that experts suggest:

CLAUDE TAITTINGER: *Mr. Taittinger's general rule is: "Never with sweets." Instead, he suggests "a Comtes de Champagne Blanc de Blancs drunk with seafood, caviar, or pâté of pheasant." Another note from Mr. Taittinger: He doesn't serve Champagne with cheese because, he says, "The bubbles do not go well." He prefers red wine with cheese.*

CHRISTIAN POL ROGER: *With Brut non-vintage: light hors d'oeuvres, mousse of pike. With vintage: pheasant, lobster, other seafood. With rosé: a strawberry dessert.*

in these glasses as it did in the old-fashioned model, and these shapes also enhance the smell and aromas of the wine in the glass.

What's the difference between Champagne and sparkling wine?

As I've already mentioned, Champagne is the wine that comes from the Champagne region of France. In my opinion, it is the best sparkling wine in the world, because the region has the ideal combination of elements conducive to excellent sparkling winemaking. The soil is fine chalk, the grapes are the best grown anywhere for sparkling wine, and the location is perfect. This combination of soil, climate, and grapes is reflected in the wine.

Sparkling wine, on the other hand, is produced in many areas, and the quality varies from wine to wine. The Spanish produce the popular Codorniu and Freixenet—both excellent values and good sparkling wines, known as *cavas*. The German version is called *Sekt*. Italy has *spumante*, which means "sparkling." The most popular Italian sparkling wine in the United States is Asti Spumante.

New York State and California are the two main producers of sparkling wine in this country. New York is known for Great Western, Taylor, and Gold Seal. California produces many fine sparkling wines, such as Chandon, Korbel, Piper-Sonoma, Schramsberg, Mumm Cuvée Napa, Roederer Estate, Domaine Carneros, Iron Horse, Scharffenberger, and "J," by Jordan Winery. Many of the larger California wineries also market their own sparkling wines.

Is there a difference between the way Champagne and sparkling wines are made?

Sometimes. All authentic Champagnes and many fine sparkling wines are produced by Méthode Champenoise, described earlier in this chapter, and which, as you now know, is laborious, intensive, and very expensive. If you see a bottle of sparkling wine for $3.99, you can bet that the wine was not made by this process. The inexpensive sparkling wines are made by other methods. For example, in one method the secondary fermentation takes place in large tanks. Sometimes these tanks are big enough to produce 100,000 bottles of sparkling wine.

DOMAINE CHANDON is owned by the Moët-Hennessy Group, which is responsible for the production of Dom Pérignon in France. In fact, the same winemaker is flown into California to make the blend for the Domaine Chandon.

ABOUT 20% OF the sparkling wines made in the United States are made by the Méthode Champenoise.

PIPER-HEIDSIECK has sold the Piper-Sonoma and its vineyards to Jordan Winery. Jordan will now produce the wines for Piper-Sonoma.

ANOTHER FORTIFIED wine is Madeira. Although it is not as popular as it once was, Madeira wine was probably the first wine imported into America. It was favored by the colonists, including George Washington, and was served to toast the Declaration of Independence.

TWO OTHER famous fortified wines are Marsala (from Italy) and Vermouth (from Italy and France).

THE NEUTRAL grape brandy, when added to the wine, raises the alcohol content to 15% to 20%.

FOR YOU historians, Puerto de Santa María is where Christopher Columbus's ships were built and where all the arrangements were made with Queen Isabella for his journey of discovery.

THE PALOMINO grape accounts for 90% of the planted vineyards in Sherry.

SHERRY

THE TWO GREATEST FORTIFIED WINES in the world are Port and Sherry. These wines have much in common, although the end result is two very different styles.

What exactly is fortified wine?

Fortified wine is made when a neutral grape brandy is added to wine to raise the wine's alcohol content. What sets Port apart from Sherry is when the winemaker adds the neutral brandy. It's added to Port during fermentation. The extra alcohol kills that yeast and stops the fermentation, which is why Port is relatively sweet. For Sherry, on the other hand, the brandy is added after fermentation.

Where is Sherry made?

Sherry is produced in sunny southwestern Spain, in Andalusia. An area within three towns makes up the Sherry triangle. They are:

JEREZ DE LA FRONTERA

PUERTO DE SANTA MARÍA

SANLÚCAR DE BARRAMEDA

Which grapes are used to make Sherry?

There are two main varieties:

Palomino (this shouldn't be too difficult for horse lovers to remember)
Pedro Ximénez (named after Peter Siemons, who brought the grape from Germany to Sherry)

What are the different types of Sherry?

Manzanilla: Dry
Fino: Dry
Amontillado: Dry to medium-dry
Oloroso: Dry to medium-dry
Cream: Sweet

What are the unique processes that characterize Sherry production?

Controlled oxidation and fractional blending. Normally a winemaker guards against letting any air into the wine during the winemaking process. But that's exactly what makes Sherry—the air that oxidizes the wine. The winemaker places the wine in barrels and stores it in a bodega.

What's a bodega?

No, I'm not talking about a Latino grocery store at 125th Street and Lexington Avenue in New York City. In Sherry, a *bodega* is an aboveground structure used to store wine. Why do you think winemakers would want to store the wine above ground? For the air. Sherry is an oxidized wine. They fill the barrels approximately two-thirds full, instead of all the way, and they leave the bung (cork) loosely in the barrel to let the air in.

THE ANGEL'S SHARE

When Sherry is made, winemakers let air into the barrels, and some wine evaporates in the process. Each year they lose a minimum of 3 percent of their Sherry to the angels, which translates into seven thousand bottles per day lost through evaporation!

Why do you think the people of Sherry are so happy all the time? Besides the excellent sunshine they have, the people breathe in oxygen and Sherry.

So much for controlled oxidation. Now for fractional blending. Fractional blending is carried out through the Solera System.

What's the Solera System?

The Solera System is an aging and maturing process that takes place through the dynamic and continuous blending of several vintages of Sherry that are stored in rows of barrels. At bottling time, wine is drawn out of these barrels—never more than one-third the content of the barrel—to make room for the new vintage. The purpose of this type of blending is to maintain the "house" style of the Sherry by using the "mother" wine as a base and refreshing it with a portion of the younger wines.

HERE'S ANOTHER abbreviation for you—PX. Do you remember TBA, QbA, AOC, and DOC? If you want to know Sherry, you may have to say "PX," which stands for the Pedro Ximénez grape.

PX IS USED to make Cream Sherry, like Harveys Bristol Cream, among others. Cream Sherry is a blend of PX and Oloroso.

SHERRY ACCOUNTS for less than 3% of Spanish wine production.

IN TODAY'S Sherry, only American oak is used to age the wine.

SOME SOLERAS can be a blend of 10 to 20 different harvests.

I'M SURE you're familiar with these four top-selling Sherries: Harveys Bristol Cream, Dry Sack, Tio Pepe, and La Ina.

TO CLARIFY the Sherry and rid it of all sediment, beaten egg whites are added to the wine. The question always comes up: "What do they do with the yolks?" Did you ever hear of flan? That's the puddinglike dessert made from all the yolks. In Sherry country, this dessert is called *tocino de cielo*, which translated means "the fat of the angels."

OF THE SHERRY consumed in Spain, 90% is Fino and Manzanilla. As one winemaker said, "We ship the sweet and drink the dry."

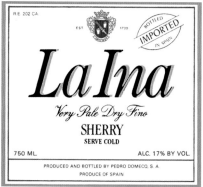

How do I buy Sherry?

Your best guide is the producer. It's the producer, after all, who buys the grapes and does the blending. Ten producers account for 60 percent of the export market. The top Sherry producers are:

GONZÁLEZ BYASS
CROFT
PEDRO DOMECQ
HARVEYS
SANDEMAN

WILLIAMS & HUMBERT
SAVORY AND JAMES
OSBORNE
EMILIO LUSTAU
HIDALGO

How long does a bottle of Sherry last once it's been opened?

Sherry will last longer than a regular table wine, because of its higher alcoholic content, which acts as a preservative. But once Sherry is opened, it will begin to lose its freshness. To drink Sherry at its best, you should consume the bottle within two weeks of opening it and keep the opened bottle refrigerated. Manzanilla and Fino Sherry should be treated as white wines and consumed within a day or two.

FOR FURTHER READING

I recommend *Sherry* by Julian Jeffs.

WINE AND FOOD

MAURICIO GONZÁLEZ: *He believes that Fino should always be served well chilled. He enjoys having Fino as an apéritif with Spanish tapas (hors d'oeuvres), but he also likes to complement practically any fish meal with the wine. Some of his suggestions: clams, shellfish, lobster, prawns, langoustines, fish soup, or a light fish such as salmon.*

JOSÉ IGNACIO DOMECQ: *He suggests that very old and rare Sherry should be served with cheese. Fino and Manzanilla can be served as an apéritif or with light grilled or fried fish, or even smoked salmon. "You get the taste of the smoke better than if you have it with a white wine." Amontillado is not to be consumed like a Fino. It should be served with light cheese, chorizo (sausage), ham, or shish kebab. It is a perfect complement to turtle soup or a consommé. According to Mr. Domecq, dry Olor-oso is known as a sporty drink in Spain—something to drink before hunting, riding, or sailing on a chilly morning. With Cream Sherry, Mr. Domecq recommends cookies, pastries, and cakes. Pedro Ximénez, however, is better as a topping for vanilla ice cream or a dessert wine before coffee and brandy.*

PORT

PORT COMES FROM THE DOURO region in northern Portugal. In fact, in recent years, to avoid the misuse of the name "Port" in other countries, the true Port from Portugal has been renamed "Porto" (for the name of the port city from which it's shipped).

Just a reminder: Neutral grape brandy is added to Port during fermentation, which stops the fermentation and leaves behind up to 9 to 11 percent residual sugar. This is why Port is on the sweet side.

What are the two types of Port?

Wood Port: This type includes *Ruby Port*, which is dark and fruity, blended from young non-vintage wines (Cost: $); and *Tawny Port*, which is lighter and more delicate, blended from many vintages, aged in casks—sometimes up to forty years and longer. (Cost: $$/$$$)

Vintage Port: This wine is aged two years in wood and will mature in the bottle over time. (Cost: $$$$)

Is every year a vintage year for Port?

No, it varies from shipper to shipper. And in some years, no vintage Port is made at all. For example, in 1994, 1997, 2000, and 2003, four of the recent vintages for Port, most producers declared a vintage. On the other hand, in 1990 and 1993, Port, in general, was not considered vintage quality.

WOOD PORT VS. VINTAGE PORT

The biggest difference between wood Port (Ruby and Tawny) and vintage Port is this: The wood Port is ready to drink as soon as it is bottled and it will not improve with age. Vintage Port, on the other hand, gets better as it matures in the bottle. A great vintage Port will be ready to drink fifteen to thirty years after the vintage date, depending upon the quality of the vintage.

PORT WINE has been shipped to England since the 1670s. During the 1800s, to help preserve the Port for the long trip, shippers fortified it with brandy, resulting in Port as we know it today.

AS WITH SHERRY, Port evaporation is a problem—some 15,000 bottles evaporate into the air every year.

PORT IS usually 20% alcohol. Sherry, by comparison, is usually around 18%.

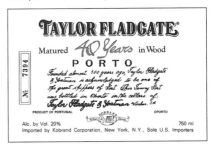

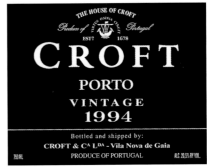

IN A TYPICAL year, 60% of the Port is Tawny and Ruby; 30% is vintage character; 7% is old Tawny; and 3% is vintage.

THE FIRST vintage Port was recorded in 1765.

OTHER PORT STYLES

LBV ("Late Bottled Vintage"): A wood Port made from a single vintage, bottled four to six years after the harvest. Similar in style to vintage Port, but lighter, ready to drink on release, no decanting needed.

QUINTA MEANS individual vineyard.

THE BRITISH are known to be Port lovers. Traditionally, upon the birth of a child, parents buy bottles of Port to put away for the baby until its 21st birthday, not only the age of maturity of a child, but also that of a fine Port.

"The 1994 vintage is the greatest for Port since the legendary 1945."
—JAMES SUCKLING, author, *Vintage Port*

COLHEITA: also from a single vintage, but wood-aged a minimum of seven years.

VINTAGE CHARACTER: Similar style to LBV, but a blend of vintages from the better years.

How do I buy Port?

Once again, as with Sherry, Port's grape variety should not dictate your choice. Find the style and the blend you prefer, but even more important, look for the most reliable producers. Of the Port available in the United States, the most important producers are:

A. A. FERREIRA	NIEPOORT & CO., LTD.
C. DA SILVA	QUINTA DO NOVAL
CHURCHILL	RAMOS PINTO
COCKBURN	ROBERTSON'S
CROFT	SANDEMAN
DOW	TAYLOR FLADGATE
FONSECA	W. & J. GRAHAM
HARVEYS OF BRISTOL	WARRE & CO.

BEST BETS FOR VINTAGES OF PORT

1963*   1970*   1977*   1983*   1985   1991*
1992   1994*   1997*   2000*   2003*

Note: * signifies exceptional vintage

Should vintage Port be decanted?

Yes, because you are likely to find sediment in the bottle. By making it a practice to decant vintage Port, you'll never be bothered by sediment.

How long will Port last once it's been opened?

Port has a tendency to last longer than ordinary table wine because of its higher alcohol content. But if you want to drink Port at its prime, drink the contents of the open bottle within one week.

FOR FURTHER READING

I recommend *The Port Companion* by Godfrey Spence and *Vintage Port: The Wine Spectator's Ultimate Guide* by James Suckling.

Matching Wine and Food

BY KEVIN ZRALY AND ANDREA IMMER

YOU'VE JUST TASTED your way through eight classes in this book and discovered at least a shopping cart's worth of wines to really enjoy. And for what purpose? Food! The final stop on the wine odyssey—and the whole point of the trip—is the dinner table. Quite simply, wine and food were meant for each other. Just look at the dining habits of the world's best eaters (the French, the Italians, the Spanish): Wine is the seasoning that livens up even everyday dishes. Salt and pepper shakers are a fixture of the American table, but in Europe it's the wine bottle.

ARE YOU a menu maven or a wine-list junkie? Personally, I look at the wine list first, choose my wine, and then make my meal selection.

WINE-AND-FOOD MATCHING BASICS

FIRST, FORGET EVERYTHING YOU'VE EVER heard about wine-and-food pairing. There's only one rule when it comes to matching wine and food: The best wine to pair with your meal is whatever wine you like. No matter what!

If you know what you want, by all means have it. Worried that your preference of a Chardonnay with a sirloin steak might not seem "right"? Remember, it's your own palate that you have to please.

What's wine-and-food synergy?

Sounds like a computer game for gourmets, right? If up until now you haven't been the wine-with-dinner type, you're in for a great adventure. Remember, the European tradition of wine with meals was not the result of a shortage of milk or iced tea. Rather, it results from what I call wine-and-food synergy—when the two are paired, both taste better.

How does it work? In the same way that combining certain foods improves their overall taste. For example, you squeeze fresh lemon onto your oysters, or grate Parmesan cheese over spaghetti marinara, because it's the combination of flavors that makes the dish.

CHARDONNAY IS a red wine masquerading as a white wine, which, in my opinion, makes it a perfect match for steak.

HOW DO I make my wine and food decision?
1. What kind of wine do I like?
2. Texture of food (heavy or light)
3. Preparation (grilled, sautéed, baked, etc.)
4. Sauce (cream, tomato, wine, etc.)

Now apply that idea to food-and-wine pairing; foods and wines have different flavors, textures, and aromas. Matching them can give you a new, more interesting flavor than you would get if you were washing down your dinner with, say, milk (unless you were dining on chocolate-chip cookies).

Do I have to be a wine expert to choose enjoyable wine-and-food matches?

Why not just use what you already know? Most of us have been tasting and testing the flavors, aromas, and textures of foods since before we got our first teeth, so we're all food experts! As we'll show you, just some basic information about wine and food styles is all you'll need to pick wines that can enhance your meals.

What about acidity?

Acid acts as a turbocharger for flavor. It enhances and lengthens the flavor of the dish. Watch television's Food Network. They're always using lemons and limes—acidic ingredients. Even dishes that aren't "sour" have a touch of an acid ingredient to pump up the flavor. As chef Emeril Lagasse says, "Kick it up a notch!"

What role does texture play?

There's an obvious difference in texture or firmness between different foods. Wine also has texture, and there are nuances of flavor in a wine that can make it an adequate, outstanding, or unforgettable selection with the meal. Very full-style wines have a mouth-filling texture and bold, rich flavors that make your palate sit up and take notice. But when it comes to food, these wines tend to overwhelm most delicate dishes (and clash with boldly flavored ones). Remember, we're looking for harmony. A general rule is: The sturdier or fuller in flavor the food, the more full-bodied the wine should be.

Once you get to know the wines, matching them with food is no mystery. Here is a list with some suggestions based on the texture of the wine and the foods they can match.

A FAIL-SAFE food: When in doubt, order roast chicken, which acts as a blank canvas for almost any wine style—light, medium, or full-bodied.

DO YOU drink your tea with milk or lemon? The milk coats your mouth with sweetness, whereas the lemon leaves your tongue with a dry crispness.

PROBABLY ONE of the reasons that classic French cuisine is noted for its subtlety is because the French want to let their wines "show off." This is an especially good idea if the wine is a special or "splurge" bottle.

White Wines

LIGHT-BODIED WHITES	MEDIUM-BODIED WHITES	FULL-BODIED WHITES
Alsace Pinot Blanc	Pouilly-Fumé	Chardonnay*
Alsace Riesling	Sancerre	Chablis Grand Cru
Chablis	White Graves	Meursault
Muscadet	Chablis Premier Cru	Chassagne-Montrachet
German Kabinett and Spätlese	Mâcon-Villages	Puligny-Montrachet
Sauvignon Blanc*	Pouilly-Fuissé	Viognier
Orvieto	St-Véran	
Soave	Montagny	
Verdicchio	Sauvignon Blanc*/ Fumé Blanc	
Frascati	Chardonnay*	
Pinot Grigio	Gavi	
Pinot Gris	Gewürztraminer	

Matching Foods

Sole	Snapper	Salmon
Flounder	Bass	Tuna
Clams	Shrimp	Swordfish
Oysters	Scallops	Lobster
	Veal paillard	Duck
		Roast chicken
		Sirloin steak

MY FAVORITE white wine for picnics is German Riesling Kabinett/Spätlese. On a hot summer day, I can think of no better white wine than a chilled German Riesling. The balance of fruit, acid, and sweetness as well as the lightness (low alcohol) make these wines a perfect match for salads, fruits, and cheese. For those who prefer a drier style Riesling, try Alsace, Washington State, or the Finger Lakes region of New York.

"WHAT'S YOUR favorite wine for Thanksgiving?" is one of the most-asked wine-and-food questions I get that I don't have a definitive answer for. The problem with Thanksgiving is that not just the turkey but everything else that is served with it (sweet potatoes, cranberry, butternut squash, stuffing) can create havoc with wine. This is also the big family holiday in the United States, and do you really want to share your best wines with Uncle Joe and Aunt Carol? Try "user-friendly" wines—easy drinking, inexpensive wines from reliable producers.

Note that starred wines are listed more than once. That's because they can be vinified in a range of styles from light to full, depending on the producer. When buying these, if you don't know the style of a particular winery, it's a good idea to ask the server or wine merchant for help.

MY FAVORITE red wine for picnics is Beaujolais. I'll never forget my first summer in France, sitting outside a bistro in Paris and being served a chilled Beaujolais. A great Beaujolais is the essence of fresh fruit without the tannins, and its higher acidity blends nicely with all picnic fare.

MY FAVORITE red wine for lunch is Pinot Noir. Since most of us have to go back to work after lunch, the light, easy-drinking style of a Pinot Noir will not overpower the usual luncheon fare of soups, salads, and sandwiches.

MY FAVORITE wine for lamb is Bordeaux or California Cabernet Sauvignon. In Bordeaux they have lamb with breakfast, lunch, and dinner! Lamb has such a strong flavor, it needs a strong wine. The big, full-bodied Cabernet Sauvignons from California and Bordeaux blend in perfectly.

PINOT NOIR is a white wine masquerading as a red wine, which makes it a perfect wine for fish and fowl. Other choices include Chianti Classico and Spanish Riojas (Crianza and Reserva). For barbecued shrimp in the middle of the summer, I opt for chilled Beaujolais.

BITTERNESS IN wine comes from the combination of high tannin and high alcohol, and these wines are best served with food that is either grilled, charcoaled, or blackened.

Red Wines

LIGHT-BODIED REDS	MEDIUM-BODIED REDS	FULL-BODIED REDS
Bardolino	Cru Beaujolais	Barbaresco
Valpolicella	Côtes du Rhône	Barolo
Chianti	Crozes-Hermitage	Bordeaux (great châteaus)
Rioja-Crianza	Burgundy Premiers and Grands Crus	Châteauneuf-du-Pape
Beaujolais	Bordeaux (Crus Bourgeois)	Hermitage
Beaujolais-Villages	Cabernet Sauvignon*	Cabernet Sauvignon*
Burgundy (Village)	Merlot*	Merlot*
Bordeaux (proprietary)	Zinfandel*	Zinfandel*
Pinot Noir*	Chianti Classico Riserva	Syrah/Shiraz*
	Dolcetto	Malbec*
	Barbera	
	Rioja Reserva and Gran Reserva	
	Syrah/Shiraz*	
	Pinot Noir*	
	Malbec*	

Matching Foods

Salmon	Game birds	Lamb chops
Tuna	Veal chops	Leg of lamb
Swordfish	Pork chops	Beefsteak (sirloin)
Duck		Game meats
Roast chicken		

Note that starred wines are listed more than once. That's because they can be vinified in a range of styles from light to full, depending on the producer. When buying these, if you don't know the style of a particular winery, it's a good idea to ask the server or wine merchant for help.

Do sauces play a major role when you're matching wine and food?

Yes, because the sauce can change or define the entire taste and texture of a dish. Is the sauce acidic? Heavy? Spicy? Subtly flavored foods let the wine play the starring role. Dishes with bold, spicy ingredients can overpower the flavor nuances and complexity that distinguish a great wine.

Let's consider the effect sauces can have on a simple boneless breast of chicken. A very simply prepared chicken paillard might match well with a light-bodied white wine. If you add a rich cream sauce or a cheese sauce, then you might prefer a medium-bodied or even a full-bodied white wine. A red tomato-based sauce, such as a marinara, might call for a light-bodied red wine.

No-Fault Wine Insurance

Drinking wine with your meals should add enjoyment, not stress; but it happens all too often. You briefly eye the wine list or scan the wine-shop shelf, thinking well, maybe . . . a beer. In the face of so many choices, you end up going with the familiar. But it can be easy to choose a wine to enjoy with your meal.

From endless experimentation at home and in the restaurant, I've come up with a list of "user-friendly" wines that will go nicely with virtually any dish. What these wines have in common is that they are light- to medium-bodied, and they have ample fruit and acidity. The idea here is that you will get a harmonious balance of flavors from both the wine and the food, with neither overwhelming the other. Also, if you want the dish to play center stage, your best bets are wines from this list.

THE ADDITION of salt highlights both the tannins and the alcohol in wine.

Cooking with Wine

Try to use the same wine or style that you are going to serve.

Spicy Sauces

Try something with carbon dioxide, such as a Champagne or a sparkling wine.

User-Friendly Wines

ROSÉ WINES	WHITE WINES	RED WINES
Virtually any rosé or white Zinfandel	Pinot Grigio	Chianti Classico
	Sauvignon Blanc/ Fumé Blanc	Rioja Crianza
	German Riesling Kabinett and Spätlese	Beaujolais-Villages
	Pouilly-Fumé and Sancerre	Côtes du Rhône
	Mâcon-Villages	Pinot Noir
	Champagne and sparkling wines	Merlot

These wines work well for what I call "restaurant roulette"—where one diner orders fish, another orders meat, and so on. They can also match well with distinctively spiced ethnic foods that might otherwise clash with a full-flavored wine. And, of course, all these wines are enjoyable to drink on their own.

WINE AND CHEESE—FRIENDS OR FOES?

As in all matters of taste, the topic of wine and food comes with its share of controversy and debate. Where it's especially heated is on the subject of matching wine and cheese.

But wait! Isn't it common wisdom that wine and cheese are "naturals" for each other? For me, a good cheese and a good wine will enhance the flavors and complexities of both.

The key to this match is in carefully selecting the cheese; therein lies the controversy. Some chefs and wine-and-food experts caution that some of the most popular cheeses for eating are the least appropriate for wine because they overpower it—a ripe cheese like Brie is a classic example.

The "keep-it-simple" approach applies again here. I find that the best cheeses for wines are the following: Parmigiano-Reggiano, fresh Mozzarella, Pecorino, Talleggio, and Fontina from Italy; Chèvre, Montrachet, Tomme, and Gruyère from France; Dutch Gouda; English or domestic Cheddar; domestic aged or fresh goat cheese and Monterey Jack; and Manchego from Spain.

My favorite wine-and-cheese matches:

Chèvre/fresh goat cheese—Sancerre, Sauvignon Blanc

Montrachet, aged (dry) Monterey Jack—Cabernet Sauvignon, Bordeaux

Pecorino or Parmigiano Reggiano—Chianti Classico Riserva, Brunello di Montalcino, Cabernet Sauvignon, Bordeaux, Barolo, and Amarone

Manchego—Rioja, Brunello di Montalcino

What to drink with Brie? Try Champagne or sparkling wine. And blue cheeses, because of their strong flavor, overpower most wines except—get ready for this—dessert wines! The classic (and truly delicious) matches are Roquefort cheese with French Sauternes, and Stilton cheese with Port.

MY FAVORITE cheese with wine is Parmigiano-Reggiano. Now we are really getting personal! I love Italian food, wine, and women (I even married one), but Parmigiano-Reggiano is not just to have with Italian wine. It also goes extremely well with Bordeaux, California Cabernets, and even the lighter Pinot Noirs.

SWEET SATISFACTION: WINE WITH DESSERT, WINE AS DESSERT

I REMEMBER MY FIRST TASTE of a dessert wine—a Sauternes from France's Bordeaux region. It was magical! Then there are also Port, Cream Sherry, Beerenauslese, to name a few—all very different wines with one thing in common: sweetness. Hence the name "dessert" wines—their sweetness closes your palate and makes you feel satisfied after a good meal. But with wines like these, dessert is just one part of the wine-and-food story.

"Wine with dessert?" you're thinking. At least in this country, coffee is more common, a glass of brandy or liqueur if you're splurging. But as more and more restaurants add dessert wines to their by-the-glass offerings, perhaps the popularity will grow for these kinds of wine. (Because they're so rich, a full bottle of dessert wine isn't practical unless several people are sharing it. For serving at home, dessert wines in half-bottles are a good alternative.)

I like a dessert wine a few minutes before the dessert itself, to prepare you for what is to come. But you certainly can serve a sweet dessert wine with the course.

Here are some of my favorite wine-and-dessert combinations:

Port—dark chocolate desserts, walnuts, poached pears, Stilton cheese

Madeira—milk chocolate, nut tarts, crème caramel, coffee- or mocha-flavored desserts

Pedro Ximénez Sherry—vanilla ice cream (with the wine poured over it), raisin-nut cakes, desserts containing figs or dried fruits

Beerenauslese and Late Harvest Riesling—fruit tarts, crème brûlée, almond cookies

Sauternes—fruit tarts, poached fruits, crème brûlée, caramel and hazelnut desserts, Roquefort cheese

Muscat Beaumes-de-Venise—crème brûlée, fresh fruit, fruit sorbets, lemon tart

Asti Spumante—fresh fruits, biscotti

Vouvray—fruit tarts, fresh fruits

Vin Santo—biscotti (for dipping in the wine)

MY FAVORITE wine for chocolate is Port. For me, both chocolate and Port mean the end of the meal. They are both rich, sweet, satisfying, and sometimes even decadent together.

Often, I prefer to serve the dessert wine as dessert. That way I can concentrate on savoring the complex and delicious flavors with a clear palate. It's especially convenient at home—all you have to do to serve your guests an exotic dessert is pull a cork! And if you're counting calories, a glass of dessert wine can give you the satisfying sweetness of dessert with a lot less bulk (and zero fat!).

12 BOTTLES OF wine = 1 case

BOTTLE SIZES

375 ml = 12.7 oz = half bottle
750 ml = 25.4 oz = full bottle
1.5 liters = 50.8 oz = magnum (two bottles)

How much wine should I order for my dinner party?

At a dinner party where several wines will be served, I allow one bottle for every five people, which equals approximately one 5-oz. glass per person.

Okay. But, really, I just want to know the best wine to serve with hors d'oeuvres for my dinner reception.

Champagne. One of the most versatile wines produced in the world, Champagne has a "magical effect" on guests. Whether served at a wedding or a dinner at home, Champagne remains a symbol of celebration, romance, prosperity, and fun.

The Business of Wine:
From the Winery to the Consumer

I PURCHASED MY FIRST WINE BOOK when, as a bartender during my college days, I was responsible for ordering all the wine for the restaurant where I worked. It was 1970 and, at nineteen years old, I was overwhelmed by the amount of information I needed to learn, understand, and memorize. Back then, when the selection and availability of wine was far more limited, wine knowledge began with learning all about French wines and progressed with a casual introduction to Italian, Spanish, and German wines; there was little need to know much about California wine.

Today's wine buyer has thousands of choices: California has become one of the world's leading wine producers; excellent wineries have developed in every region of the United States; and outstanding wines from Australia, Chile, Argentina, New Zealand, and South Africa have become permanent fixtures in the U.S. market.

To help readers negotiate their way through this more complicated world of wine, I've added this chapter in order to share some of the knowledge I've acquired over the last thirty years in a way that I hope will benefit readers who are interested in developing their own taste, building their own wine collection, or looking for a good bottle of wine for tonight's dinner.

So let's begin by learning how the wine industry works, examine how it came to work this way, and explore the primary ways consumers can purchase wine. Since most Americans buy wine in either retail wine and liquor stores or in restaurants, let's begin with the retail stores.

Buying wine in a retail store sounds simple enough: You walk in looking for wine. You're either shopping for a specific wine or you're looking for a new wine to try out with tonight's dinner. The point is, you want to buy wine and you're looking forward to enjoying it.

That simple shopping trip is often very frustrating, however. The typical experience leaves buyers unable to find the year, label, or type of wine they're looking for. Instead they're confronted with an almost overwhelming choice of wines, many of which they know nothing about.

Why doesn't the wine shop have the exact bottle you want? Because wine retailing is different from most other retailing in the United States.

NORTH CAROLINA liquor stores can sell only wine that is fortified (more than 15.5% alcohol).

IN VERMONT and Oregon, liquor stores cannot sell wine.

IN VIRGINIA, liquor stores can sell only Virginia wines.

WANT TO buy wine on Sunday? Nineteen states prohibit the sale of wine on Sundays.

WANT TO buy your wine with a credit card? Six states still do not allow you to use a credit card for wine purchases.

SOME STATES allow retailers to import wine but most do not.

What makes wine retailing unique?

First you have to understand that small producers from all over the world produce wine in limited quantities. Because their supply is limited, your ability to find exactly what you're looking for is chancy. The store you're shopping in might be sold out of the wine you want or might never have stocked the wine. In fact, it might never even have been offered the opportunity to purchase the wine in the first place.

Second, unlike food, clothing, or electronics, no national retail or distribution network exists for wines—and that's because of some uniquely American history.

THE LEGACY OF PROHIBITION (1920–33)

THE FOLLOWING states permit wine to be sold only in liquor stores:

Alaska
Arkansas
Delaware
Kansas
Minnesota
Mississippi
New York
Oklahoma
Pennsylvania
South Dakota
Tennessee
Utah

LAWS REGARDING THE SALE OF wine and spirits go back to 1933, to the repeal of the Twenty-first Amendment to the Constitution, which ended thirteen years of Prohibition. Prohibition taught the federal government that prohibiting the sale and consumption of alcoholic beverages created far more problems than it solved: U.S. citizens wanted their alcohol and they were going to have it. Crime rates rose and tax revenues fell. As a result, once Prohibition ended, the federal government decided to take a very cautious approach to regulating the sale and distribution of all alcoholic beverages. Instead of setting up laws on a federal level, they opted to let individual states legislate intrastate and interstate distribution.

The result of this decision is that each of the fifty states has different rules and regulations, creating an enormous challenge for wine producers—foreign and domestic—in bringing their wines to market. In New York State, for example, an individual can buy a retail liquor license to operate a retail liquor store. That shop will be allowed to sell only wine and spirits, not beer. Supermarkets in New York are allowed to sell beer, but not wine or spirits. Across the river in New Jersey, in many places you can buy food and wine in the same store. In Pennsylvania, wine and liquor stores are run by the state, not by individuals, and the state authority sets pricing and selection policies. Some states make matters even worse by allowing individual counties and even municipalities within the state to set up their own rules. As you can imagine, this makes the distribution of wines and spirits in the United States an extremely complex business.

CONTROL STATES

As it was the right and privilege of each state to decide how to control, sell, and distribute "adult" beverages, many states and jurisdictions decided to control the sale of wine, beer, and spirits at the retail and wholesale level.

These jurisdictions control the sale of distilled spirits and, in some cases, wine, through government agencies at the wholesale level. Twelve states also exercise control over retail sales for off-premises consumption either through government-operated package stores or designated outlets which the state supervises with a sales-agency relationship.

There are eighteen states that are called control states. In five of them (noted below with asterisks), the state and/or local governments control wine distribution. In Virginia and Idaho, the state controls the sale of wines produced there.

CONTROL STATES

Alabama	Michigan	Utah*
Idaho	Montana	Vermont
Iowa	New Hampshire*	Virginia
Maine	North Carolina	Washington
Maryland	Ohio	West Virginia
(Montgomery County)	Oregon	Wyoming*
Mississippi*	Pennsylvania*	

So how does wine ever get to retail stores?

Given the complexity of a fifty-state system, the wine industry has set up a three-tiered system of distribution. The system was designed to allow for areas of specialization along the cumbersome path of getting wine to consumers.

The three tiers are

Tier 1: Importer or winery

Tier 2: Wholesaler (distributor)

Tier 3: Retailer or restaurant

Tier 1—Importers and Wineries

The first tier comprises importers and wineries. A winery is self-explanatory: These are the winemakers who actually make the wines you buy in a wine shop or enjoy in a restaurant. The largest portion of all wine produced in the

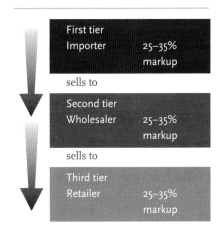

THE THREE-TIER SYSTEM

First tier
Importer — 25–35% markup

sells to

Second tier
Wholesaler — 25–35% markup

sells to

Third tier
Retailer — 25–35% markup

United States is sold by wineries directly to second-tier wholesalers.

Importers are buyers. They select wines from producers all over the world, sometimes entering into exclusive arrangements with them, negotiating prices, and shipping wines into the United States.

This first tier of wine distribution is responsible for selecting and bringing to market more than 90 percent of all wine sold in the United States.

Why do I need to know about importers?

Imagine that you own a vineyard in France and are making bottles and bottles of wine—so much wine, you can't sell all of it in France alone. You decide to sell your wine in the U.S. The most efficient way to do this is to find an importer. The importer will arrange to ship your wine from France, get it through customs, and make arrangements with wholesalers and distributors to sell and market it to retailers and restaurants throughout the United States. The best importers are very careful in selecting the wines they represent and, as a result, many of them have name recognition even at the consumer level.

Importers vary in size and territory: Some specialize in French wine, others in Italian; some deal exclusively with high-quality wines, others carry wine from many different countries, and others deal in bulk. Quality importers try to carry a full line of good wines at all price points.

As both a wine drinker and wine collector, I always check the wine label for the name of the importer, especially when I try a new wine. As I've mentioned, quality importers guard their reputations carefully by seeking out the best wines from abroad. Knowing the importer's reputation helps me assess the quality of an unknown wine. After the name of the winery, the importer's name is the most critical piece of information on a wine label. By paying attention to the importers listed on the labels of your favorite wines, you'll begin to find the ones whose tastes most often match your own. Remember those names as you explore new wines. An importer's endorsement is no guarantee that you'll enjoy the wine, but it's one of the more important criteria to consider in wine buying.

TIER 2—WHOLESALERS AND/OR DISTRIBUTORS

The second tier of wine distribution belongs to wholesalers and/or distributors. One of their functions is dealing with all the rules and regulations of the state in which they reside. Some wholesalers/distributors operate in multiple states

THERE ARE only a few import companies that deal solely with wine. Most of the larger companies are wine-and-spirit importers.

KEVIN ZRALY'S FAVORITE IMPORTERS OF HIGH-QUALITY WINE

Billington Imports (Chile and Argentina)
Chateau & Estate (Bordeaux)
Clicquot, Inc. (France)
European Cellars (France and Spain)
Fine Estates from Spain
Frederick Wildman (France and Italy)
Kermit Lynch (France)
Kobrand
Leonardo Locascio (Italy)
Martine's Wines (France)
Michael Skurnik
Neil Empson (Italy)
Paterno (France and Italy)
Robert Kacher (France)
Terry Theise (Germany)
Vineyard Brands
Wilson Daniels
W.J. Deutsch & Sons Ltd.

and have intricate knowledge of the rules and regulations in many states.

Wholesalers also play a key role in determining price. Negotiating with importers and wineries (remember, all wine is first brought to market through either importers or wineries), wholesalers negotiate how much they'll pay for each bottle they handle. They then sell directly to retail stores and restaurants.

It's not important for individual wine buyers to know the names of wholesalers. They're key players for the first and third tiers: wineries and importers, and retailers and restaurants. To the consumer, they're all but invisible.

What factors determine the price of wine?

First, the importer has made some money, negotiated a price with the producer, added his costs of shipping and marketing, and included his profit. Next, the importer sells his wine to the wholesaler. The wholesaler has to cover the cost he's paid the importer or winery as well as warehousing, shipping, delivering, other expenses, and, of course, include his profit. He then sells to the retailer and restaurateur. The retailer or restaurateur buying the wine determines the final price that you, the consumer, will pay.

Retail pricing in wine is similar to other retail businesses. There are no fixed rules and no standard markups. But general policies do exist. Full markup equals 50 percent of what the retailer pays for the wine. In a competitive marketplace, some retailers sell wines at significantly lower markups. The average markup probably runs between 25 percent and 35 percent.

Retailers can use pricing as a marketing tool: Sometimes retailers sell popular wines at a lower markup—or even at cost, where permissible—as a lure to bring customers into the store hoping that they'll buy other items at a higher markup as well. Some retailers discount prices as a matter of policy, appealing directly to the cost-conscious wine consumer. Retailers often put old or slow-selling stock on sale to clean out their inventory and make room for new wines. (Remember, most wine produced in the world is meant to be consumed within one year.)

The size and selection of the store, the store's location, and the service and knowledge of the owners and staff are also factors that determine pricing. If you are a serious wine buyer, find a good retailer in your area and form a relationship with the staff. As a regular customer, you will end up with better pricing and the most current information on the wines you're likely to enjoy.

ACQUISITIONS AND MERGERS

A major change in retail and wholesale wine buying in the United States over the last ten years—directly affecting pricing and distribution—has been the many acquisitions and mergers. Three of the biggest recent sales were of Seagrams to Pernod Ricard and Diageo in 2001; Chalone Wine Group to Diageo in 2004; and Robert Mondavi Winery to Constellation in 2004.

WHOLESALE ACQUISITIONS AND MERGERS

What used to be a small mom-and-pop wholesale business has turned into a major corporate delivery system of wines to retailers and restaurants. Look at the two top wholesalers in the country: Southern Wines and Spirits began as a wholesaler in Florida and is now operating in twelve states. The Charmer-Sunbelt Group, which began in New York, now has wholesale operations in sixteen states.

COSTCO IS the leading retailer of wine in the United States, with 400 stores and $620 million in wine sales.

KEVIN ZRALY'S PET PEEVES ABOUT
WINE RETAIL

Inconsistent pricing

Lack of knowledgeable owners
    and staff

Poor ventilation and temperature
    control

Stores all look the same

Not consumer-friendly

Disorganization

Too dependent upon critics' choices
    and not their own

Intimidating staff

QUESTIONS A GOOD RETAILER
SHOULD ASK

1. What's your price range?

2. Is this a wine for a dinner party,
   special occasion, gift, everyday
   wine?

3. Red or white?

4. What country?

5. Dry, semidry, sweet?

6. Light, medium, or full-bodied?

7. Do you have a particular grape
   variety that you enjoy?

8. If it's for a special dinner, what's the
   menu?

9. How many bottles will you need?

TIER 3—THE RETAILER AND THE RESTAURATEUR

Finally, we return to the retailer and to the restaurateur. They are the last link in the wine distribution system in the United States, the link most familiar to wine consumers all across the country, and the link most important to you.

You've now learned that there is no single way, because of the different laws of each of the fifty states, for me to be specific about how you can buy wine in your particular state, county, or municipality. From this point on, I'll describe the ways most generally available to wine buyers throughout the country and I'll give general advice about buying wine, which should be useful regardless of where you do your buying.

Wine consumers have several different options when it comes to buying wine. The most common options are:

> Retail stores
> Restaurants
> Wineries
> Wine clubs
> Wine auctions
> The Internet

What are the wine retail store options?

Keeping in mind that state laws vary, there are generally four types of outlets that sell wine at retail. They are:

> Supermarkets and grocery stores
> Drugstores
> Gas stations and convenience stores
> Wine and liquor stores

SUPERMARKETS AND GROCERY STORES

A tremendous amount of wine is sold in supermarkets. Some wine publications even track total monthly wine sales in supermarkets, broken down by varietals and style, to give an indication of overall national sales. The biggest advantage of buying wine in supermarkets is convenience: you can buy your wine at the same time and in the same place you're buying your groceries. Supermarkets often offer decent wines at reasonable prices. However, with some notable exceptions, supermarkets tend to offer a limited selection, often stocking only the most mass-produced and -marketed varieties. These can be perfectly satisfying wines, but you'll have to do your own homework by buying and trying. (See "Wine-Buying Strategies for Your Wine Cellar.") Because wine is not their primary business, these stores rarely have knowledgeable staff and are unlikely to offer any special ordering service. But if your wine buying retail choices are limited or you just want the convenience, try to shop in a supermarket whose selection shows some knowledge and imagination. Those are likely to be supermarkets with wine managers. Get to know the wine manager. Listen to his recommendations and if you find them satisfying, use him as a resource for trying new wines.

Where state laws permit, national retail chains like Target and Costco have begun selling wine. Since their core business is focused on discount, it's possible to find some good wines at very good prices.

DRUGSTORES, GAS STATIONS, AND CONVENIENCE STORES

Drugstores, gas stations, and convenience stores are useful retail outlets only when there are no other alternatives. Prices can be attractive, but selections are likely to be very limited. If you're serious about wine, these are not retailers you'll be doing a lot of business with, but for wines under twenty dollars, they will probably have something worth buying.

WINE AND LIQUOR STORES

Fortunately for the majority of wine consumers, there are retailers who specialize in wine. They read the wine trade journals; they understand vintages, producers, importers, vineyards, varietals, and blends from all over the world. They might sell wine exclusively, or they might be full-service wine, liquor, and beer stores. These retailers are the heart and soul of the wine industry. They're often owned and staffed by dedicated wine professionals who take a keen interest in all the wines they carry, who care about the tastes and demands of their customers, and who will go out of their way to help you find a bottle of that special wine you had at a very expensive restaurant the night before. These are the shops you want to haunt. You want to get to know the staff, their tastes, and you want them to know you. As they begin to know you by the wines you buy, they'll make recommendations that are likely to suit your tastes and recommend wines you might not have otherwise tried.

THE FOLLOWING 24 states permit wine sales in any outlet:
- Alabama
- Arizona
- California
- Florida
- Georgia
- Hawaii
- Idaho
- Indiana
- Iowa
- Louisiana
- Maine
- Massachusetts
- Michigan
- Missouri
- Montana
- Nebraska
- New Hampshire
- New Jersey
- New Mexico
- Ohio
- South Carolina
- West Virginia
- Wisconsin
- Wyoming

YOU CAN buy any alcoholic beverage (beer, wine, spirits) at all four types of outlets in the following states:

Arizona
California
Hawaii
Massachusetts
Michigan
Missouri
Nebraska
Nevada
New Jersey
New Mexico
West Virginia
Wisconsin
Wyoming

The best advice I can offer a wine lover is to choose a wine retailer with the same care and consideration you would use in choosing a great restaurant, an understanding therapist, a skilled doctor, an experienced lawyer, or a creative hairdresser.

BUYING WINE IN RETAIL STORES

- *Go to a store that specializes in wine.*
- *Do your homework and price comparisons before you shop.*
- *Some retailers offer discounts on case lots. Ask.*
- *Never buy a case of wine without first trying a bottle.*
- *Don't be afraid to try a trusted retailer's suggestion—it's less expensive to experiment in a retail store than in a restaurant.*
- *Get on as many mailing lists as you can.*
- *Find out about in-store tastings.*
- *Know how much you want to spend.*

When should I go to a specialty wine store?

Following is a list of wines that are difficult to find but worth seeking. This list underscores the need for the serious wine buyer to seek out a knowledgeable wine merchant, because the best of these wines can be bought only through specialty retail wine stores.

Burgundy: Burgundy is one of the most complicated wine regions on earth. If you like Chardonnay and Pinot Noir and want to invest in one of France's treasures, you will need to find a store familiar with all the intricacies of Burgundy. They not only know the important villages, but they also have a good selection of great producers, the best vintages, and proper storage conditions.

California Cabernet Sauvignons: There are more than 1,600 wineries in California and hundreds of them produce Cabernet Sauvignon. Some of the best and most sought-after Cabernets are allocated by the producers to a few select retailers. Those retailers are given an allotment of wine—even they don't have an unlimited supply. These select retailers offer these choice wines only to their preferred customers. If you don't have a strong relationship with that retailer, you won't be able to buy the wine.

Bordeaux: There are more than seven thousand châteaus in Bordeaux but American wine enthusiasts are familiar with only about fifty of them.

Bordeaux is probably the most talked about wine region on earth, both because of the quality of its wine and the size of the region. It is also the number one wine sold through auction houses, and it appreciates in value more than any other wine.

Bordeaux is also unique: Unlike most other wines of the world, the best vintage Bordeaux produced is sold as a future—that is, it is bought even before it is bottled. Retail prices per bottle of a Bordeaux château—the same exact wine—can vary by as much as $100 a bottle. Price depends on whether the retailer purchased the wine as "futures," bought it when it first arrived in the United States, or bought it the day before you want to drink it. The bottom line: Compare Bordeaux prices at different retailers before buying. Also, make sure they have the right storage conditions.

The great wines of Italy: Twenty years ago it was easy to buy Italian wines—*no problemo*! Today's Italian wines are the best ever, produced with a vast array of names on the label (the names on the label can indicate region, type of grape, or, now, reflect a proprietary wine). Many of the best now sell in excess of $100 a bottle. I'm lucky: New York has many stores that specialize in Italian wine. Find the wine retailer in your state or city with the best knowledge and widest selection of Italian wines.

Is it possible to taste wines in the store before I buy them?

This sounds like a great concept and follows my rule never to buy a case of wine until I've tried a bottle. But it's problematic. While many grocers provide samples, the types of sample offered are limited and what is offered is often provided by the producer as a form of marketing. When were you allowed to taste a banana before buying a bunch?

Sampling exists in wine shops in the form of wine tastings. When offered, they are often supported by the importer or winery; they want you to try their wine hoping you'll like it enough to buy a bottle—or more.

Quality wine retailers often host their own wine tastings, and sometimes the wine is provided by the retailer himself. Some of them even have wine classes. These retailers are committed to introducing their regular customers to new types and varieties of wine. They understand that everything in wine is about taste: If you like it, you'll buy it. But even the highest-end retailer can't let you taste everything in his stock. Doing so would cost the retailer a great deal of money when supplies are limited and prices high.

SOME OF THE BEST-VALUE WINES AVAILABLE IN THE UNITED STATES BY STYLE

Alsace Riesling
Chianti Classico Riservas
Cabernet Sauvignon (Chile)
Crozes Hermitage
Cru Bourgeois (Bordeaux)
Languedoc-Rousillon
Non-vintage Champagne
Reservas from Rioja
Rosso from Tuscany
Côtes du Rhône
Sauvignon Blanc (all regions)

Of course, those pesky state-controlled regulations also play an important role in whether a store can offer the wine consumer samples. Again, different states have different rules. Nineteen states prohibit any wine sampling in retail outlets, while fifteen other states impose a variety of restrictions. Some of the most memorable restrictions are:

- Customers may receive only one three-ounce sample;
- A licensed salesperson may purchase one drink per customer;
- Only domestic farm wineries are allowed to be sampled;
- Never on Sundays.

KEVIN ZRALY'S TOP WINE CRITICS

CRITIC	PUBLICATION
Gerald Asher	*Gourmet* magazine
Anthony Dias Blue	CBS and *Bon Appetit*
Robert M. Parker Jr.	*The Wine Advocate*
Frank Prial and Eric Asimov	*The New York Times*
Jerry Shriver	*USA Today*
Steve Tanzer	*International Wine Cellar*
Lettie Teague	*Food and Wine* magazine
Dorothy J. Gaiter and John Brecher	*The Wall Street Journal*

If I can't taste the wine, should I pay attention to wine ratings?

We Americans love to rate things. We rate cars, restaurants, sporting events, television programs, movies, books, and medical care. Almost no aspect of American consumer habits exists that isn't rated. This came about partly as a response to the enormous variety of goods and services offered to consumers; with so many choices, ratings can be useful—especially in areas with numerous options, where you have little time or inclination (or ability) to do your own research. The power of ratings to influence consumer purchasing is so great, rating systems are often developed by ad councils, growers' cooperatives, hospitals, and sometimes, the federal government.

Ratings are a fact of life in America, and it was inevitable that rating systems would come to the wine industry. If you understand how the wine rating systems work, you can use them to your advantage. Ratings began in the wine trade as a 20-point scoring system to establish uniform standards at professional wine tastings. The 20-point system assigns a numerical value to each of four qualities that professional wine tasters judge when they taste wine. As you look at how the points are allotted, you'll see what qualities professionals are looking for and how important each one is in the rating. In the 20-point system, the qualities and maximum values are:

Color and appearance	3
Smell (aroma and bouquet)	5
Taste (flavor)	9
Length and quality	3
	20 points

Consumer wine ratings began with a 100-point system developed by the wine writer Robert M. Parker Jr. In the 100-point system, every wine begins with 50 points. As the quality of the wine increases, so does the number of points it receives—all the way up to an orgasmic 100 points! Nearly all wine publications and most wine critics have now adopted the 100-point system. It's the system you're most likely to encounter in wine shops, catalogs, books, and magazines.

Opinions are divided on whether this is the best way to judge wine; personally, I have no use for rating wine by numbers. In my classes, the only vote taken is whether you like the wine or not. For the consumer, a high rating gives credibility to a wine's quality. But be cautious in relying solely on ratings: If you consider 80 points a low rating, you might ignore many well-made, reasonably priced wines that have characteristics you would find appealing without breaking the bank.

You will definitely encounter ratings as you shop for wine in retail stores, on the Internet, in catalogs, and through wine clubs. Learn to use ratings to your best advantage. Get to know the critics with rating systems, choose the ones whose tastes most match your own, and buy accordingly. But keep in mind that critics are individuals, too. As with movie critics, book reviewers, and restaurant reviewers, no one's opinion will ever exactly match your own.

KEVIN ZRALY'S BEST WINE MAGAZINES

Decanter
Wine & Spirits
Wine Enthusiast
Wine Spectator

THE FOLLOWING wineries offer some of the best-value wines available in the United States:

- Beringer
- Chateau Ste. Michelle
- Columbia Crest
- Concha y Toro
- Fetzer
- Gallo of Sonoma
- Lindemans
- Robert Mondavi
- Rosemount

What about buying wine direct from wineries? Can I have it shipped to my home?

Buying wine at wineries can be fun and exciting. A wine tour of the Napa Valley will provide you with great scenery, good food, and a real education in how wine is made. You'll gain a better understanding of why each vineyard in a similar geographic area produces a unique product. You'll discover labels you've never heard of and find varietals that are often impossible to buy anywhere but at the source. You'll meet the growers and begin to understand the kind of passion, commitment, dedication, pride, and love they have for their grapes, their fields, their vocation, and their wine. Your knowledge of wine and appreciation of its complexity will expand exponentially. I encourage all wine enthusiasts to visit as many vineyards in as many regions and countries as possible. Visiting the source is a soulful experience. Plus, you get to actually taste the wine before you buy it!

But be careful how much you buy; the law might limit you to what you can carry home. Shipping wine is subject to an equally complex set of archaic rules and regulations as apply to the sale and transportation of all alcoholic beverages. Check your state, county, or local laws to find out whether you're legally allowed to have wine shipped to your home.

If you live in Southern California, tour the North Coast wineries of Napa and Sonoma, taste some excellent wines, and decide to have them shipped to your home, you're in luck: Intrastate shipping is perfectly legal. Twelve other states allow you to ship wine from California as well. But if you live in New York and buy wine from anywhere in California, you'll have to carry it home yourself: It's against the law in New York State to ship wine back to New York from out of state. New York is one of more than twenty states that prohibit direct shipment from out of state. However, in May 2005, the U.S. Supreme Court voted 5–4 to overturn such laws, calling them discriminatory. That leaves it up to the states to determine whether to allow *all* direct shipments (both intra- and interstate)—or to discontinue the practice entirely. In the meantime, check carefully before you make plans to ship any wine across state lines!

What about wine clubs? Are they a good source for wine?

I did a quick Internet search for "wine clubs" and found more than three hundred listings. Wine clubs exist to provide you, the wine consumer, an easy way to purchase wine without leaving home. They offer many types of service: Some clubs automatically ship new wines to you each month, some offer special "club discounts"; some offer proprietary brands; some offer rare wines; and some give the wine novice an introduction to the entire world of wine by automatically selecting and shipping a selection each month of different wines: red, white, foreign, and domestic.

My own experience with clubs has been disappointing; most don't really offer a better selection than I can find at a good wine retailer, and the rules and conditions of membership often aren't worth the trouble. But if you prefer the convenience of armchair shopping, look for a club that offers exactly what you're looking for, whether it's low price, automatic selection, or a wine education by mail. The same interstate shipping rules apply to clubs that apply to all wine shipping. As you investigate club buying, first check to make sure they can legally ship wine to you.

Another option I'd encourage you to investigate is your local wine retailer. Many have existing clubs and Web sites; those that don't will often set up a club just for you. Let your retailer know what you want: Describe your favorite wine color, regions, and price range, and decide how many bottles you want each month. Some retailers even deliver your selections right to your home. What they send will be specially selected for you and your taste.

Is it a good idea to buy wines at auction?

In the last ten years interest in wine has grown to such a degree that the finest wines are becoming increasingly difficult to find in retail stores. Years ago, I had no trouble buying wines that were ten, twenty, or even thirty years old from a good wine retailer. Today, I am lucky to find anything over five years old. Why? Supply and demand. Most good, aged wines are now sold at auction. Christie's started a wine auction division in 1966 and Sotheby's followed suit in 1970.

I asked Peter D. Meltzer, the auction correspondent for *Wine Spectator* magazine, if buying wine at auction was a good idea for consumers. His answer was conditional: Wine auctions are an excellent way to acquire fine and rare bottlings in a variety of formats that are not readily available

MORE AND more, wine lovers are turning to auctions to buy their wine: Worldwide auction sales totaled $33 million in 1994; within ten years that figure had more than tripled. In 2004, worldwide auctions passed the $100 million mark. New York had the largest share, at $65 million.

through traditional distribution channels. Mature wines often sell for less at auction than more recent releases typically found in retail stores. Auction prices often fall below retail and, occasionally, wholesale prices. Plus, mixed lots (mixed bottles in less than case lots) enable buyers to sample a wide cross section of wines without having to purchase any one bottle by the case. This creates a great educational "tasting kit." But you have to know what you're looking for, and have a good understanding of vintages, varietals, producers, and pricing. If you plan to buy wine at auction, you must do your homework first.

According to Mr. Meltzer, these are the most important strategies to master to buy wine successfully at auction

TWO-THIRDS of all wine sold at auction comes from the great châteaus of Bordeaux.

- Familiarize yourself with retail catalogs and recent prices paid for wines from the major auction houses. You wouldn't want to pay more at auction than the retailer next door charges; knowing what similar wines have sold for at recent auctions gives you an idea how much to bid on the wine you want.
- Carefully study condition reports and provenance information included in the auction catalog before considering a bid. Avoid lots that have not been stored in temperature- and humidity-controlled storage facilities. Remember, with few exceptions, you are buying as is.
- Try to attend pre-sale tastings, where offered, to sample as many of your potential bids as possible.
- Remember to factor the buyer's fee into your bidding strategy plus any applicable sales tax.
- Don't engage in bidding wars. You may win the bottle but lose the price war.
- Stay awake. There's always a point in large auctions where people seem to nod off. These are the moments when bargains present themselves to the wary. Late afternoon is often the best time for best buys.
- Small lots (three to four bottles) of premium wines often sell for proportionally less than complete, twelve-bottle cases. Large offerings (two to three dozen bottles) are often not as good a bargain as small lots.
- Wines in their original wooden case tend to be more expensive than those repacked in cardboard. Unless you plan to resell your wine, take advantage. The wooden case is nice, but not worth the extra cost.

What are futures in wine?

Think of the commodities market: Brokers race around the trading floor at the Board of Trade in Chicago buying and selling agricultural crops months, even years, before the crops are actually harvested. They're betting on future crop yields and market demand, both of which determine final prices once the crop is harvested. It's a form of gambling, with the broker hoping the price paid today for a bushel of next summer's corn will be less than the price per bushel when the corn is harvested.

Wine futures are somewhat similar. When you buy wine futures, you pay a retailer today for wine that hasn't matured and won't be ready for drinking for some years (and in the case of extraordinary wines, will actually improve for decades). You'll be able to buy the wine at a lower opening price, and you're betting that the wine will age well enough to be of greater value than what you originally paid.

Wine futures started in France. As in the example of the commodities market above, it began as a way wine brokers could buy wine at lower prices before it was even bottled. It provided benefits for both the producers and the brokers: It gave producers immediate cash to help cover their operating costs and provided brokers greater opportunity to make more money. Brokers were gambling that the wine value would increase enough to recoup their original costs and yield tidy profits.

I now understand a little bit about the wine futures market, but generally speaking, is wine a good investment?

It wasn't long ago that outstanding California wines couldn't find any buyers except serious wine collectors. Serious wine collectors are always in pursuit of new wines, looking for wines that they believe are underappreciated and undervalued. These same collectors, after tasting the extraordinary Cabernet vintages of the early 1990s, realized the potential for these wines in the fine-wine market. They bought all they could get. They brought the world's attention and focus to California wines, introducing the larger market of individual consumers to California's outstanding product, simultaneously increasing the value of their own California wine holdings. Now, because of the keen noses of those early collectors, the latest great vintage from the best producers of California Cabernet Sauvignon was already sold, just as it was entering the market. Nearly the entire production was bought by "new" wine collectors who are buying wines either to

TOP BORDEAUX FUTURES

Château Lafite Rothschild
Château Latour
Château Margaux
Château Haut-Brion
Château Léoville-Las-Cases
Château Pichon-Lalande
Château Cos d'Estournel
Château Palmer
Château Lynch Bages
Château La Mission-Haut-Brion
Château Cheval Blanc
Château Ausone
Château Le Pin
Château Pétrus
Château La Conseillante
Château Lafleur

BEST BORDEAUX VINTAGES

1961	1986	1996
1966	1988	2000
1970	1989	2003
1982	1990	2004
1985	1995	

TOP PORT FUTURES

Taylor Fladgate
Fonseca
Warre
Graham
Dow
Quinta do Noval

BEST PORT VINTAGES

1963	1994	2000
1977	1997	2003

enjoy at a later date or to sell the wines at auction five years from now at a profit. They are investing in wine.

Investment in wine for profit is a relatively new phenomenon. Even the great Bordeaux châteaus didn't make a large profit until twenty years ago. In 1982, the illustrious wine critic Robert M. Parker Jr. declared the 1982 Bordeaux vintage one of the best Bordeaux ever produced. This created an enormous demand for the wine, which was quickly bought up by collectors and "investors." It was a great call on Parker's part, and the 1982 vintage Bordeaux did, indeed, live up to his description. It aged remarkably well and ten years later sold for nearly double its 1982 price. This has had a profound impact on the wine industry. What was once a quiet little hobby of wine collectors, connoisseurs, and savvy retailers has now become big business.

Market conditions today are different from what they were even five years ago for another reason: In the last ten years, there have only been four great investment-grade vintages in Bordeaux and five great vintages of California wine. Investment-grade wines aren't produced with predictable regularity. Like any speculative venture, investing in wine is risky: You need to be sure you're willing to take a loss if you decide to buy wine solely as an investment. Plus, you'll need to make sure you have the right conditions in which to store your investment. And, of course, until recently, it was illegal in many states for individuals to sell wine without a license. You'll need to check your local laws.

By all means, buy wine by the case and buy futures if you can afford them. Even if you don't make any money, you'll still have the wine, and while it may not have brought you great wealth, it will be there for you to open, pour, and enjoy.

With that said, I am still investing my money on certain wines I believe will continue to increase in value. Here is my list:

BLUE CHIPS

1. The great châteaus of Bordeaux (Médoc) 1995, 1996, 2000, and 2003
2. The best producers of Napa Cabernet Sauvignon 1997, 1999, 2001, 2002, and 2003
3. The Rhône Valley, France, especially the great producers of Hermitage 1997, 1998, 1999, and 2003, and Châteauneuf du Pape 1998, 2000, 2001, and 2003
4. Vintage Port 1994, 1997, 2000, and 2003

OTHER GOOD CHOICES

5. Top Italian Super Tuscan 1997, 1999, 2001, and 2004
6. Best Estates of Burgundy 1999 and 2002
7. Barolos and Barbarescos 1996, 1997, 1998, 1999, 2000, 2001, and 2004

What are good wines to buy now and cellar for your child's twenty-first birthday?

Wines from the following regions and countries are the ones to look for:

2004	Napa Cabernet Sauvignon, Piedmont
2003	Rhône (North and South). Sauternes, Bordeaux, Port
2002	Napa Cabernet Sauvignon, Germany*, Burgundy**, Sauternes
2001	Napa Cabernet Sauvignon, Sauternes, Germany*, Rioja and Ribera del Duero
2000	Bordeaux, Châteauneuf-du-Pape, Piedmont, Amarone, Port
1999	Piedmont, Rhône (North), California Zinfandel, Burgundy**
1998	Bordeaux (St-Émilion/Pomerol), Rhône (South), Piedmont (Barolo, Barbaresco)
1997	Napa Cabernet Sauvignon, Tuscany (Chianti, Brunello), Piedmont, Amarone, Port, Australian Shiraz
1996	Burgundy, Piedmont, Bordeaux (Médoc), Burgundy**, Germany*, vintage Champagne
1995	Bordeaux, Rhône, Rioja, Napa Cabernet Sauvignon, vintage Champagne
1994	Port, Napa Cabernet Sauvignon and Zinfandel, Rioja
1993	Napa Cabernet Sauvignon and Zinfandel
1992	Port, Napa Cabernet Sauvignon and Zinfandel
1991	Rhône (North), Port, Napa Cabernet Sauvignon
1990	Bordeaux, Napa Cabernet Sauvignon, Rhône, Burgundy**, Tuscany (Brunello), Piedmont, Amarone, Sauternes, Champagne, Germany*
1989	Bordeaux, Rhône, Piedmont, Rioja
1988	Sauternes, Rhône (North), Piedmont
1987	Napa Cabernet Sauvignon and Zinfandel
1986	Bordeaux, Sauternes, Napa Cabernet Sauvignon
1985	Bordeaux, Port, Rhône (North), Champagne, Piedmont, Amarone

*Auslese and above   **Grand Cru

Wine-Buying Strategies for
Your Wine Cellar

2004 Top 10 Imported Wine
Brands in the United States

1. Yellow Tail (Australia)
2. Concha y Toro (Chile)
3. Riunite (Italy)
4. Lindemans (Australia)
5. Rosemount Estate (Australia)
6. Casarsa (Italy)
7. Bolla (Italy)
8. Georges Duboeuf (France)
9. Cavit (Italy)
10. Ecco Domani (Italy)

Buying and selecting wines for your cellar is the most fun and interesting part of wine appreciation—besides drinking it, of course! You've done all your studying and reading on the wines you like, and now you go out to your favorite wine store to banter with the owner or wine manager. You already have an idea what you can spend and how many bottles you can safely store until they're paired with your favorite foods and friends.

Wine buying has changed dramatically over the last twenty years. Many liquor stores have become wine-specialty stores, and both the consumer and retailer are much more knowledgeable. Even twenty years ago, the wines of California, Australia, and Chile were not the wines the consumer cared to buy. Back then, the major players were the wines of France and Italy. Today there's so much more diversity in wine styles and wine prices, it's almost impossible to keep up with every new wine and new vintage that comes on the market. You can subscribe, among many publications, to *Wine Spectator*; *The Wine Enthusiast*; *Wine & Spirits*; or *Wine Advocate*, Robert M. Parker Jr.'s newsletter, to help you with your choices, but ultimately you'll find the style of wine to suit your own personal taste.

In this book I don't recommend specific wines from specific years because I don't believe that everyone will enjoy the same wines, or that everyone has the same taste buds as I do. I think it's very important that every year the consumer have a general overview of what's hot and what's not. Here are some of my thoughts and strategies for buying wine this year.

There is, and will continue to be, an abundance of fine wine over the next few years. The vintage years of 1995, 1996, 2000, 2003, and 2004 in Bordeaux; 1999, 2000, 2001, and 2004 in Piedmont and Tuscany; 2001, 2002, and 2003 in Germany; 2003 in the Rhône Valley; 1999 and 2002 in Burgundy reds; 2003 in Chile and Argentina; and 2001 in Australian Shiraz will give us great wines to drink over the next few years. The 2001, 2002, and 2003 vintages for California Cabernet Sauvignon and Chardonnay are generally excellent. The 1994 and 2000 vintage Ports are available. Although many of these wines are high-priced, there still remain hundreds of wines under fifteen dollars that you can drink now or cellar for the future.

Anyone can buy expensive wines! In an average year I taste some three thousand wines. The real challenge is finding the best values—the ten-dollar bottle that tastes like a twenty-dollar bottle. The following is a list of my buying strategies for my own wine cellar. This is by no means a complete roster of great wines, but most of these are retasted every year and have been consistently good.

Everyday Wines
($10 and under)

Argentina

Bodegas Norton Malbec

Bodegas Esmeralda Malbec
Mendoza Alamos

Trapiche Malbec

Australia

Jacob's Creek Shiraz/Cabernet

Lindemans Chardonnay Bin 65

Oxford Landing Sauvignon Blanc

Penfolds Semillon/Chardonnay

Rosemount Chardonnay or
Shiraz/Cabernet (Diamond Label)

Yellow Tail

California

Beringer Merlot Founders Estate

Buena Vista Sauvignon Blanc

Fetzer Merlot Eagle Peak

Fetzer Sauvignon Blanc or Syrah

Forest Glen Cabernet Sauvignon or
Shiraz

Forest Ville Selections Cabernet or
Chardonnay

Monterey Vineyard Cabernet
Sauvignon

Napa Ridge Merlot

R.H. Phillips Cabernet Sauvignon
Barrel Cuvée

Robert Mondavi Woodbridge
Selections

Round Hill Chardonnay

Chile

Caliterra Cabernet Sauvignon or
Merlot

Carmen Carmenere

Santa Rita Cabernet Sauvignon 120

Walnut Crest Merlot

France

Beaujolais-Villages Louis Jadot or
Georges Duboeuf

Château Bonnet Blanc

Côtes du Rhône Guigal

Côtes du Rhône Parallele "45"
Jaboulet

Fortant de France Merlot or Syrah

Hugel Gentil

J. Vidal-Fleury Côtes du Rhône

La Vieille Ferme Côtes du Ventoux

Les Jemelles Syrah or Merlot

Louis Latour Ardèche Chardonnay

Mâcon-Villages (most producers)

Maître d'Estournel

Michel Lynch

Réserve St-Martin Merlot

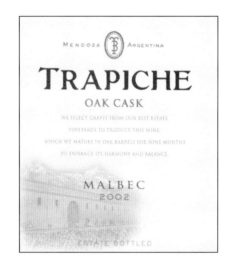

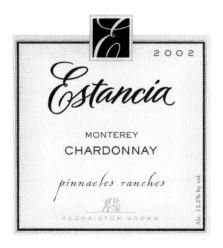

Italy

Chiarlo Barbera d'Asti

Montepulciano Red,
Casal Thaulero

Spain

Bodegas Montecillo Cumbrero

Marques de Cáceres Crianza

Washington State

Columbia Crest Semillon-
Chardonnay

Covey Run Fumé Blanc

Hogue Chardonnay Columbia Valley

Hogue Fumé Blanc

Once-a-Week Wines

($10 to $20)

Argentina

Bodegas Cantena Zapata
Malbec Alamos

Bodegas Weinert Carrascal

Navarro Correas
Cabernet Sauvignon
"Collection Privada"

Australia

Banrock Station
Chardonnay

Black Opal Cabernet Sauvignon
and Shiraz

Lindemans Shiraz Bin 50 or
Cabernet Sauvignon Bin 45

Penfolds Bin 389

Penfolds Chardonnay, Shiraz,
and Cabernet Sauvignon

Rosemount Show Reserve
Chardonnay

Wolf Blass
Chardonnay

California

Amberhill Cabernet Sauvignon

Beaulieu Merlot Costal

Benziger Chardonnay,
Merlot, or Cabernet Sauvignon

Beringer Cabernet Sauvignon
Founders Estate

Beringer Chardonnay

Carmenet Cabernet Sauvignon

Chateau Souverain Chardonnay

Chateau Souverain Merlot

Chateau St. Jean Chardonnay and
Sauvignon Blanc

Cline Cellars Zinfandel

Eshcol Cabernet and
Chardonnay

Estancia Chardonnay or
Cabernet Sauvignon

Ferrari-Carano Fumé Blanc

Fetzer Barrel Select Cabernet
Sauvignon or Zinfandel

Fetzer Sundial Chardonnay

Forest Glen Merlot

Frog's Leap Sauvignon Blanc

Gallo of Sonoma Chardonnay,
Cabernet Sauvignon,
Pinot Noir,
and Merlot

Geyser Peak Sauvignon Blanc

Hawk Crest Chardonnay,
Cabernet Sauvignon,
or Merlot

Kendall-Jackson Chardonnay
Vintners Reserve, Syrah, or
Cabernet Sauvignon

Laurel Glen Quintana
Cabernet Sauvignon

Liberty School
Cabernet Sauvignon

Louis Martini
Cabernet Sauvignon

Markham Merlot and
Sauvignon Blanc

Mason Sauvignon Blanc

Meridian Chardonnay or Cabernet
Sauvignon

Ravenswood Zinfandel Napa Valley

Ridge Zinfandel (Sonoma)

Rosenblum Zinfandel Vintners
Cuvée

Saintsbury Chardonnay

Sebastiani Chardonnay, Sonoma

Silverado Sauvignon Blanc

Simi Cabernet Sauvignon

Simi Sauvignon Blanc or
Chardonnay

St. Francis Merlot

St. Supery Sauvignon Blanc

Chile

Casa Lapostolle Cabernet Sauvignon
or Merlot Cuvée Alexandre

Concha y Toro Casillero del Diablo,
Cabernet Sauvignon, Puente Alto

Cousiño Macul Antiguas-Reserva
Cabernet Sauvignon

Los Vascos Reserve Cabernet
Sauvignon

Montes Merlot

Santa Rita Cabernet Sauvignon
Casa Real

France

Alsace Riesling—Trimbach, Hugel,
or Zind-Humbrecht

Château de Bellevue Morgon, Jadot

Château de Sancerre, Lapostolle

Château Greysac

Château La Cardonne

Château Larose Trintaudon

Château Meyney

Côtes du Rhône Reserve Perrin

Crozes-Hermitage Les Jalets,
Jaboulet

Domaine Leroy Bourgogne Rouge

Fleurie, Georges Deboeuf

Ladoucette Pouilly-Fumé

Mercurey, Faiveley

Pouilly-Fuissé, Georges Deboeuf

St-Veran Louis Jadot

Germany

Kabinett/Spätlese—Wehlener
Sonnenuhr by J.J. Prüm or
Niersteiner Olberg by Strub

Italy

Allegrini Valpolicella Classico

Anselmi Soave

Antinori Sangiovese Santa Cristina

Boscaini Pinot Grigio

Castello Banfi Toscana Centine

Lungarotti Rubesco

Marco Felluga Pinot Grigio, Collio

Michele Chiarlo Barbera d'Asti

Pighin Pinot Grigio

Rosso di Montalcino Col d'Orcia

Ruffino Chianti Classico Riserva

Taurino Salice Salentino

New Zealand

Brancott Chardonnay or
Sauvignon Blanc

Glazebrook Sauvignon Blanc

Goldwater Sauvignon Blanc

Kim Crawford Sauvignon Blanc

Nobilo Sauvignon Blanc

Saint Clair Sauvignon Blanc

Stoneleigh Chardonnay and
Sauvignon Blanc

Ports

Fonseca Bin #27

Sandeman Founders Reserve

Spain

Bodegas Muga Reserva

Conde de Valdemar Crianza

Sparkling Wines

Bouvet Brut

Codorniu Brut Classico

Cristalino Brut

Freixenet Brut

Korbel

Washington State

Canoe Ridge Merlot

Chateau St. Michelle
Riesling Eroica

Columbia Crest Chardonnay,
Merlot, and Cabernet Sauvignon

Covey Run Chardonnay
and Merlot

Hogue Cabernet Sauvignon
and Merlot

Once-a-Month Wines

($20 to $50)

Argentina

Catena Cabernet Sauvignon Alta

Salentein Malbec

Australia

Penfolds Shiraz Bin 28

California

Cabernet Sauvignon

Artesa

Beaulieu Rutherford

Beringer Knights Valley

Clos du Val

The Hess Collection

Geyser Peak Reserve

Jordan

Joseph Phelps

Mondavi

Raymond

Ridge

Whitehall Lane

Chardonnay

Arrowood Grand Archer

Beringer
Private Reserve

Chalone

Cuvaison

Ferrari-Carano

Kendall-Jackson
Grand Reserve

Mondavi

Pine Ridge, Carneros

Sonoma-Cutrer

Merlot

Clos du Bois

Frei Brothers

Shafer

Pinot Noir

Acacia

Au Bon Climat

Byron

Calera

Etude

Mondavi

Morgan

Saintsbury (Carneros)

Sparkling

Chandon Reserve

Domaine Carneros

Iron Horse

Roederer Estate

Syrah

Clos du Bois

Fess Parker

Justin

Zinfandel

Ridge Geyserville

Rosenblum-Continente

Seghesio Old Vine

Chile

Concha y Toro Cabernet
Sauvignon Don Melchor

Errazúriz Don Maximiano
Founders Reserve

Veramonte Primus

Viña Montes Cabernet
Sauvignon Apalta

France

Château Carbonnieux Blanc

Château de Sales

Château Fourcas-Hosten

Château Fuissé, Pouilly-Fuissé

Château Gloria

Château Les Ormes de Pez

Château Olivier Blanc

Château Phélan-Ségur

Château Pontesac

Château Sociando-Mallet

Olivier Leflaive Puligny-Montrachet

Pascal Jolivet Pouilly-Fumé

Italy

Antinori Badia a Passignano
Chianti Classico

Antinori Chianti Classico Tenute
Marchese Riserva

Badia a Coltibuono Chianti
Classico Riserva

Col d'Orcia Brunello di Montalcino

Mastroberardino Taurasi

Melini Chianti Classico
Riserva Massovecchio

Oregon

Argyle Pinot Noir

Willamette Valley Vineyards
Pinot Noir

South Africa

Hamilton Russell Pinot Noir
and Chardonnay

Spain

Alvaro Palacios Priorat
Les Terrasses

Bodega Montecillo Reserva

C.U.N.E. Contino Reserva

La Rioja Alta Viña
Ardanza

Pesquera

Washington State

Canoe Ridge Chardonnay

Chateau St. Michelle
Dr. Loosen Chardonnay
and Cabernet Sauvignon

L'Ecole No. 41
Cabernet Sauvignon

Once-a-Year Wines
($$$$+)

It's easy to buy these kinds of wine when money is no object! Any wine retailer
would be more than happy to help you spend your money!

Creating an Exemplary Restaurant Wine List

W HEN I FIRST CONCEIVED the idea for this book in the early 1980s, I had two purposes in mind. One was that my wine students were telling me that they needed an easier-to-understand text than the one I was using, and two, that there was a tremendous need in the hotel and culinary schools in the United States for a beginning guide to wine.

If you are a consumer, you may find this chapter to be interesting reading, since it was written for the young student who is about to embark on a career in the restaurant or hotel business.

Today the *Windows on the World Complete Wine Course* is used at top educational institutions such as the Culinary Institute of America, Cornell University, Michigan State University, University of Nevada (Las Vegas), Florida International University, and more than 100 other schools specializing in the hospitality industry.

Anyone who is even marginally aware of market trends knows that the popularity of wine has increased dramatically. Wine lists are no longer the province of an elite group of high-ticket, white-tablecloth culinary temples. There are ever-increasing ranks of customers who actively seek to enjoy wine in restaurants of all price levels.

To attract these potential customers, many a restaurateur has toyed with the idea of revamping and expanding his wine list. Yet, when confronted with the stark reality of such a task, many panic and accept the judgment of others, who have their own profit motives in mind. Once the restaurateur has acknowledged that it's time to start carrying more than house red, white, and rosé wines, he must lay the groundwork for building a list.

To illustrate: The hypothetical restaurant to which you've just taken the deed is a picturesque 100-seat establishment located in a moderate-size city. Your restaurant is open for both lunch and dinner, and doesn't possess any definite ethnic identity, falling under that umbrella label of "Continental/American."

The following is a step-by-step procedure in question-and-answer format for building a wine list for your restaurant. Remember, the most important aspects of your wine list are that it should complement your menu offerings, be attractively priced, offer an appealing selection, and be easy for the customer to select from and understand.

What's your competition?

Before you consider which wineries to choose, or fret about whether to have 40 or 400 wines, take the time to investigate your market. Visit both the restaurants that attract the clientele you're aiming for (your target market) and the ones above and below your scale. Study how they merchandise wine, how well their staff serves it, and obtain a copy of their wine list—provided it's not chained to the sommelier's neck. Go during a busy dinner hour and observe how many bottles of wine are nestled in ice buckets or present on tables. Get a feeling for your competition's commitment to wine.

Can wine distributors offer help?

Yes. Contact the various suppliers in your area and explain to them what your objectives are. Ask them to suggest a hypothetical wine list—you're under no obligation to use it. Many wine distributors have specially trained people to work along with restaurateurs on their wine lists. They can also suggest ways of merchandising and promotion. Use them as a resource.

What's your storage capacity?

Wine requires specific storage conditions: an ideal temperature range of 55°F to 60°F, away from direct sunlight and excessive vibration. Your wine storage does not belong next to the dishwashing machine or the loading dock. How large a space do you have? Does it allow room for shelving? You'll want to store the bottles on their sides. How accessible is the wine to service personnel?

What are your consumers' preferences?

Preliminary research reveals that 75 percent of the wine consumed in the United States is domestic and 25 percent is imported. The consumer preferences for our hypothetical restaurant's audience are predominantly American and French wines.

How long should your list be?

This is, in part, determined by storage space and capital investment. For our hypothetical restaurant, we decided to feature sixty wines on the list. Initially, this might seem like a lot for a 100-seat restaurant, but consider that those wines will be divided among sparkling, red, white, and rosé, and encompass the regions of France, the United States, Italy, Spain, Germany, Chile, and Australia. Sixty is almost the minimum number that will allow you the flexibility to offer a range of types and tastes and wine for special occasions, as well as for casual quaffing. We want our customers to know that wine matters in our restaurant.

What proportion of red to white?

In my wine school I always ask my students about their wine preferences. Ten years ago, the majority of my students preferred white wine, but today I find that my students have a decided preference for red wines. Because of this preference, I have decided to feature thirty-one reds and twenty-three whites, with six sparkling wines.

How should prices be set?

Don't plan on paying your mortgage with profits from your wine list! Pricing is dictated according to your selections. Aim for 60 percent of these wines to be moderately priced. Why? Because this is the price category in which the highest volume of sales will take place. For our purposes, mid-priced wines sell for between twenty-five and thirty-five dollars. Therefore, we want thirty-six of our wines priced in this range. Of the remaining wines, 20 percent (twelve wines) would be priced less than twenty-five dollars, and 20 percent more than thirty-five dollars.

The percentage of profit realized on wine is less than that realized on cocktails. However, the dollar-value profit is greater since the total sale is much more. Too many restaurateurs have intimidated much of the potential wine market by stocking only very rare, expensive wines and pricing them into the stratosphere. You want a wine list that will enable all your customers to enjoy a bottle (or two) of wine with their meal without having to float a bank loan. The bulk of your customers are looking for a good wine at a fair price—not a rare vintage wine at $400 a bottle.

What's your capital investment?

Determine with your accountant the amount of money you'll initially invest. Decide whether you want an inventory that will turn over in thirty to sixty days, or if you wish to make a long-term investment in cellaring wines. The majority of restaurants make short-term wine investments.

What will it actually cost?

Once we've decided on the number of wines on the list, and the general pricing structure, it's easy to determine what it will cost for one case of each wine. With some wines—the ones we anticipate will be very popular—our initial order will be for two cases, and for the more expensive wines, we'll start off with a half case. Our sixty-selection wine list will require an initial investment of approximately $8,500. Here's how we arrived at that "ballpark" figure:

LOW-PRICED WINES	
12 cases @ $75 per case average	$900.00
MEDIUM-PRICED WINES	
36 cases @ $130 per case average	$4,680.00
HIGH-PRICED WINES	
12 cases @ $240 per case average	$2,880.00
TOTAL	$8,460.00

What goes on the wine list?

There are many different styles of wine list. Some opt for long descriptions of the wine's characteristics and feature facts and maps of viticultural regions. For our restaurant, we're going to adopt a very straightforward approach.
- The list is divided into categories by type, and each type is divided into regions.
- The progression is: sparkling wine, white, red, and blush.

Each entry on the wine list should have the following information:
- *Bin number*—This simplifies inventory and reordering, and assists both customer and staff with difficult pronunciation.
- *Name of wine*—Be precise.
- *Vintage*—This is often omitted on wine lists by restaurateurs who want to be able to substitute whatever is available. This practice is resented by

anyone with a passing interest in wine, and with today's laser-printed wine lists, it is, in my opinion, unacceptable.

- **Shipper**—This information is very important for French wines, particularly those from Burgundy.

The type, style, and color of the paper you choose for your wine list are personal decisions. However, double-check all spelling and prices before the list is sent to the printer. It is very embarrassing when your customers point out spelling errors.

Which categories of wine should be used?

Our wine list includes six sparkling wines (three French, two American, and one Spanish). There are twenty-three white wines, thirty red wines, and one blush, for a grand total of sixty. Here is one example of how the categories might be broken down. Of course, each restaurant should choose the wines according to availability and price.

Should I buy wine without tasting it?

Tasting the wines for the list is of utmost importance. If you've decided to feature a Chardonnay, contact your distributors and ask to taste all the Chardonnays that conform to your criteria of availability and price. Tasting the wines blind will help you make selections on the basis of quality rather than label. These tastings represent quite an investment of time. To choose a wine list of sixty wines, you could easily taste three times that many.

Once you've narrowed the field, try pairing the wines with your menu offerings. If possible, include your entire staff in these tastings, from managers to waiters to chefs. The more familiar they are with the wines on the list and the foods they complement, the better they'll be able to sell your selections.

Recheck the availability of your selected wines. Place your orders. Remember, you don't have to buy twenty-five cases of each wine.

Your restaurant's open—what's next?

This is a guideline to establishing an initial list. It is important to update and revise the list to meet the requirements of your customers and the ever-changing wine market.

Once your list has been implemented, it's imperative that you track wine

Building a Basic Restaraunt Wine List

WHITE AND SPARKLING WINES (29)	RED AND BLUSH WINES (31)

WHITE AND SPARKLING WINES (29)

FRENCH (8)

1 Mâcon Blanc
1 Chablis (Premier Cru)
1 Meursault
1 Puligny-Montrachet
1 Pouilly-Fuissé
1 Pouilly-Fumé or Sancerre
1 Alsace (1 Riesling or
 Gewürztraminer)
1 Bordeaux (1 Graves or Sauternes)

AMERICAN (12)

2 Sauvignon Blanc/Fumé Blanc
10 Chardonnay

ITALIAN (1)

1 Pinot Grigio

AUSTRALIAN (1)

1 Chardonnay

GERMAN (1)

1 Rhein or Mosel

SPARKLING (6)

3 French Champagne
 (2 Non-vintage, 1 Prestige Cuveé)
2 American Sparkling
 (2 different price categories)
1 Spanish Sparkling

RED AND BLUSH WINES (31)

FRENCH (7)

1 Beaujolais
2 Burgundy (such as
 Nuits-St-Georges, Pommard,
 Volnay)
3 Bordeaux (different price
 categories)
1 Rhône Valley (Côtes du
 Rhône, Châteauneuf-du-Pape,
 or Hermitage)

AMERICAN (18)

3 Merlot
3 Pinot Noir
2 Zinfandel
10 Cabernet Sauvignon

ITALIAN (2)

1 Chianti Classico Riserva
1 Barolo or Barbaresco

AUSTRALIAN (1)

1 Shiraz

SPANISH (1)

1 Rioja Reserva

CHILEAN (1)

1 Cabernet Sauvignon

BLUSH (1)

1 White Zinfandel

sales to determine how successful the list has been. Analyze your wine list with respect to the following factors:

- The number of bottles sold per customer (divide the number of bottles sold by the number of covers).
- Per-person check average for wine.
- How much white wine to red (by percentage)—you might find that you need more or fewer whites, or more or fewer reds.
- The average price of a bottle of wine sold in the first three months.
- The ten most popular wines on the list.
- Instruct your staff to report any diner's request for a wine that's not on your list.

The steps involved in compiling our hypothetical list of sixty wines are the same steps that are used in compiling larger, more ambitious lists. Obviously, this list highlights only the major areas—sixty wines barely scratch the surface of what's available. True, with this size restriction we're unable to give great depth of selection, but it's still a list where the average customer, including myself, would find something appealing.

THE PROGRESSIVE WINE LIST

IN THE MID-'90S AT WINDOWS ON THE WORLD, we changed our wine list into a progressive wine list.

We decided that Americans were more comfortable ordering wines by the specific grape varieties than by country and region. We featured the three major grape varieties for white wines—Riesling, Sauvignon Blanc/Fumé Blanc, and Chardonnay, and the three major grape varieties for reds—Cabernet Sauvignon, Pinot Noir, and Merlot. Then, we took all the wines and listed them by the major grape from which they are produced. For other wines made from other grape varietals, we created a separate heading on our wine list called "Worldly Wines."

We took it a step further and placed the wines on the list in order, from the lightest style to the heaviest style wines. This type of list is known as a "Progressive Wine List." There is a distinct advantage to this kind of wine list. By placing your lighter-bodied wines first and your heavier-bodied wines next, it helps your waitstaff to better recommend wines for the food the customer has chosen. To create a Progressive Wine List for your restaurant, you would lead off with the Rieslings, from the lightest to the heaviest style wines, then the Sauvignon

Blancs/Fumé Blancs, and then the Chardonnays. For the red wines, you would begin with the Pinot Noirs, the Merlots, and then the Cabernet Sauvignons.

What about wine by the glass?

In my opinion, the most significant change in the twenty years since the first edition of this book has been the selling of wines by the glass. This is a home run for everyone—the consumer now has the opportunity to try different wines at different price points without buying a bottle. The waitstaff gets to learn more about different styles of wines by the glass than they do about wines listed on the wine list, plus they don't have to deal with the opening of a bottle since most of these wines are coming from the bar.

For the restaurant owner, you have a happier customer, a happier staff, faster service, and the potential to make more revenue and profits with an effective wine-by-the-glass program.

A note on pricing wines by the glass: The bottle of wine holds approximately twenty-five ounces; some restaurants get five 5-ounce pours from each bottle and others get six 4-ounce pours. My rule of thumb is to sell a glass for what the bottle costs me.

How many wines by the glass should I offer?

No matter how many wines you serve by the glass, whether it's only one or twenty, you must cork and store your wines (red and white) in the refrigerator overnight.

If you are interested in a wine-by-the-glass program, I suggest you start with six wines—three whites and three reds available at a low, medium, and high price point for each category. It is also a good idea (especially on your busy nights) to offer some very special, rare wine by the glass, just as a chef will add specials to his or her menus.

If you plan to have more than ten wines by the glass, invest in a wine preservation system. With under ten, if you are selling an opened bottle of wine within forty-eight hours and you follow the overnight refrigeration procedure, you can probably do without a preservation system and still maintain the quality of the wine.

If you're a consumer, you now have an idea what's involved in creating a balanced wine list. For restaurateurs, the logistic of creating a wine list may seem Olympian. This chapter was offered to take some of the mystery out of this task.

Wine Service and Wine Storage in Restaurants and at Home

CONGRATULATIONS! HAVING REACHED THIS POINT, you've read about wine through all eight classes, and then how to combine wine with food, how to buy wine (and find the best values), and even how to create a restaurant wine list.

The last step in this process is serving the wine. Whether you are hosting a meal at a restaurant or at home, the goal of proper wine service should be to get the most enjoyment from your wine while eliminating any of the "performance anxieties" that would interfere with that enjoyment.

WINE IN RESTAURANTS

KEVIN ZRALY'S PET PEEVES OF RESTAURANT WINE SERVICE

- Not enough wine lists
- Incorrect information, i.e., wrong vintage and producer
- High markups
- Untrained staff
- Lack of corkscrews
- Out-of-stock wines
- Improper glassware
- Overchilled whites and warm reds

IN A RESTAURANT, I strongly recommend that you order all your wines at the beginning of the meal and have them opened so you're not sitting there without wine when your main course arrives. Even better, call the restaurant ahead of time and preorder your wines.

WINE SERVICE RITUAL

In most restaurants, the wine service ritual is as intimidating to the service staff as it is to the new wine consumer.

Picture this scenario: You've ordered your bottle of wine. The server now presents you with the bottle.

What do you do?

First, make sure that the wine presented to you at the table is the same wine you ordered from the wine list and is the correct vintage. Now the fun begins. The server opens the wine and presents you with the cork.

SOME WINERIES, especially in California, are now using synthetic corks to seal their wine. Since 1993, St. Francis Winery in Sonoma has sealed its wine with a synthetic cork. And Napa Valley's Plump Jack Winery released their $135/bottle 1997 Reserve Cabernet Sauvignon with a screw cap! Stay tuned for more.

SOME FACTORS that contribute to the making of a bad wine are
- Faulty corks
- Poor selection of grapes
- Bad weather
- Bad winemaking
- High alcohol and tannin (bitterness)
- Herbaceousness
- Bacteria and yeast problems
- Unwanted fermentation in the bottle
- Hydrogen sulfide (rotten-egg smell)
- Excess sulfur dioxide
- Poor winery hygiene
- Bad barrels
- Poor storage

AN OXIDIZED wine smells like Sherry or Madeira.

What are you supposed to do with the cork?

Nothing! After thirty years of being in the wine and restaurant industry, I have no idea why we give the customer the cork. In the movies, the bon vivant used to sniff the cork and wave it around ceremoniously. That looks good on film, but why would anyone want to smell a wet winey cork?!

If you really want to find out whether a wine is good, all you have to do is pour it in your glass, swirl it, and smell it. It's all in the smell!

The Magical Mystery Taste Test

Now you have to taste the wine. So many steps, so little time. While everyone at the dinner table is looking at you, the server pours the first taste of wine. Will Mikey like it?

At this point I urge my students to remember that the first taste of wine is always a shock to your taste buds. If you are unsure, take a second taste to confirm your first impression. If you really want to impress your guests, simply smell the wine and nod your approval.

When should you send wine back in a restaurant?

Whenever you feel there is something wrong with the wine. Most restaurants will not have a problem with people sending a bottle of wine back, even though most of them sent back will be in good shape. For those of you who have heard about servers who recommend a wine to a table and add, "If you don't like it, I'll drink it myself," believe me, they do drink it, especially the good stuff!

What are the main reasons for sending wine back?

The first reason is that the wine is spoiled or oxidized. It has lost its fruit smell and taste, usually because of poor storage of the wine or the wine has passed its prime and should have been consumed earlier.

The second reason is that the wine is corked. It is estimated that 3 to 5 percent of all the world's wines are corked, meaning that the cork that was used to seal the bottle was defective. You'll know immediately if a wine is corked because the smell of the wine is not of fruit, but is more like a dank, wet cellar or moldy newspaper.

Is it necessary to spend a lot of money for wine in restaurants?

I've been in the restaurant business most of my life and also a customer in restaurants at least three times per week. So you might find it interesting that I never order a bottle of wine that costs more than fifty dollars (unless someone else is paying!). I do not believe that a restaurant is a great place for experimentation with wine because of the higher markup charged at most restaurants. We all know of great restaurants in our area that charge too much for wine and those that offer a fair markup. I find it more interesting to find a ten-dollar bottle of wine that tastes like a twenty-dollar bottle, a twenty-dollar bottle that tastes like a forty-dollar bottle, and so on. I go to the restaurants with the best wine prices. Restaurants with only high-priced wines and a limited choice of wines under fifty dollars do not get my credit card!

What is the tipping policy for sommeliers in restaurants?

As a sommelier (wine steward), I always appreciated receiving a gratuity for my knowledge and service. Although it should not be automatic, remember that "tips" (an acronym for "To Insure Proper Service") should definitely benefit your return to the restaurant.

A sommelier can make your dining experience better by

- Not trying to sell you the most expensive wine on the list (unless, of course, you ask)
- Matching your food selection properly
- Decanting the wine
- Giving special wine suggestions that are not on the list
- Being attentive to your table
- Taking the label off the bottle (as a remembrance)
- Making your reservation and getting you a good table

Depending on service, I will tip anywhere from five to twenty dollars above the regular waiter gratuity for the sommelier.

DID YOU KNOW?

The wine-tasting ritual goes back to the days of kings, when royal tasters had to sample wine to make sure it did not contain poison before it was served to the king and his table. Unfortunately there was a high turnover rate of royal tasters!

TODAY'S ROYAL tasters are called sommeliers, which is the French word for wine steward. At the real ritzy restaurants, they are clad in tuxedos (a little bit more intimidation) and are usually seen wearing a chain with a little cup at the end of it. The cup is called a *tastevin* and is used by true sommeliers to taste the wine for you.

When everyone orders something different, what's the most versatile wine to complement dinner?

One of the biggest dilemmas my students confront is dining out with a large group and having to choose a wine to match a wide assortment of meat, fish, and vegetarian selections.

I usually order "safe" wines. My two favorite choices for a white wine are a Chardonnay without oak, such as a Mâcon from France or a slightly oak-aged Chardonnay from California or Australia.

As for the reds, my number one choice is definitely a Pinot Noir, most likely from California or Oregon, but if I can find a red Burgundy for under fifty dollars, that would also be one of my choices. Other red choices would be Brunello di Montalcino and Chianti from Italy, and Reservas and Gran Reservas from Rioja, Spain.

These selections work well with meat, fish, and vegetarian choices.

WINE BY THE GLASS

In my opinion, the best thing that has happened to wine appreciation for both the consumer and the restaurateur is wine by the glass. If I'm going to do any experimentation in a restaurant, it will definitely be in a restaurant that has a good selection of wines by the glass. This also solves the age-old challenge of what wine to order when one person orders fish and another orders meat. You're no longer stuck with one bottle to accommodate everyone's different menu choices.

Another good thing about wine by the glass is that you get a hassle-free wine experience. That means:

1. You don't have to decipher the wine list. You don't even have to ask for it.
2. You don't have to approve the label.
3. You don't have to smell the cork.
4. You don't have to go through the tasting ritual.

THE AVERAGE temperature of a refrigerator is 38°F to 45°F.

TEMPERATURE

One of the biggest complaints in restaurant wine service is that the white wines are served too cold, but for me, being a red wine drinker, my biggest complaint is that the red wines are served too warm.

White wines served too cold will hide the true character and flavor of the wine. Red wines served too warm change the balance of the components and hinder the true taste of the wine, increasing the sensation of alcohol and tannin over the fruit, especially in California wines.

In my own dining-out experience at least 50 percent of the time the wine is served at an improper temperature. It's easier to solve the problem for a white wine by leaving it in the glass and letting it warm up, but to chill down a red wine I have to order a bucket filled with ice and water and leave my wine in it for five to ten minutes to bring it to the correct temperature. I strongly recommend that you follow the same method, even though it may be a hassle. I can assure you that you'll enjoy your wines more.

QUICK TIPS ON TEMPERATURES FOR SERVING WINE

1. Great Chardonnays are best at warmer temperatures (55°F to 60°F) than whites made from Sauvignon Blanc or Riesling (45°F to 55°F).
2. Champagnes and sparkling wines taste better well chilled (45°F).
3. Lighter reds, such as Gamay, Pinot Noir, Tempranillo, and Sangiovese bring out a better balance of fruit to acid when served at a cooler temperature (55°F to 60°F) than wines such as Cabernet Sauvignon and Merlot (60°F to 65°F).

WINE AT HOME

STORAGE

I'm sure not everything you bought for your new wine cellar is going to be there five years from now, but some wines do improve with age, and you must protect your investment. The fun of wine collecting is trying wines at different stages in their growth.

Warmer temperatures prematurely age wine. How important is it to have proper storage for your new wine collectibles? Well, let me put it another way. Without proper storage, you will never know how good the wine could have been!

In wine collecting it seems as if it's always the cart before the horse. First I'll buy the wines, then I'll think about where I'm going to put them. Which of course is the wrong way to begin wine collecting. I've often asked my students

WHERE DO you store your wines? If you live in a château, I'm sure you have a beautiful wine cellar, but if you live in an apartment with an average temperature of 70°F and your wines are stored with your shoes, this is not good news for the health of your wine.

IF YOU leave a bottle of wine in a 70°F room, as opposed to in a 55°F room, you are actually prematurely aging the wine twice as quickly.

how many of them live in châteaus and how many of them live in *apartamentos*? The *apartamento* people usually store their fine wines in the first door as you enter their *apartamento* next to their muddy shoes. If you are an apartment dweller and you have fine wine, you should look into wine storage in your area or buy a château!

While the optimum temperature is 55°F, I would rather the wine be a consistent 65°F all year long than swing in temperature from 55°F to 75°F. That is the worst scenario and can be very harmful to the wine. And just as warm temperatures will prematurely age the wine, temperatures too cold can freeze the wine, pushing out the cork and immediately ending the aging process.

When all else fails, especially for those living in a cozy apartment, put your wines in the refrigerator—both whites and reds—rather than risk storing them in warm conditions.

The second consideration in long-term wine storage (five years or more) is humidity. If the humidity is too low, your corks will dry out. If that happens, wine will seep out of the bottle. Again, if wine can get out, air can get in. Too much humidity, and you are likely to lose your labels. Personally, I'd rather lose my labels than lose my corks. My own wine cellar ranges from 55°F to 60°F and the humidity stays at a fairly constant 75 percent. Humidity and temperature are the most important things when it comes to wine storage, but I would also be careful regarding off smells and excessive vibration.

National statistics show that most wine purchased at retail stores will be consumed within three days of purchase, but for those of you who are collecting, you must protect your investment—whether you have a dozen bottles or two thousand.

SPILL THE WINE

Try an equal mixture of liquid soap and hydrogen peroxide to take out red wine stains.

Should my wines be stored horizontally or vertically?

Wine bottles should be stored horizontally, at up to a ten-degree angle, especially for long-term aging. The reason very simply is that when the bottle of wine is stored on its side, the wine will be in contact with the cork. This prevents any oxygen, the major enemy of wine, from getting into the bottle. If the wine is kept in a vertical position, the chances are great that the cork will dry out, the wine will evaporate, and the oxygen getting in will quickly spoil your wine.

P.S. Whoever wrote that it is important to turn the bottle of wine once a month was probably a beer drinker.

How long should I age my wine?

The Wall Street Journal recently came out with an article stating that most people have one or two wines that they've been saving for years for a special occasion. This is probably not a good idea!

More than 90 percent of all wine—red, white, and rosé—should be consumed within a year. With that in mind, the following is a guideline to aging wine from the best producers in the best years:

WHITE

California Chardonnay	3–8+ years
French White Burgundy	2–10+ years
German Riesling (Auslese, Beerenauslese, and Trockenbeerenauslese)	3–30+ years
French Sauternes	3–30+ years

RED

Bordeaux Châteaus	5–30+ years
California Cabernet Sauvignon	3–15+ years
Argentine Malbec	3–15+ years
Barolo and Barbaresco	5–25+ years
Brunello di Montalcino	3–15+ years
Chianti Classico Riservas	3–10+ years
Spanish Riojas (Gran Reservas)	5–20+ years
Hermitage/Shiraz	5–25+ years
California Zinfandel	5–15+ years
California Merlot	2–10+ years
California/Oregon Pinot Noirs	2–5+ years
French Red Burgundy	3–8+ years
Vintage Ports	10–40+ years

There are always exceptions to the rules when it comes to generalizing about the aging of wine (especially considering the variations in vintages), hence the plus signs in the table above. I have had Bordeaux wines more than a hundred years old that were still going strong. It is also not unlikely to find a great Sauternes or Port that still needs time to age after its fiftieth birthday.

But the above age spans represent more than 95 percent of the wines in their categories.

P.S. The oldest bottle of wine still aging in Bordeaux is a 1797 Lafite Rothschild.

What's the best way to chill a bottle of wine quickly?

The best technique that I have found for chilling white wines on short notice is to submerge the bottle in a mixture of ice, water, and salt. Within ten minutes the wine is ready for drinking.

THE CORKSCREW

How many of you have seen other people break a cork or even push the cork in the bottle when opening wine?

Many times this happens because people either use the wrong corkscrew or they open the wine incorrectly.

Of the many different kinds of corkscrews and cork-pullers available, the most efficient and easiest tool to use is the pocket model of the Screwpull, a patented device that includes a knife and a very long screw. Simply by turning in one continuous direction, the cork is extracted effortlessly. This is the best type of corkscrew for home use, and because it is gentle, it is best for removing long, fragile corks from older wines.

The corkscrew most commonly used in restaurants is the "waiter's corkscrew." Small and flat, it contains a knife, screw, and lever, all of which fold neatly into the handle.

How do I open a bottle of wine?

When opening a bottle of wine, the first step is to remove the capsule. You can accomplish this best by cutting around the neck on the underside of the bottle's lip. Once you remove the capsule, wipe the top of the cork clean—often dust or mold adheres to the cork while the wine is still at the winery, and before the capsule is put on the bottle. Next, insert the screw and turn it so that it goes as deeply as possible into the cork. Don't be afraid to go through the cork. I'd rather get a little cork in my wine than not get the cork out of the bottle.

The most important technique in opening a bottle of wine is once you have lifted the cork one-quarter of the way out, stop and turn the screw farther into the cork. Now pull the cork three-quarters of the way out. This is the point where most people feel they're in control and start pulling and bending the cork. And of course, they end up leaving a little bit of the cork still in the bottle. The best method at this point is to use your hand to wiggle out the cork.

Just to make you feel better: I still break at least a dozen corks a year.

TO DECANT, PERCHANCE TO BREATHE

Does a wine need to breathe?

This is one of the most controversial subjects among my wine friends, and everyone seems to have a different answer or angle regarding the question.

I think most of my peer group would agree that simply opening a bottle of wine an hour or two before service will not really help the wine. It also will not hurt the wine. It is probably a good idea if you are having a dinner party at home to open your wines before your guests arrive.

What is bothersome to me is when a waiter in a restaurant asks me whether I would like my wine to breathe before he or she serves it. A waiter once told me that the wine I had ordered needed at least thirty minutes' "breathing" before I could drink it. Not only did I disagree, but as a restaurant director, I certainly hope that the customer is ordering a second bottle thirty minutes later.

The major question still remains, though. Does a wine improve when it is taken out of the bottle and put into your decanter or glass? There are many schools of thought. I've had students swear to me that certain wines tasted much better after three hours in the decanter than when first served from the bottle. On the other hand, many studies with professional wine people have shown no discernible difference between most wines opened, poured, and consumed immediately and those that have been in a decanter over an extended period of time.

One thing for sure is that very old wine (more than twenty-five years) should be opened and consumed immediately. One of the most interesting wine experiences I ever had was in the late seventies, and involved a bottle of a 1945 Burgundy. When I opened the wine, the room filled with the smell of great wine. The first taste of the wine was magnificent. Unfortunately, fifteen minutes after opening the bottle, everything about the wine changed, especially the taste. The wine started losing its fruit, and the acidity overpowered the fruit.

WHEN IN France, do as the French. My experience in visiting the French wine regions is that in Burgundy (Pinot Noir) they very rarely decant, but in Bordeaux (Cabernet Sauvignon and Merlot) they almost always decant.

MY PRIMARY reason for decanting a bottle of wine is to separate the wine from the sediment.

I HAVE had good and bad experiences with decanting. I must admit that some wines did get better, but many older wines, especially when exposed to air, actually deteriorated quickly. Words of wisdom: If you decide to decant an older bottle of wine, do it immediately before service, not hours ahead of time, to make sure that the wine will not lose its flavor by being exposed to the air for an extended period of time.

What happened? Oxygen is the culprit here. Just as buried treasure is taken from the sea and kept in salt water in order not to expose it to oxygen, wine is destroyed by exposure to oxygen. If I had decanted that wine first and left it to "breathe," I would never have had that first fifteen minutes of pleasure. This probably will not happen every time you open an old bottle of wine, but it is very important to be aware of how fragile older wines can be.

So what's my advice after opening thousands and thousands of bottles of wine? Open it up, pour it in a glass, and enjoy the wine!

Which wines do I decant?

The three major wine collectibles are the ones that most likely will need to be decanted, especially as they get older and throw more sediment. The three major wine collectibles are:

1. Great châteaus of Bordeaux (ten years and older)
2. California Cabernets (eight years and older)
3. Vintage Port (ten years and older)

How do I decant a bottle of wine?

1. Completely remove the capsule from the neck of the bottle. This will enable you to see the wine clearly as it passes through the neck.
2. Light a candle. Most red wines are bottled in very dark green glass, making it difficult to see the wine pass through the neck of the bottle. A candle will give you the extra illumination you need and add a theatrical touch. A flashlight would do, but candles keep things simple.
3. Hold the decanter (a carafe or glass pitcher can also be used for this purpose) firmly in your hand.
4. Hold the wine bottle in your other hand, and gently pour the wine into the decanter while holding both over the candle at such an angle that you can see the wine pass through the neck of the bottle.
5. Continue pouring in one uninterrupted motion until you begin to see the first signs of sediment.
6. Stop decanting once you begin to see sediment. At this point, if there is still sediment left, leave the wine standing until it settles. Then continue decanting.

GLASSWARE

Whether you're dining out or you're at home, the enjoyment of food and wine is enhanced by fine silver, china, linen, and, of course, glassware. The color of wine is as much a part of its pleasure and appeal as its bouquet and flavor. Glasses that alter or obscure the color of wine detract from the wine itself. The most suitable wineglasses are those of clear glass with a bowl large enough to allow for swirling.

A variety of shapes are available, and personal preferences should guide you when selecting glasses for home use. Some shapes, however, are better suited to certain wines than to others. For example, a smaller glass that closes in a bit at the top helps concentrate the bouquet of a white wine and also helps it keep its chill. Larger, balloon-shaped glasses are more appropriate for great red wines.

The most suitable Champagne glasses and the ones more and more restaurants are using are the tulip or the Champagne flute. These narrow glasses hold between four and eight ounces, and they allow the bubbles to rise from a single point. The tulip shape also helps to concentrate the bouquet.

How should I wash my wineglasses?

For your everyday drinking of wine, wash your glasses in the dishwasher. But I've had many a great wine spoiled because of the detergent used. Therefore, my special wine glasses are not put into the dishwasher. They are washed by hand without any soap or detergent. Glasses are susceptible to scents, so mine are carefully dried hanging from a rack, not upside down on a counter or cloth.

THE BEST wineglasses are made by Riedel. The Riedel family, Austrian glassmakers, has been on a crusade for more than 25 years to elevate wine drinking to a new level with their specially designed varietal glassware. They have designed their glasses to accentuate the best components of each grape variety. Riedel glassware comes in three different styles. The top of the line is the handcrafted Sommelier series. Next comes the Vinum. For your everyday meal—for those of you who do not want to spend a tremendous amount of money on glassware—they also produce the less expensive Overture series.

Award-Winning Wine Lists

I STRONGLY BELIEVE THAT A restaurant with a great wine list will also have excellent food and service. Try one of these restaurants and see what I mean.

The restaurants below were chosen by *Wine Spectator*, the largest-selling wine newspaper in the United States, for having the best lists in the world. (Each restaurant shown here has been honored as such from the date given.)

Alberobello, Italy
Il Poeta Contadino (since 1997)

Altamonte Springs, Florida
Maison & Jardin Restaurant
(since 1995)

Anaheim, California
Mr. Stox (since 1983)

Aspen, Colorado
Montagna at the Little Nell (since 1997)

Big Sur, California
Sierra Mar (since 1993)

Boston, Massachusetts
The Federalist (since 2001)

Boulder, Colorado
Flagstaff House Restaurant (since 1983)

British Columbia
Sooke Harbour House (since 2000)

Cáceres, Spain
Atrio (since 2003)

Carmel, California
Casanova Restaurant (since 1990)
Pacific's Edge Restaurant (since 1991)

Carmel Valley, California
Marinus Restaurant (since 2001)

Chappaqua, New York
Crabtree's Kittle House Inn (since 1994)

Chestertown, New York
Friends Lake Inn (since 1997)

Chicago, Illinois
Charlie Trotter's (since 1993)
The Dining Room at the Ritz-Carlton (since 1982)
Italian Village Restaurant (since 1984)

Costigliole d'Asti, Italy
Guido Ristorante (since 1996)

East Rutherford, New Jersey
Park and Orchard Restaurant (since 1991)

Eureka, California
Restaurant 301 at the Hotel Carter (since 1998)

Florence, Italy
Enoteca Pinchiorri (since 1984)

Fullerton, California
The Cellar (since 1992)

Highland Park, Illinois
Carlos' Restaurant (since 1990)

Houston, Texas
Rotisserie for Beef and Bird (since 1988)

Kansas City, Missouri
JJ's (since 1996)
Starker's Restaurant (since 1992)

Lake Louise, Alberta, Canada
Post Hotel Dining Room (since 2002)

Las Vegas, Nevada
Aureole (since 2000)
Picasso (since 2003)
Piero Selvaggio Valentino (since 2002)

Los Angeles, California
Patina Restaurant (since 1994)

Mill Valley, California
El Paseo Restaurant (since 1987)

Monte Carlo, Monaco
Le Louis XV–Alain Ducasse (since 1995)

Monterey, California
The Sardine Factory (since 1982)

Nantucket, Massachusetts
Topper's at the Wauwinet (since 1996)

Nashville, Tennessee
The Wild Boar Restaurant (since 1993)

Nassau, Bahamas
Graycliff (since 1988)

New Orleans, Louisiana
Brennan's Restaurant (since 1983)
Emeril's (since 1999)

New York, New York
Alain Ducasse at the Essex House
    (since 2003)
Daniel (since 2002)

Felidia Ristorante (since 1988)
Montrachet (since 1994)
Sparks Steak House (since 1981)
Tribeca Grill (since 2002)
"21" Club (since 2003)
Veritas (since 2000)

Ontario, Canada
Via Allegro Ristorante (since 2003)

Ormalingen, Switzerland
Landgasthof & Vinothek Farnsburg
    (since 1992)

Palm Beach, Florida
L'Escalier at the Florentine Room
    (since 1981)

Paris, France
Alain Ducasse au Plaza Athénée (since 1998)
La Tour d'Argent (since 1986)
Le Cinq (since 2003)
Michel Rostang (since 1993)
Taillevent (since 1984)

Raleigh, North Carolina
The Angus Barn (since 1989)

Roanne, France
Troisgros (since 1996)

Sag Harbor, New York
The American Hotel (since 1981)

San Diego, California
The WineSellar & Brasserie (since 1989)

San Francisco, California
The Carnelian Room (since 1982)
Fifth Floor (since 2001)
Restaurant Gary Danko (since 2001)
Rubicon (since 1998)

Santa Barbara, California
Wine Cask (since 1994)

Santa Monica, California
Valentino (since 1981)

Santa Teresa, New Mexico
Billy Crews Dining Room (since 1986)

Saratoga, California
The Plumed Horse (since 1987)

Scottsdale, Arizona
Mary Elaine's (since 2000)

Seattle, Washington
Canlis (since 1997)

Siasconset, Massachusetts
The Chanticleer Inn (since 1987)

Singapore
Les Amis (since 1996)

St Moritz, Switzerland
Hotel Waldhaus am See (since 1998)

Ste-Marguerite du Lac Masson, Quebec, Canada
Bistro à Champlain (since 1988)

Strasbourg, France
Au Crocodile (since 1993)

Sylt-Westerland, Germany
Restaurant Jörg Muller (since 1993)

Tampa, Florida
Bern's Steak House (since 1981)

Tokyo, Japan
Enoteca Pinchiorri-Tokyo (since 1994)

Toronto, Canada
Opus Restaurant on Prince Arthur (since 2002)

Tucson, Arizona
Anthony's in the Catalinas (since 1993)

Tyngsboro, Massachusetts
Silks at Stonehedge Inn (since 1996)

Vonnas, France
Georges Blanc (since 1987)

Washington, D.C.
Galileo da Roberto Donna (since 1997)

Washington, Virginia
The Inn at Little Washington (since 1995)

West Dover, Vermont
The Inn at Sawmill Farm (since 1992)

West Indies
Malliouhana (since 1999)

Wiesbaden, Germany
Ente (since 1985)

Wilmington, Vermont
The Hermitage Inn (since 1984)

Zurich, Switzerland
Restaurant Riesbächli (since 1990)

Frequently Asked Questions About Wine

What happens when you can't finish the whole bottle of wine?

This is one of the most frequently asked questions in wine school (although I have never had this problem).

If you still have a portion of the wine left over, whether it be red or white, the bottle should be corked and immediately put into the refrigerator. Don't leave it out on your kitchen counter. Remember, bacteria grow in warm temperatures, and a 70°F+ kitchen will spoil wine very quickly. By refrigerating the wine, most wines will not lose their flavor over a forty-eight-hour period. (Some people swear that the wine even tastes better, although I'm not among them.)

After forty-eight hours the wine will begin to oxidize. This is true of all table wines with an 8 to 14 percent alcohol content. Other wines, such as Ports and Sherries, with a higher alcohol content of 17 to 21 percent, will last longer, but I wouldn't suggest keeping them longer than two weeks.

Another way of preserving wine for an even longer period of time is to buy a small decanter that has a corked top and fill the decanter to the top with the wine. Or go to a hobby or craft store that also carries home winemaking equipment and buy some half bottles and corks.

Remember, the most harmful thing to wine is oxygen, and the less contact with oxygen, the longer the wine will last. That's why some wine collectors also use something called the Vacu-Vin, which pumps air out of the bottle. Other wine collectors spray the bottle with an inert gas such as nitrogen, which is odorless and tasteless, and which preserves the wine from oxygen.

Remember, if all else fails, you'll still have a great cooking wine!

Why do I get a headache when I drink wine?

The simple answer may be overconsumption! Seriously though, more than 10 percent of my students are medical doctors, and none of them has been able to give me the definitive answer to this question.

Some people get headaches from white wine, others from red, but when it comes to alcohol consumption, dehydration certainly plays an important role in how you feel the next day. That's why for every glass of wine I consume, I will have two glasses of water to keep my body hydrated.

There are many factors that influence the way alcohol is metabolized in your system. The top three are:

1. Health
2. DNA
3. Gender

Research is increasingly leaning toward genetics as a reason for chronic headaches.

For those of you who have allergies, different levels of histamines are present in red wines; these can obviously cause discomfort and headaches. I myself am allergic to red wine and I "suffer" every day.

Many doctors have told me that food additives contribute to headaches. There is a natural compound in red wine called tyramine, which is said to dilate blood vessels. Further, many prescription medicines warn about combining with alcohol.

Regarding gender, due to certain stomach enzymes, women absorb more alcohol into their bloodstream than men do. A doctor who advises women that one glass of wine a day is a safe limit is likely to tell men that they can drink two glasses.

Do all wines need corks?

It is a time-honored tradition more than two centuries old to use corks to preserve wine. Most corks come from cork oak trees grown in Portugal and Spain.

The fact is that most wines could be sold without using cork as a stopper. Since 90 percent of all wine is meant to be consumed within one year, a screw cap will work just as well, if not better, than a cork for most wines.

Just think what this would mean to you—no need for a corkscrew, no broken corks, and, most important, no more tainted wine caused by contaminated cork.

I do believe that certain wines—those with potential to age for more than five years—are much better off using cork. But also keep in mind, for those real wine collectors, that a cork's life span is approximately twenty-five to thirty years, after which you'd better drink the wine or find somebody to recork it.

Some wineries now use a synthetic cork made from high-grade thermoplastic that is FDA-approved and also recyclable. These corks form a near-perfect seal, so leakage, evaporation, and off flavors are virtually eliminated. They open with traditional corkscrews and allow wine to be stored upright.

But the trend today is to use the Stelvin Screw Cap. Wineries around the world, especially in California (Bonny Doon, Sonoma Cutrer, etc.), Australia, and New Zealand, use Stelvin.

What is a "corked" wine?

This is a very serious problem for wine lovers! There are some estimates that 3 to 5 percent of all wines have been contaminated and spoiled by a faulty cork. The principal cause of corked wine is TCA, short for 2,4,6-trichloranisole.

When we find such a bottle at the Wine School, we make sure that every student gets a chance to smell a "corked" wine. It's a smell they won't soon forget!

Some of my students describe it as a dank, wet, moldy, cellar smell, and some describe it as a wet cardboard smell. It overpowers the fruit smell in the wine, making the wine undrinkable. It can happen in a ten-dollar bottle of wine or a thousand-dollar bottle of wine.

What's that funny-looking stuff attached to the bottom of my cork?

Tartaric acid, or tartrates, is sometimes found on the bottom of a bottle of wine or the cork. Tartaric acid is a harmless crystalline deposit that looks like glass or rock candy. In red wines, the crystals take on a rusty, reddish-brown color from the tannin.

Most tartrates are removed at the winery by lowering the temperature of the wine before it is bottled. Obviously this does not work with all wines, and if you keep your wine at a very cold temperature for a long period of time (for example, in your refrigerator), you can end up with this deposit on your cork.

Cool-climate regions like Germany have a greater chance of producing the crystallization effect.

Does the age of the vine affect the quality of the wine?

You will sometimes see on French wine labels the term *Vieilles Vignes* ("old vines"). By law, the term requires the wine be made from grapes on vines that are twenty years or older. In California, I've tasted many Zinfandels that were made from vines that were more than seventy-five years old. Many wine tasters, including myself, believe that these old vines create a different complexity and taste than do younger vines.

In many countries, grapes from vines three years old or younger cannot be made into a winery's top wine. In Bordeaux, France, Château Lafite Rothschild produces a second wine, called Carruades de Lafite Rothschild, which is made from the vineyard's youngest vines (less than fifteen years old).

As a vine gets older, especially over thirty years, it starts losing its fruit-production value. In commercial vineyards, vines will slow down their production at about twenty years of age, and most vines are replanted by their fiftieth birthday.

What are the hot areas in wine?

It seems as if most countries are catching the wine craze. Here are some areas where I have seen major growth and improvement in quality, especially with certain grape varieties over the last twenty years

> **New Zealand:** Sauvignon Blanc and Chardonnay
> **Chile:** Cabernet Sauvignon
> **Argentina:** Malbec
> **Hungary:** Tokaji (one of the greatest dessert wines in the world)
> **Austria:** Gruner Veltliner
> **Portugal:** Not just Port anymore! Try Bacca Velha and you'll see what I mean.
> **South Africa:** Sauvignon Blanc, Pinot Noir, and Syrah

And what will you be writing about in the year 2025?

Argentina, the United States, and Australia.

Besides the wine recommended in your book, can you recommend other wines from other countries?

Every year when I finish writing a new edition, people invariably ask me, "What did you add to the book this year to make it better?" My philosophy is, what did I learn this year that the beginning and intermediate wine person do not need to know; thus, every year my book gets more concise.

Of course, this is very unfair to great winemakers around the world whose countries or regions are not covered in my book. Here are some of the other great winemakers of the world:

South Africa: Hamilton Russell, Kanonkop, Thelema, Glen Carlou
New Zealand: Cloudy Bay, Goldwater, Brancott, Morton Estate
Italy: Lungarotti, Mastroberardino, Jermann
Austria: Franz Prager, Kracher
Hungary: Royal Tokaji, Disznoko
Israel: Yarden
France: Mas de Daumas Gassac
Lebanon: Chateau Musar
Canada: Inniskilin

What are the most important books for your wine library?

Thank you for buying my wine book, which I hope you have found useful for a general understanding of wine. As with any hobby, there is always a thirst for more knowledge.

I hope that you noticed that at the end of each chapter, I recommended specific wine books for the different wine regions.

The following is a list of general books I consider required reading if you want to delve further into this fascinating subject:

The Essential Wine Book, Oz Clarke
Oz Clarke's New Encyclopedia of Wine
Oz Clarke's Wine Atlas
Great Wine Made Simple, Andrea Immer
Hugh Johnson's Modern Encyclopedia of Wine
World Atlas of Wine, Hugh Johnson
The Wine Bible, Karen MacNeil
Wine for Dummies, Ed McCarthy and Mary Ewing Mulligan
Oxford Companion to Wine, Jancis Robinson
The New Sotheby's Wine Encyclopedia, Tom Stevenson

Since the above volumes are sometimes encyclopedic in nature, I always carry with me two pocket guides to wine:

Hugh Johnson's Pocket Encyclopedia of Wine
Oz Clarke's Pocket Wine Guide

Where can I get the best wine service in the United States?

The James Beard Awards have recognized the following restaurants with the Outstanding Wine Service Award:

1993	Charlie Trotter's, Chicago
1994	Valentino, Santa Monica
1995	Montrachet, New York
1996	Chanterelle, New York
1997	The Four Seasons, New York
1998	The Inn at Little Washington, Washington (Virginia)
1999	Union Square Café, New York
2000	Rubicon, San Francisco
2001	French Laundry, Yountville, California
2002	Gramercy Tavern, New York
2003	Daniel, New York
2004	Babbo, New York
2005	Veritas, New York

The past winners for Wine and Spirits Professional of the Year Award are:

1992	Andre Tchelistcheff, Beaulieu Winery
1993	Kevin Zraly, Windows on the World, New York
1994	Randall Grahm, Bonny Doon Vineyard, Santa Cruz
1995	Marvin Shanken, *Wine Spectator*
1996	Jack and Jaimie Davies, Schramsberg Vineyards, Calistoga
1997	Zelma Long, Simi Winery, Healdsburg
1998	Robert M. Parker Jr., *The Wine Advocate*
1999	Frank Prial, *The New York Times*
2000	Kermit Lynch, Berkeley
2001	Gerald Asher, *Gourmet*
2002	Andrea Immer, French Culinary Institute
2003	Fritz Maytag, Anchor Brewing Co.
2004	Karen MacNeil, Culinary Institute of America
2005	Joseph Bastianich, Italian Wine Merchants, New York

What's the difference between California and French wines, and who makes the better wines?

You really think I'm going to answer that? California and France both make great wines, but the French make the best French wines!

From production strategy to weather, each region's profile is distinct. California wines and French wines share many similarities. They also have many differences. The greatest similarity is that both France and California grow most of the same grape varieties. The biggest differences are soil, climate, and tradition.

The French regard their soil with reverence and believe that the best wines only come from the greatest soil. When grapes were originally planted in California, the soil was not one of the major factors in determining which grapes were planted where. Over the last twenty years, this has become a much more important aspect for the vineyard owners in California, and it's not unheard of for a winemaker to say that his/her best Cabernet Sauvignon comes from a specific area.

As far as weather goes, the temperatures in Napa and Sonoma are different from those of Burgundy and Bordeaux. The fact is, that while European vintners get gray hair over pesky problems like cold snaps and rainstorms in the growing season, Californians can virtually count on abundant sunshine and warm temperatures.

Tradition is the biggest difference between the two, and I'm not just talking about winemaking. For example, vineyard and winery practices in Europe have remained virtually unchanged for generations; and these age-old techniques—some of which were written into law—define each region's own style. But in California, where few traditions exist, vintners are free to experiment with modern technology and create new products based on consumer demand. If you've ever had a wine called Two Buck Chuck, you know what I mean.

It is sometimes very difficult for me to sit in a tasting and compare a California Chardonnay and a French white Burgundy, since they have been making wines in Burgundy for the last 1,600 years and the renaissance of California wines is not yet 40 years old.

I buy both French and California wines for my personal cellar, and sometimes my choice has to do totally with how I feel that day: Do I want to end up in Bordeaux or the Napa Valley?

The Best of the Best:
An Opinionated Tribute

THE BEST WINE WRITERS IN THE WORLD

Books: Hugh Johnson

When I started the study of wine in 1970, I began with three books: Alexis Lichine's *Wines of France*, Frank Schoonmaker's *The Encyclopedia of Wine*, and Hugh Johnson's *Wine*. For most beginners, these books would be overwhelming. For me, I wanted more!

Alexis and Frank are no longer with us, but Hugh Johnson has carried the torch with his *Modern Encyclopedia of Wine*, *The World Atlas of Wine*, *How to Enjoy Your Wine*, and his *Pocket Encyclopedia of Wine*. Indeed, he's my favorite wine writer overall.

Three of my other favorite wine book writers are also Brits: Jancis Robinson, Clive Coates, and Oz Clarke. My favorite book writers on American wines are James Laube and Matt Kramer.

Newspapers: *The New York Times, The Wall Street Journal, USA Today*

Three major newspapers with three completely different styles of writing—just like wine!

As long as I've been involved with wine, Frank Prial has been at *The New York Times*. Not only is he a great reporter, but his realistic approach to wine and wine writing connects to his reader, both beginner and advanced. He's never been afraid of controversy, and, as many have said, he tells it like it is. Eric Asimov now shares the "Wine Talk" column with Frank Prial, and they have added wine ratings (one star to four stars, as for the restaurant reviews) to the column.

Jerry Shriver, the food-and-wine writer for *USA Today*, does a tremendous amount of research on all his articles, asks the right questions, and ends up with a thorough and detailed yet easy-to-understand report on whatever he covers.

Dorothy J. Gaiter and John Brecher of *The Wall Street Journal* bring a wide-ranging, down-to-earth, and even interactive approach to their column. They're the best at answering readers' questions.

Food Magazines: Anthony Dias Blue—*Bon Appétit*

For twenty of my thirty years in wine, Andy has been the wine writer for *Bon Appétit* magazine. He has a commonsense approach to wine and is always trying to find the ten-dollar bottle of wine that tastes like a twenty-dollar bottle of wine. His book *American Wine* was one of the first comprehensive guides to wines of the United States. He also has a syndicated show on CBS radio and is the director of the *Bon Appétit* "Wine and Spirits Focus" around the country.

Another must-read for the serious wine aficionado is Gerald Asher, whose column "Wine Journal" has been appearing in *Gourmet* since 1972.

Lettie Teague, wine editor of *Food and Wine* magazine, has a fabulous dry sense of humor mixed with a healthy skepticism. Alan Richmond, who is the husband of Lettie Teague, has probably won more wine- and food-writing awards than anyone. He is a long-time writer for *GQ*, and his articles also appear in *Bon Appétit*. He's funny, direct, and extremely knowledgeable.

THE BEST WINE PUBLICATION

Wine Spectator

I remember meeting with Marvin Shanken when he purchased *Wine Spectator* in 1979. Back then it was a worthwhile publication with very few subscribers. Marvin is a great businessman; over the last twenty-five years he has taken the magazine from a few hundred subscribers to upwards of 380,000. It is a must-read for the consumer, and the articles and ratings are extremely important to all segments of the wine industry.

His ability to maintain his editorial staff of wine writers, many of whom have been with him for more than twenty years, is a phenomenal accomplishment in the ever-changing world of wine. His magazine features great wine writers and editors such as James Laube, Per-Henrik Mansson, Kim Marcus., Thomas Matthews, James Molesworth, Bruce Sanderson, Harvey Steiman, and James Suckling.

A totally different format and point of view is *Decanter* magazine. This British publication includes feature articles by Brits Michael Broadbent, Steven Spurrier, Hugh Johnson, and Clive Coates. An American, Norm Roby, covers the California scene.

The Wine Enthusiast magazine is the passion of the owner, editor, and publisher, Adam Strum, who also owns *The Wine Enthusiast* catalogue of wine accessories. The magazine is seasoned with experienced writers such as Steve Heimoff and Roger Voss, along with such contributing editors as Alexis Bespaloff and Jeff Morgan, and coverage of spirits by F. Paul Pacult.

Wine and Spirits magazine, the brainchild of owner, publisher, and editor Joshua Greene, features the talents of senior editor Tara Q. Thomas, columnists Fiona Morrison, M.W., and Bill St. John, and contributing editor Anthony Giglio.

THE BEST WINE TASTER IN THE WORLD

Robert M. Parker Jr.

We both started studying wines around the same time but took different paths. He has basically changed the way wines are tasted and rated in the world through his 100-point scoring system. I know of no other human being who has tasted more wines than Mr. Parker—ten thousand a year, according to him! All his reviews are published in the *Wine Advocate*, with more than forty thousand subscribers. Whether you like his assessments or not, you have to admire his stamina, perseverance, and red tongue!

Another prolific wine taster is Michael Broadbent. Through the wine department at Christie's Auction House, he has possibly tasted more older wines than Mr. Parker, describing the wines without using a numbering system but in his own poetic, British fashion.

THE BEST WINE IMPORTER IN THE UNITED STATES

Kobrand

Chances are good you've heard of Tattinger Champagne, Jadot Burgundy, Sassicia, Taylor-Fladgate, Fonseca, Cakebread, and St. Francis. These are just some of the great wines of the Kobrand portfolio. They have been in

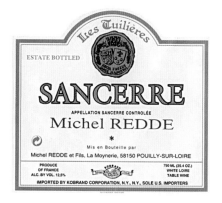

business for more than sixty years and have always been professional, charitable, and one of the best importers when it comes to wine education. Other great wine importers include Frederick Wildman & Sons Ltd. and Paterno Imports.

THE BEST WINERY IN CALIFORNIA (TIE)

Robert Mondavi

Beringer Winery

Based on tradition, availability, and quality at all price levels, it's a tie between the Robert Mondavi Winery and the Beringer Winery. I wonder what Napa Valley would be like today without the foresight of the Beringer and Mondavi families. Beringer represents the "old" and the "new" California. Robert Mondavi created the "new."

Obviously, Best Winery in California was one of the toughest decisions for me to make, considering that there are more than 1,600 wineries in California. Many of them make better and more expensive wines than these two wineries, but both Robert Mondavi and the Beringer Winery have been able to produce great wines consistently.

THE BEST WINE TO AGE

The Great Châteaus of Bordeaux

Many great wine regions on Earth produce red wines that will age for thirty or more years. But nowhere on Earth is there a region that produces both red and white wines that you can drink 100 years later!

THE BEST BOTTLE SIZE FOR AGING

Magnum

This is not just my opinion—my friends who collect and make wine all say that their best wines will last longer and mature more slowly in a magnum (the equivalent of two bottles) than in a 750 ml.

One of the theories for this difference in bottle-size aging is the amount of air that is in the bottle (the air between the wine and the cork) versus the quantity of wine.

It's also more fun to serve a magnum at a dinner party.

THE BEST WINE IN THE WORLD

Château Latour

I'm often asked, if I had to choose only one wine, which would it be? Jokingly, I try to get out of answering the question by simply saying, "Red"! After tasting more than twenty-five thousand different wines and different vintages over my thirty-year career, it's not an easy answer. That said, if I were on a desert island, I'd like to have with me *cases* of Château Latour.

Made primarily of Cabernet Sauvignon and coming from, in my opinion, the best wine region on Earth—Bordeaux—it has rarely disappointed me, even in "off" vintages. I've been lucky to have tasted every vintage of Château Latour as far back as 1900 and a few from the 1800s. The smell and taste of an aged Latour cannot be described in words or numbers, but only with fond memories.

THE BEST SOMMELIER IN THE UNITED STATES (TIE)

Larry Stone, Rubicon, San Francisco

Roger Dagorn, Chanterelle, New York

A lot of students ask me whether or not they should consult the sommelier for their wine selections. The answer is sometimes yes and sometimes no. It can be tricky—I've heard horror stories, like when my best friend got his check and the bottle recommended by the sommelier cost $500! With any sommelier, you must let them know how much you are willing to spend and hope they have the knowledge to help you.

The French word *sommelier* basically means "wine waiter"—someone who will be at the restaurant to help you with your wine selection. A lot of somme-

"If it's a California wine you wish, Mr. Larry will assist you."

© The New Yorker Collection 1981, James Stevenson from cartoonbank.com. All rights reserved.

liers, like myself, became wine directors, but both Larry and Roger will be there at your table when you are ready to order your wine.

Both of these guys are master sommeliers, which involves an extensive amount of research and testing.

THE BEST RESTAURANT WINE CELLAR DESIGN

Aureole, Las Vegas

I still have fond memories of my first visit to the wine cellar at the "21" Club in my early days as a student of wine. Back then, it was a hidden room that had been part of a speakeasy during the tumultuous Prohibition years. Today, you can actually dine there.

At Windows on the World, we created the Cellar in the Sky. When it was in existence, this private cellar—107 stories above Manhattan—accommodated thirty-six people who were surrounded by wine bottles.

But today, the most dramatic wine cellar in the United States is the Wine Tower. The $1.2 million construction was designed by Adam D. Tahini at Aureole, Las Vegas. It is four stories (forty-two feet) high and fourteen feet square and can hold almost ten thousand bottles at a perfect 55°F temperature. Even if you don't gamble, it's worth the trip to Las Vegas to see this monument to wine.

THE BEST WINE REGIONS FOR A VACATION

Napa Valley, California

Tuscany, Italy

Bordeaux, France

A great vacation for me is great wine, fabulous restaurants, perfect climate, proximity to the ocean, beautiful scenery (am I asking too much yet?), and nice people! These three wine regions fulfill my needs.

"You see? I've always told you California wines weren't so bad."

© The New Yorker Collection 1957, Ed Fisher from cartoonbank.com. All rights reserved.

THE BEST PLACE FOR CABERNET SAUVIGNON

Bordeaux, France (Médoc)

Runner-up—California

In my opinion the greatest wines of the world are the Châteaus of Bordeaux. The primary grape of the Médoc wine is Cabernet Sauvignon. These are not only the best wines for investment, they are some of the best wines to age. With some seven thousand Châteaus, there's plenty of wine to choose from at all different price points.

THE BEST PLACE FOR PINOT NOIR

Burgundy, France

Runners-up—Oregon, California

Burgundy is a region deep in history and tradition. Vines have been planted there for over a thousand years, and the sensuous Pinot Noir is the only red grape allowed (other than Beaujolais).

The only problems with a great Pinot Noir from Burgundy are its price tag and availability.

THE BEST PLACE FOR RIESLING

Germany

Runner-up—Alsace, France

Many professionals and wine connoisseurs believe that the best white wine made in the world is Riesling. It is definitely one of the best wines to go with food, especially with lighter-style fish dishes, such as sole and flounder.

I still think that the consumer is confused by the Riesling grape variety and thinks that all Rieslings are sweet. The reality is that 99 percent of all Alsace Rieslings are dry, and most of the German Rieslings I would classify as off-dry or semisweet.

Even though I probably drink more Alsace Rieslings than German Rieslings, the diversity of style of the German wines—dry, off-dry, semisweet, and very sweet—is the reason I would rank German Rieslings as the best in the world.

THE BEST PLACE FOR SAUVIGNON BLANC

Loire Valley, France

Runner-up—New Zealand

The Sauvignon Blanc produced in the Loire Valley is best known by its regional names, Sancerre and Pouilly-Fumé. The best of the New Zealand Sauvignon Blancs are sold under the producer's name.

The stylistic differences between the Sauvignon Blancs of the Loire Valley and New Zealand are striking. While both Sauvignon Blancs are medium in body with high acidity, and while both work well with fish and poultry, the New Zealand Sauvignon Blancs have what some would call a very aggressive bouquet or aroma that you either like or don't like, which continues in the taste. I like it!

THE BEST PLACE FOR CHARDONNAY

Burgundy, France

Runner-up—California

As much as I like the best producers of California Chardonnay, the elegance and balance of fruit, acidity, alcohol, and oak in a white Burgundy wine are unmatched in the world. From the non-oak-aged Chablis to the barrel-fermented and barrel-aged Montrachets, to the light, easy-drinking Mâcons and the world-famous Pouilly-Fuissé, there is a style and price for everyone.

THE BEST PLACE FOR MERLOT

Bordeaux, France (St-Émilion, Pomerol)

Runner-up—California

The great châteaus of St-Émilion and Pomerol both produce wines made primarily of the Merlot grape. The major difference between the two is the price and availability. St-Émilion is a much larger region than Pomerol, with many more châteaus, offering a better price/value relationship than Pomerol. So for my money I'd go with St-Émilion, based on its lower price and also because today it is the most progressive of all the Bordeaux wine regions.

THE BEST "FUN" CORK

Frog's Leap Winery, Napa, California

I have great admiration for winemakers who produce great wine and have fun at the same time. John Williams, the owner and winemaker of Frog's Leap, and one of the premier winemakers in California, adds humor to drinking, with the inscription "Ribit" on every Frog's Leap cork.

THE BEST AFTER-DINNER WINE

Port

You don't need to drink a lot of Port to get the full enjoyment. One glass of this sweet and fortified (20 percent alcohol) wine ends a meal with a satisfying taste.

Most of the Port that I consume—whether it be Ruby, Tawny, or Vintage—I drink between September and March, the cooler months in the Northeast. For me, the best way to enjoy Port is when it's twenty degrees (or colder) and snowing outside—after the kitchen and all the dishes have been cleaned, your children are tucked away into their dream world, and you are sitting in front of your fireplace with your golden retriever by your side!

THE BEST WINE EVENT

Wine Spectator's New York Wine Experience

There are many great wine events in the United States. In the year 2006, *Wine Spectator* will celebrate the twenty-fifth anniversary of its New York Wine Experience. I have to admit a certain bias since I was cofounder of the event. What makes this wine weekend the best is that it was established on three principles:

1. Only the best wineries of the world are invited.

2. The winemaker or owner must be present.

3. All proceeds go to scholarships.

Twenty-five years later, this biannual event has maintained the highest quality of wines, seminars, and speakers of any wine event in the world.

Windows on the World:
A Personal History

BY KEVIN ZRALY

WINDOWS ON THE WORLD

WINDOWS ON THE WORLD OPENED its elevator doors for the first time on April 12, 1976, as a private luncheon club. The press had been writing about its opening for months, speculating on whether the whole project—both the restaurant and the World Trade Center complex that housed it—could be pulled off. After all, never before had a project this large been attempted. The World Trade Center was not only designed to include the tallest building in the world, it was going to be one of the largest urban centers ever built, with more than 40,000 World Trade Center office workers and 150,000 commuters passing through the complex every day.

All eyes were on Joe Baum, the man in charge of food services for the World Trade Center complex and mastermind behind the Windows on the World Restaurant. Joe had created some of New York's most successful landmark restaurants, including The Four Seasons, La Fonda del Sol, and the Forum of the Twelve Caesars.

He was known in the industry as a maverick, a restaurant genius, and a pit bull, and was often called all these names at the same time. In 1970, Joe Baum had signed a contract with the Port Authority of New York and New Jersey to design and manage all the restaurant and food-service areas of the World Trade Center. Joe and his associates, Michael Whiteman and Dennis Sweeney, conceived and organized twenty-two restaurants that were to be located throughout the complex.

Joe had grandiose ideas for the restaurant on top of the World Trade Center—ideas that would cost a lot of money.

"One evening in 1975, my father Joe came home late for a family dinner. After another marathon day of creating and planning, he was full of excitement and teeming with enthusiasm. 'What do you think if we called the place Windows on the World?' he asked. In my infinite wisdom I thought, Not bad, but will people remember the name?"

—CHARLES BAUM

"The building wasn't finished when we first went up to the 107th floor. We stepped out of the elevator into a cavernous, undifferentiated space; onto a million sheets of plywood, ducking under scaffolds, the winds blowing, inching closer and closer to the edge to take in the view. I was petrified, and then I saw it: the shocking beauty of the city my father loved."

—HILARY BAUM

Joe Baum on top of Two World Trade Center, overlooking One World Trade Center and Windows on the World

The Cellar in the Sky Restaurant

"As one of the first to join the 'Baum Squad,' I caught Joe's contagious fervor about Windows on the World right away and always knew it would be a smash success. And having the opportunity to work with Joe's 'kitchen cabinet'—James Beard, Craig Claiborne, Albert Stockli, Pierre Franey, Jacques Pépin, and Albert Kumin—was an education in itself. But nothing in my life will ever compare to opening day in April of 1976, a day of such excitement and wonder over this uber-restaurant."

—DENNIS SWEENEY

In the early '70s, New York City was in the midst of a severe fiscal crisis, and many New Yorkers were against building the World Trade Center to begin with. So Joe called his former classmate from Cornell, Curt Strand, president of Hilton International, to partner with the Port Authority, and together they formed a company called Inhilco.

Hilton International named Joe Baum president of Inhilco. With the backing of the Port Authority, more than $17 million was spent developing Windows on the World. Their main focus was the 107th floor of One World Trade Center, which they divided into five parts: The Restaurant (which seated nearly three hundred guests); The City Lights Bar; Hors D'Oeuvrerie, which served everything except the main course; The Cellar in the Sky, a glass-enclosed working wine cellar that seated just thirty-six guests and served a seven-course, five-wine, one-seating dinner; and six private banquet rooms capable of accommodating more than three hundred people. All together, Windows on the World spanned one acre, 107 stories up in the sky.

Joe Baum was a master contractor. He hired the best culinary talent available. He asked James Beard and Jacques Pépin to help develop the menus, Warren Platner to design the restaurant, Milton Glaser to design all the graphics, and Barbara Kafka to select everything from glassware to table settings. Joe also hired top restaurant managers, including his partner in other great New York restaurants, Alan Lewis, and a staff that would do anything Baum requested.

Joe was looking for a young American to run his wine department. I was lucky enough to be hired as the first cellar master at Windows on the World. I took the job after consulting with friends, many of whom warned me about leaving my job as a wine salesman to work at Windows. They gave me three reasons not to take the job

1. In 1976, no one went downtown after 6 p.m.
2. Rooftop restaurants weren't considered quality operations.
3. Joe Baum had the reputation of being difficult to work with.

On all three counts, I learned it just wasn't so. In fact, I knew it was going to be a great restaurant and job when I asked Joe about creating the wine list.

He said: "It's very simple. I want you to create the biggest and the best wine list that New York has ever seen—and don't worry about how much it costs!" There I was, a twenty-five-year-old kid in a candy store—only it sold wine!

In May of 1976, before Windows on the World's official opening, the cover of *New York* magazine read: THE MOST SPECTACULAR RESTAURANT IN THE WORLD—HOW A BRILLIANT RESTAURATEUR CREATED A MASTERPIECE ON THE 107ᵀᴴ FLOOR OF THE WORLD TRADE CENTER. The article was written by the illustrious Gael Greene. Some of the superlatives from that article included: "a miracle," "a masterpiece," "a dream," "a triumph," and "almost unreal." It went on, "No other sky-high restaurant quite prepares you for the astonishment of the horizon."

The World Trade Center and Windows on the World also became symbols for the financial turnaround of New York City and their completion played a key role in the revitalization of lower Manhattan. This was underscored the year Windows on the World opened, 1976, which was also America's bicentennial year. Imagine an unobstructed view from the 107th floor of the spectacularly refurbished Statue of Liberty and the entire New York Harbor with its flotilla of tall ships. What a sight it was! Seeing the bicentennial fireworks from Windows became the hottest ticket in the world.

On that memorable July Fourth evening, I went alone to the top of One World Trade Center (the broadcast antennae and barriers had not yet been erected) and watched all the fireworks displays within a sixty-mile radius. I knew I'd made the right decision to work at Windows on the World: I remember thinking that life didn't get much better than this. I was serving wine to kings, queens, presidents, sports heroes, and movie stars. During the next five years, I met every celebrity I had ever heard of or read about.

Windows on the World was an instant success and was booked months in advance.

The Windows on the World Wine School has operated continuously for the last twenty-nine years, since the opening of the restaurant in 1976, even during times of uncertainty. The Wine School started with a small group of ten lunch club members in 1976. Club members started inviting their friends, who then invited their friends. Soon the friends of club members outnumbered the club members. Still, the class list kept growing. In 1980 we opened

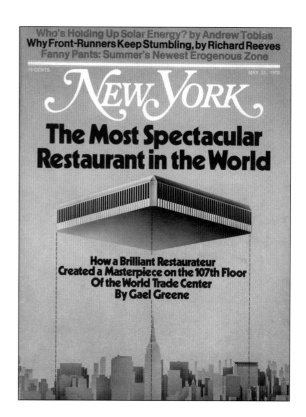

New York magazine cover, May 1976

"On July 4, 1976, Windows on the World was filled with celebrities for the bicentennial fireworks display. I was given the very pleasant task of escorting Princess Grace of Monaco. As we watched the extravaganza over the Statue of Liberty, Princess Grace held my hand very tightly because the fireworks made her somewhat nervous. I asked if the moment reminded her of To Catch a Thief and her very famous, very passionate scene with Cary Grant, set to the backdrop of fireworks. She was astounded I knew the film and the scene. So I told her that if she wanted to watch the film again, she could that night, because it was being shown at 11:30, on Channel 2."

—MELVIN FREEMAN, Page, 1976–93 and 1996–2001

"Windows on the World was a miracle to conceive and open. In the early '70s, rooftop restaurants were failing—it seemed like an impossible dream. But with the genius of Joe Baum, and the determination of many individuals, including myself, to have a restaurant on top of the World Trade Center, the dream became a reality."

—GUY TOZZOLI, Director, World Trade Center Association, 1970 to present

"Even more than high school and college, my 'education' at Windows on the World University has stood me well in tackling the challenges of the world at large."

—MICHAEL SKURNIK, Assistant Cellarmaster, 1977–78

"It has been the greatest privilege for me to be part of Windows on the World and its wonderful team members, from the inception of the one-acre restaurant complex back in 1974 and during its first 12 years of operation. Windows on the World wore a smile of confidence from the day it opened. Overnight, the restaurants and banquet rooms gained worldwide recognition. Its attention to detail, its definite philosophy about wine and food, and its innovative approach to wine merchandising and education, were Windows' greatest assets. Windows became a 'premier' destination—a place to celebrate, host a party, or entertain in style for business or romance."

—TONI AIGNER, President, Inhilco, 1978–90

"I moved to New York in June 1990 and worked in the wine department of Windows during 1991 and 1992. . . . My greatest memories are the nights when the view north over the city captured all the excitement and energy of New York." —BRUCE SANDERSON, Assistant Cellarmaster, 1991–92

the Wine School to the public. Since then, more than sixteen thousand students have attended classes.

So what made Windows on the World so great? Was it the sixty-second elevator ride? Was it the menu concept? Was it the youthful, energetic staff? Was it the extensive and outrageously low-priced wine list? Or was it the most spectacular view in the world?

For me, it was all of the above.

I continued as cellar master and, over the next four years, Windows on the World sold more wine than any other restaurant in the United States—and probably the world. The first five years of Windows on the World had been nonstop.

In 1980, I was named wine director for Windows on the World and Hilton International, and in 1981, I cofounded the New York Wine Experience, which is a celebration of the best wines from all over the world. The New York Wine Experience was held for the first three years at Windows on the World. Events like this, combined with our superb, well-priced wine list, helped establish Windows on the World as a true destination for wine lovers. We drew amateur wine enthusiasts as well as professionals; we attracted students and teachers alike; anyone seriously interested in wine stopped up for a bottle or two and a meal, including many who wanted to work in our wine cellar.

In 1985, my book, *Windows on the World Complete Wine Course*, made its debut, putting the Wine School in print for the first time. Over the next eight years, Windows continued to be one of the most successful restaurants in the world, the Wine School enrollment continued to grow, and the book became the best-selling wine book in the United States.

By the time Windows' fifteenth anniversary rolled around in 1991, both the restaurant and lower Manhattan had experienced their share of ups and downs. In 1987, Wall Street suffered a steep drop in stock market prices, which affected the restaurant business for several years. That same year, Ladbroke, a hotel and gaming company, bought out Hilton International and became the owner of Windows. As the stock market recovered, so did the businesses in lower Manhattan. By then, however, the notion of opening a fine restaurant near the financial district was no longer a novelty, and business at Windows faced quite a bit of competition from the proliferation of restaurants in its neighborhood.

FRIDAY, FEBRUARY 26, 1993—THE BOMBING AT THE WTC

THE FIRST TERRORIST ATTACK ON the World Trade Center took place on February 26, 1993, at 12:18 P.M. Six people were killed, including one of our employees who worked in the receiving department in the World Trade Center basement. Food and wine author Andrea Immer, cellar master at the time, escorted all our patrons down 107 flights of stairs to safety.

Windows on the World shut down after the bombing, leaving more than 400 food-service people without jobs. Within six months I was the last Windows on the World employee on the payroll. Windows on the World lay dormant from February 26, 1993, until June 1996. My wine school coordinator and I were the only people allowed to enter Windows on the World after the 1993 bombing. It was a very lonely time.

Although the restaurant was closed from 1993 until 1996, with the help of Andrea Immer; Johannes Tromp, the director of Windows on the World; and Jules Roinnel, the director of The World Trade Center Club, the Wine School kept going. After the 1993 bombing, American Express gave us a temporary office across the street from the World Trade Center. Our view was of One World Trade Center and we would often stand at the windows watching tow trucks remove car after car—all destroyed—from the underground World Trade Center garages.

"I remember the first terrorist attack in 1993. We walked down the stairs with our lunch guests. I returned to work with Kevin when we reopened in 1996. I will never forget the extraordinary joy of seeing and touching those wines again, and welcoming our wine students back, and just being 'home,' where everything sparkled, most of all, the people."
—ANDREA IMMER, Cellarmaster, 1992–93

"Windows on the World was brilliantly conceived and truly unique. Being a Dutch immigrant managing the complex of restaurants and private dining rooms, with its 440 culinary and hospitality professionals high above Manhattan, was an unforgettable experience. I feel honored to have been a temporary guardian of this magnificent New York City institution."
—JOHANNES TROMP, Director, 1989–93

"Windows was silent when I ran the Wine School, but I relished its solitude. I roamed its floors, inspected its rooms, absorbed all that was left frozen in time. Like Jack Nicholson in The Shining, I could sense the energy it embodied, feel its buzz, envision its diners, find myself immersed in the dream. But unlike Jack's, my visions embodied warmth and peace. The space lived and breathed even when empty and will continue to do so in our hearts." —REBECCA CHAPPA, Wine School Coordinator, 1994–95

"When I reflect on the 22 years I spent at Windows, no singular event immediately comes to mind but rather a series of images: the faces of children pressed up against the windows, the sun setting over the Statue of Liberty, and the laughter and joy of thousands of guests who created a lifetime of cherished memories." —JULES ROINNEL, Director, the World Trade Center Club, 1979–2001

World Trade Center, view from New Jersey

"Windows was the kind of place that let you come as you are, or wanted to be. You could be formal or relaxed, fancy or plain, intimate or gregarious. . . .Tourists, workers, lovers, families, dancers, and partygoers: Windows welcomed the world to the Trade Center."

—TIM SHEEHAN, Port Authority of NY/NJ

"Despite its ultimate destruction, my recollections of Windows are those of triumph. We opened it in 1976 during the depths of New York's recession, and its astounding success symbolized the city's commercial and social recovery. We re-created it after the 1993 terrorist attack on the World Trade Center and established a triumphant return as the country's largest-grossing restaurant. Windows triumphed by proving that a rooftop restaurant wasn't by definition a tourist trap. It triumphed by providing interior excitement that was better than the view. It triumphed by proving that quality beats gimmickry and that great design outlasts ephemeral themes. Most of all, it triumphed because its employees loved the place as much as its customers."

—MICHAEL WHITEMAN

"At Windows, Joe Baum led us to the promised land; an adventure in imagination, the pursuit of the unexpected and enormous scale. There has never been anything else like it."   —MILTON GLASER, Designer

"What I remember most about Windows on the World is the employee cafeteria. It was in that room that friends congregated to eat, talk, and enjoy the view of the three bridges below us. It was here where laughter and happiness prevailed. Windows was my family in New York, my world that I loved so dearly."

—INEZ RIBUSTELLO, Beverage Manager, 1999–2001

Both the Windows logo designed for the reopening in 1996 and the original logo on page 243 were created by Milton Glaser.

During the spring semester of 1993, Andrea Immer and I moved the school to the top of Seven World Trade Center. It remained there for the rest of 1993 and all of 1994. From 1994 to mid-1995, we held classes in the oval room on the forty-fourth floor of One World Trade Center, and from mid-1995 until the restaurant reopened in 1996, we operated from the newly reopened Vista Hotel (Marriott). I'm proud the Wine School remained open during those difficult years. It kept the memory of Windows alive and became a symbol to everyone that Windows would come back.

Following the 1993 bombing, the Port Authority concluded that both the 106th and 107th floors needed structural repairs, and meanwhile they would begin a search for a new operator for the restaurants. Again, requests for proposals went out, and this time more than thirty restaurant operators expressed interest in taking over Windows on the World. A review committee was formed by the Port Authority to examine each proposal and make recommendations. They narrowed it down to three entries: Alan Stillman, of the Smith & Wollensky Restaurant Group, owners of Smith & Wollensky, the Post House, The Manhattan Ocean Club, Park Avenue Café, Cité, and Maloney & Porcelli; Warner LeRoy, of Tavern on the Green, Maxwell's Plum, and later, the Russian Tea Room; and Joe Baum, the original creator of Windows on the World, who was then operating the Rainbow Room.

The Port Authority awarded the contract to Joe Baum, and the renaissance of Windows on the World began. Both Andrea Immer and I were brought back: Andrea to develop the wine list and beverage program, and I to continue with the Wine School. In all, the new staff totaled more than 400 employees and represented some 25 nationalities.

The reopening of Windows on the World in June of 1996—twenty years almost to the month after its first opening—was accomplished with Joe Baum's usual kinetic energy, *joie de vivre*, and theatrical hoopla. Joe and his partners, the Emil family, reconceived the restaurant to make it the ultimate American-style food and wine experience. They took a big risk by committing to American cooking, but it paid off. Their willingness to do so made Windows the best it ever was. Windows on the World received two stars from *The New York Times*, three stars from *Crain's*, a 22 in *Zagat*, and ranked in the top listing in *Wine Spectator* for overall dining.

Sadly, as Windows resumed its place on top of the world—having achieved high marks for both quality and service—Joe Baum died. That was in October 1998.

Over the next three years, Windows on the World remained a premier destination for wine, dining, and special events. One important change for me was the closing of The Cellar in the Sky, that intimate, romantically lit dining room lined with wine bottles. The Cellar in the Sky had been an integral part of the old Windows on the World, but by 1996 restaurants around the country were also doing food and wine pairings. It was time to replace The Cellar with something new. That something new was a restaurant called Wild Blue. Wild Blue was a

Chef/Director Michael Lomonaco and Chef Michael Ammirati in the Windows on the World kitchen

"There I saw the world from one and all other Windows of opportunity. . . . There my future began, from educating myself to educating my kids. There I learned the art of hospitality and traveled to teach others, those in the industry who remain and those who will be remembered."
—CARLOS A. GARCIA, Chief Executive Steward, 1976–86 and 1996–2001

"Windows on the World was an opportunity for Joe Baum, me, and everyone who worked with us to explore their dreams and pursue their ambitions in a spectacular environment."
—DAVID EMIL, Owner, 1993–2001

"Directing what was perhaps the most famous restaurant operation in the world challenged my intellectual and emotional being every day. The greatest of these challenges was, by the single element of location, that we would have the privilege of serving the most diverse clientele of any restaurant in the world and, in turn, employing the most diverse workforce of any restaurant in the world. The social interaction and collaboration of so many unique human beings, on both sides of the equation, was the Windows on the World experience. To have had the opportunity to be an integral part of the success of that collaboration made it an incredibly rewarding experience. In this respect, we truly were the Windows on the World." —GLENN VOGT, General Manager, 1997–2001

"Windows on the World was an inviting and hospitable place. . . . At Windows, everything seemed possible: fine wine, great food, and conviviality. There, floating high above the Earth, we never forgot we were citizens of the World. We welcomed one and all to dine, drink, and enjoy the sweetness of life."
—MICHAEL LOMONACO, Executive Chef/Director, 1997–2001

Overlooking the Brooklyn Bridge

*"On Monday, September 10, I was hosting my
class called 'Spirits in the Skybox,' a name
that has haunting implications. When we
finished, my co-host and I invited a few friends
and some members of the press to join us for a
quick drink in the bar. I usually have cocktails,
but this time we ordered Champagne. There
was no particular celebration; the group just
seemed to click, so we had several more
bottles of Champagne and food. A woman DJ
began spinning records. Someone in our group
knew her, so we stayed and ended the evening
dancing. I awoke Tuesday morning to the
horror of the terrorist attack that finished off
that medium-sized city called the World Trade
Center. I will cherish the gift I was given of
that last spontaneous celebration in Joe
Baum's majestic Windows on the World. We
were unknowingly lifting our glasses that night
in farewell to all those friends and colleagues
we would lose the following day."*

—DALE DEGROFF, Master Mixologist,
1996–2001

staff to show off their culinary skills. Wild Blue received four stars from *Crain's*, a 25 in *Zagat*, a spot in the top-ten list of New York restaurants in *Wine Spectator*, and a rating as one of New York's best by *Esquire*.

Windows was the best it could be on September 10, 2001. It was generating more than $37 million in revenues and was the number one dollar-volume restaurant in the United States. Of that $37 million, upwards of $6 million came from the sale of wines from among our 1,400 different selections. We were enthusiastic about our future and were excitedly preparing for our twenty-fifth anniversary celebration in October 2001.

On September 11, 2001, the world changed. What began as a beautiful, pristine September morning ended in a dark nightmare of death and destruction. Seventy-two coworkers, one security officer, and six construction workers, who were building the new wine cellar at Windows on the World, died in the worst terrorist attack in American history.

For me, the day is still incomprehensible. The loss of my friends and coworkers remains heavy in my heart. The World Trade Center complex was my New York City. It was my neighborhood. I shopped there. I stayed at the Marriott Hotel with my family. I lost my home and community of twenty-five years, a community I watched being built.

Windows on the World no longer exists, but the reflections of those windows will remain with me forever.

Afterword:
Looking Back, with Gratitude

I WILL ALWAYS REMEMBER:

- working with and learning from John Novi at the Depuy Canal House, 1970–76

- my first visit to a winery, in 1970

- my first wine classes, in 1971 (one where I was a student and the other where I was the teacher)

- hitchhiking to California to visit the wine country in 1972

- teaching a two-credit course as a junior in college (open only to seniors) in 1973

- Father Sam Matarazzo, my early spiritual leader

- living and studying wine in Europe, 1974–75

- planting my own vineyard (three-time failure): 1974, 1981, 1992; making my own wine in 1984 (so-so)

- the excitement of opening Windows on the World in 1976

- the support and friendship of Jules Roinnel, going back to our earliest days together at Windows

- wine tastings with Alexis Bespaloff

- Curt Strand and Toni Aigner of Hilton International

- evening, late-night, and early-morning wine discussions with Alexis Lichine in Bordeaux

- the adviser and great listener Peter Sichel, whose generosity of spirit inspired the way I teach and share my wine knowledge

- sharing great old vintages with Peter Bienstock

- touring the world of Bordeaux with wine expert Robin Kelley O'Connor

- those who are no longer here to share a glass of wine: Craig Claiborne, Joseph Baum, Alan Lewis, and Raymond Wellington

- creating and directing the New York Wine Experience from 1981–91

- witnessing the success of Michael Skurnik, who worked with me at Windows in the late 1970s and quickly rose to fame as a great importer of wines

- watching my former student Andrea Immer turn into a superstar wine-and-food personality and author

- the Food Network's *Wines A to Z* with Alan Richmond

- reading and enjoying the observations of the great wine writers and tasters (listed throughout the book)

- having the opportunity to meet all the passionate winemakers, vineyardists, and owners of the great wineries of the world

- the wine events, wine dinners, and tastings around the country that I have had the privilege of attending

- all the groups that have invited me to entertain and educate their clients about wine

- writing the first chapter of this book with Kathleen Talbert in 1983

- the original Sterling Publishing team of Burton Hobson and Lincoln Boehm

- the new Sterling Publishing team of Charles Nurnberg, Steven Magnuson, Andrew Martin, Leigh Ann Ambrosi, and Chris Vaccari

- all my editors over the last two decades, especially Felicia Sherbert, Stephen Topping, and Hannah Reich

- the team assembled especially for this anniversary edition: Laurie Kahn, Rena Kornbluh, Julie Schroeder, Jeff Ward, Becky Maines, Mike Hollitscher, Pip Tannenbaum, and Sara Cheney

- Karen Nelson for twenty years of beautiful cover designs

- Jim Anderson, who designed the original edition; and Richard Oriolo for capturing my spirit in subsequent editions

- Barnes & Noble, for always supporting my book

- Carmen Bissell, Raymond DePaul, and Faye Friedman for their help with the Wine School

- all my pourers at the school over the last thirty years

- having a great relationship with my New York City wine-school peers, especially Harriet Lembeck (Beverage Program); Mary Ewing-Mulligan (International Wine Center); and Robert Millman and Howard Kaplan (Executive Wine Seminars)

- the 16,000 students who attended the Windows on the World Wine School, which celebrates its thirtieth anniversary in 2006

- the Baum–Emil team, who re-created Windows on the World in 1996

- conducting the Sherry-Lehmann/Kevin Zraly Master Wine Class with Michael Aaron, Michael Yurch, and the rest of the Sherry-Lehmann team

- Michael Stengel, Joe Cozza, Vanessa Wehner, Kathleen Duffy, and all those nice people at the Front Desk (especially Tineka) at the Marriott Marquis Hotel NYC

- Jennifer Redmond, who assisted with the Wine School both in New Paltz and in New York City

- John and Linda Bono of Headington Wines & Liquors in New York City
- Alan Stillman, founder, chairman, and CEO of the Smith & Wollensky Restaurant Group
- the changing role of women in the wine industry (thank God!)
- being honored for "loving wine" by the James Beard Foundation
- teaching wine at Cornell University and the Culinary Institute of America
- being a member of the Culinary Institute's Board of Trustees
- Frank Prial and Florence Fabricant of *The New York Times* for their continual support
- Robert M. Parker Jr., who so generously donated his time and talents to aid the families of September 11th
- special wine friends who have "helped" me deplete my wine cellar over the years: Harvey and Lori Marshak, Charles Rascoll and Debbie Howe, and Steven Kolpan
- those who have tried to keep me organized in my business life: Ellen Kerr, Claire Josephs, Lois Arrighi, Sara Hutton, Andrea Immer, Dawn Lamendola, Catherine Fallis, Rebecca Chapa, Gina D'Angelo-Mullen, and Michelle Woodruff
- Ann Kiely for paying the bills on time
- Herb Schutte, my distributor analyst
- my wife of 15 years, Ana Fabiano (a former student who needed extra help after class!)
- my four best vintages: Anthony (1991), Nicolas (1993), Harrison (1997), and Adriana (1999)
- my parents, Charles and Kathleen
- my sisters, Sharon and Kathy
- everyone who worked at Windows on the World, especially my colleagues in the wine department
- my continuing grief at the loss of those friends and coworkers who lost their lives on September 11th

A Final Note

If this were an award-acceptance speech, I probably would have gotten the hook after the first three bullet points. Still, I'm sure I've forgotten to name at least one or two folks—an occupational hazard of consuming so much wine! So, to everyone I've ever known, from grammar school on:

May all your vintages be great!

Glossary and Pronunciation Key

Acid: One of the four tastes of wine. It is sometimes described as sour, acidic, or tart and can be found on the sides of the tongue and mouth.

Aloxe Corton (ah-LOHSS cor-TAWN): A village in the Côte de Beaune in Burgundy, France.

Alsace (al-sas): A major white wine–producing region in northeastern France.

Amarone (ah-ma-ROH-nay): An Italian wine from Veneto made by a special process in which grapes are harvested late and allowed to "raisinate," thus producing a higher alcohol percentage in the wine and sometimes a sweet taste on the palate.

Amontillado (ah-mone-tee-YAH-doe): A type of Sherry.

AOC: Abbreviation for Appellation d'Origine Contrôlée; the French government agency that controls wine production there.

AP number: The official testing number displayed on a German wine label that shows the wine was tasted and passed government quality-control standards.

Aroma: The smell of the grapes in a wine.

Auslese (OUSE-lay-zeh): A sweet white German wine made from selected bunches of late-picked grapes.

AVA: Abbreviation for American Viticultural Area.

Barbaresco (bar-bar-ESS-coh): A full-bodied, DOCG red wine from Piedmont, Italy; made from the Nebbiolo grape.

Barbera (bar-BEAR-ah): A red grape grown in Piedmont, Italy, and California.

Barolo (bar-OH-lo): A full-bodied DOCG red wine from Piedmont, Italy; made from the Nebbiolo grape.

Beaujolais (bo-zho-LAY): A light, fruity red Burgundy wine from the region of Beaujolais; in terms of quality, the basic Beaujolais.

Beaujolais Nouveau (bo-zho-LAY noo-VOH): The "new" Beaujolais that's produced and delivered to retailers in a matter of weeks after the harvest.

Beaujolais-Villages (bo-zho-LAY vil-lahj): A Beaujolais wine that comes from a blend of grapes from designated villages in the region; it's a step up in quality from regular Beaujolais.

Beaune (BONE): French city located in the center of the Côte d'Or in Burgundy.

Beerenauslese (bear-en-OUSE-lay-zeh): A full-bodied, sweet white German wine made from the rich, ripe grapes affected by "botrytis."

Bitter: One of the four tastes.

Blanc de Blancs (blahnk duh blahnk): A white wine made from white grapes.

Blanc de Noir (blahnk duh nwahr): A white wine made from red grapes.

Botrytis cinerea (boh-TRY-tiss sin-eh-RAY-ah): A mold that forms on the grapes, known also as "noble rot," which is necessary to make Sauternes and the rich German wines *Beerenauslese* and *Trockenbeerenauslese.*

Bouquet: The smell of the wine.

Brix (bricks): A scale that measures the sugar level of the unfermented grape juice (*must*).

Brunello di Montalcino (brew-NELL-oh dee mon-tahl-CHEE-no): A high-quality DOCG red Italian wine from the Tuscany region.

Brut (BRUTE): The driest style of Champagne.

Cabernet Franc (cah-burr-NAY frahnk): A red grape of the Bordeaux region and the Loire Valley of France.

Cabernet Sauvignon (cah-burr-NAY so-vee-NYOH): The most important red grape grown in the world, yielding many of the great wines of Bordeaux and California.

Carmenre: A grape grown in Chile, sometimes mistaken for Merlot.

Chablis (shah-BLEE): The northernmost region in Burgundy; a wine that comes from Chardonnay grapes grown anywhere in the Chablis district.

Chambolle-Musigny (shahm-BOWL moos-een-YEE): A village in the Côte de Nuits in Burgundy, France.

Champagne: The region in France that produces the only sparkling wine that can be authentically called Champagne.

Chaptalization: The addition of sugar to the must (fresh grape juice) before fermentation.

Chardonnay (shahr-dun-NAY): The most important and expensive white grape, now grown all over the world; nearly all French white Burgundy wines are made from 100 percent Chardonnay.

Chassagne-Montrachet (shahs-SAHN-ya mown-rah-shay): A village in the Côte de Beaune in Burgundy, France.

Château (shah-TOH): The French "legal" definition is a house attached to a vineyard having a specific number of acres with winemaking and storage facilities on the property.

Château wine: Usually the best-quality Bordeaux wine.

Châteauneuf-du-Pape (shah-toh-nuff-dew-POP): A red wine from the southern Rhône Valley region of France; the name means "new castle of the Pope."

Chenin Blanc (SHEH-nin blahnk): A white grape grown in the Loire Valley region of France and in California.

Chianti (kee-AHN-tee): A DOCG red wine from the Tuscany region of Italy.

Chianti Classico (kee-AHN-tee class-ee-ko): One step above Chianti in terms of quality, this wine is from an inner district of Chianti.

Chianti Classico Riserva (key-AHN-tee class-ee-ko re-ser-va): The best-quality level of Italian Chianti, which requires more aging than Chianti and Chianti Classico.

Cinsault (san-SO): A red grape from France's Rhône Valley.

Classified châteaux: The châteaux in the Bordeaux region of France that are known to produce the best wine.

Concord: A red grape used to make some American and Eastern states' wines.

Colheita (coal-AY-ta): The term meaning "vintage" in Portuguese.

Cosecha (coh-SAY-cha): The term meaning "harvest" in Spanish.

Côte de Beaune (coat duh BONE): The southern portion of the Côte d'Or in Burgundy, known especially for fine white wines.

Côte de Nuits (coat duh NWEE): The northern portion of the Côte d'Or in Burgundy, known especially for fine red wines.

Côte d'Or (coat DOOR): The district in Burgundy that is known for some of the finest wines in the world.

Côte Rôtie (coat roe-TEE): A red wine from the northern Rhône Valley region of France.

Côtes-du-Rhône (coat dew ROAN): The Rhône Valley region of France; also the regional wine from this district.

Cream Sherry: A type of Sherry made from a mixture of Pedro Ximénez and Oloroso.

Crianza (cree-AHN-za): A wine aged a year in oak and a year in the bottle. It is the most basic and least expensive quality level of Rioja wine.

Crozes-Hermitage (crows air-mee-TAHZH): A red wine from the northern Rhône Valley region of France.

Cru Beaujolais (crew bo-zho-LAY): The top grade of Beaujolais wine, coming from any one of ten designated villages in that region of France.

Cru Bourgeois (crew bour-ZHWAH): A list of 247 châteaus in Bordeaux that have been recognized for their quality.

Decanting: The process of pouring wine from its bottle into a carafe to separate the sediment from the wine.

Dégorgement (day-gorzh-MOWN): One step of the Champagne method used to expel the sediment from the bottle.

Demi-sec (deh-mee SECK): A Champagne containing a high level of residual sugar.

DOC: Abbreviation for Denominazione di Origine Controllata, the Italian government agency that controls wine production.

DOCG: Abbreviation for Denominazione di Origine Controllata e Garantita; the Italian government allows this marking to appear only on the finest wines. The G stands for "guaranteed."

Dolcetto (dohl-CHET-toh): A red wine from Piedmont, Italy, that is lighter in style than a Barolo or Barbaresco.

Dosage (doh-SAHZH): A combination of wine and cane sugar that is used in making Champagne.

Edelfäule (EH-del-foy-luh): A German name for the mold that forms on the grapevines when the conditions permit it. (See also *Botrytis cinerea* and "Noble Rot.")

Estate-bottled: Wine that's made, produced, and bottled by the vineyard's owner.

Extra dry: Less dry than brut Champagne.

Fermentation: The process by which grape juice is made into wine.

Fino (FEE-noh): A type of Sherry.

First growth: The highest-quality Bordeaux château wine from the Médoc Classification of 1855.

Flor: A type of yeast that develops in some Sherry production.

Fortified wine: A wine such as Port or Sherry that has additional grape brandy that raises the alcohol content.

Gamay (gah-MAY): A red grape used to make Beaujolais wine.

Garnacha (gar-NAH-cha): A red grape grown in Spain. It is the same as the Grenache grape grown in the Rhône Valley region of France,

Gevrey Chambertin (zhehv-RAY sham-burr-TAN): A village in the Côte de Nuits in Burgundy, France.

Gewürztraminer (geh-VERTZ-tra-MEE-ner): The "spicy" white grape grown in Alsace, California, and Germany.

Gran Reserva: A Spanish wine that's had extra aging.

Grand Cru (grawn crew): The highest classification for wines in Burgundy.

Grand Cru Classé (grawn crew clas-SAY): The highest level of the Bordeaux classification.

Graves (grahv): A region in Bordeaux producing dry red and white wines.

Grenache (greh-NOSH): A red grape of the Rhône Valley region of France.

Gutsabfüllung: A German word for an estate-bottled wine.

Hectare: A metric measure that equals 2.471 acres.

Hectoliter: A metric measure that equals 26.42 U.S. gallons.

Halbtrocken: The German term meaning "semidry."

Hermitage (air-mee-TAHZH): A red wine from the northern Rhône Valley region of France.

Jerez de la Frontera (hair-eth day la fron-TAIR-ah): One of the towns in Andalusia, Spain, where Sherry is produced.

Jug wine: A simple drinking wine from California that is sold in "jug" bottles.

Kabinett (kah-bee-NETT): A light, semi-dry German wine.

Liebfraumilch (LEEB-frow-milch): An easy-to-drink white German wine; it means "milk of the Blessed Mother."

Liqueur de Tirage (lee-KERR deh teer-AHZH): A blend of sugar and yeast added to Champagne to begin the wine's second fermentation.

Loire (LWAHR): A major wine-producing region in northwestern France.

Long-vatted: A term for a wine fermented with the grape skins for a long period of time to acquire a rich red color.

Mâcon Blanc (mac-CAW blahnk): The most basic white wine from the Mâconnais region of Burgundy, France.

Mâcon-Villages (mac-CAW vee-LAHZH): A white wine from designated villages in the Mâconnais region of France; a step above the Mâcon Blanc quality.

Malbec: The major red grape grown in Argentina. It is also grown in Bordeaux.

Manzanilla (mahn-than-NEE-ya): A type of Sherry.

Margaux (mar-GO): A village and district in the Bordeaux region in France.

Mechanical harvester: A machine used on flat vineyards. It shakes the vines to harvest the grapes.

Médoc (may-DOCK): A district in the Bordeaux region in France.

Merlot (mehr-LOW): The red grape grown primarily in the Bordeaux region of France and in California.

Méthode Champenoise (may-TUD shahm-pen-WAHZ): The method by which Champagne is made.

Meursault (mehr-SOH): A village in the Côte de Beaune in Burgundy, France.

Microclimate: A term that refers to an area that has a climate within a climate. While one area may be generally warm, it may contain a cooler *microclimate* or region.

Morey-St-Denis (mor-RAY san duh-NEE): A village in the Côte de Nuits in Burgundy, France.

Mosel-Saar-Ruwer (MO-z'l sahr roo-ver): A region in Germany that produces a light-style white wine.

Müller-Thurgau (MEW-lurr TURR-gow): A cross between the Riesling and the Silvaner grapes of Germany.

Muscadet (moos-cah-DAY): A light, dry wine from the Loire Valley of France.

Muscat Beaumes-de-Venise (mus-CAT bome deh ven-EASE): A sweet wine from the Rhône Valley region of France.

Must: Grape juice before fermentation.

Nebbiolo (nehb-bee-OH-loh): A red grape grown in Piedmont, Italy, which produces some of the finest Italian wine, such as Barolo and Barbaresco.

"Noble Rot": See *Botrytis cinerea*.

Non-vintage Champagne: Champagne made from a blend of vintages (more than one year's crop); it is more typical of the house style than vintage Champagne.

Nose: The term used to describe the bouquet and aroma of wine.

Nuits-St-Georges (nwee san ZHORZH): A village in the Côte de Nuits in Burgundy, France.

Official Classification of 1855: A classification drawn up by wine brokers of the best Bordeaux, Médoc, and Sauternes châteaus.

Pauillac (PAW-yak): A village and district in the Bordeaux region of France.

Pessac-Leognan (pes-sack lee in yawn): An inner district of the Graves region in Bordeaux, France, making both red and white wine.

Petite Sirah: A red grape grown primarily in California.

Pfalz (faults): A wine region in Germany.

Phylloxera (fill-LOCK-seh-rah): A root louse that kills grape vines.

Piedmont (peed-MON-tay): One of the most important wine districts in Italy.

Pinot Blanc: A white grape grown primarily in the Alsace region of France.

Pinot Grigio (PEE-noh GREE-jee-o): The most popular white wine from Italy made from the grape variety called Pinot Grigio, aka Pinot Gris in France and the United States

Pinot Meunier (PEE-noh muhn-YAY): A red grape grown primarily in the Champagne region of France.

Pinot Noir (PEE-noh nwahr): All red French Burgundy wines, except Beaujoulais, are made from 100 percent Pinot Noir grapes. It is also very successful in California and Oregon.

Pomerol (palm-muh-roll): A district in the Bordeaux region of France.

Pommard (poh-MAR): A village in the Côte de Beaune in Burgundy, France.

Pouilly-Fuissé (pooh-yee fwee-SAY): The highest-quality French white Mâconnais wine made from 100 percent Chardonnay.

Pouilly-Fumé (pooh-yee fooh-MAY): A dry white wine from the Loire Valley region of France made from Sauvignon Blanc.

Premier Cru: A wine that has special characteristics that comes from a specific designated vineyard in Burgundy, France, or is blended from several such vineyards.

Priorat: A major wine region in Spain.

Proprietary wine: A wine that's given a brand name like any other product and is marketed as such, e.g., Riunite, Mouton-Cadet.

Puligny-Montrachet (pooh-lean-yee mown-rah-SHAY): A village in the Côte de Beaune in Burgundy, France.

Qualitätswein (kval-ee-TATES-vine): A German term meaning "quality wine."

Qualitätswein mit Prädikat (kval-ee-TATES-vine mitt pray-dee-KAHT): The highest level of quality German wine.

Reserva/Riserva: A term that means a wine has extra aging; it is often found on Spanish, Portuguese, and Italian wine labels.

Reserve: A term sometimes found on American wine labels. Although it has no legal significance, it usually indicates a better-quality wine.

Residual sugar: An indication of how dry or sweet a wine is.

Rheingau (RHINE-gow): A region in Germany.

Rheinhessen (RHINE-hess-en): A region in Germany.

Rheinpfalz (RHINE-faults): A region in Germany. The official name has now been changed to Pfalz.

Ribera del Duero (ree-BAY-rah dell dway-roh): A winegrowing region in Spain.

Riddling: One step of the Champagne-making process in which the bottles are turned gradually each day until they are upside down, with the sediment resting in the neck of the bottle.

Riesling: A white grape grown in Alsace, France, and the United States.

Rioja (ree-OH-ha): A wine region in Spain.

Ruby Port: A dark and sweet fortified wine blended from non-vintage wines.

Sancerre (sahn-SEHR): A dry white wine from the Loire Valley region of France.

Sangiovese (san-jo-VAY-zay): A red grape grown primarily in Tuscany, Italy.

Sauternes (soh-TURN): A sweet white wine from the Bordeaux region of France.

Sauvignon Blanc (SOH-veen-yown blahnk): A white grape grown primarily in the Loire Valley, Graves, and Sauternes regions of France, in Washington State, New Zealand, and California (where the wine is sometimes called Fumé Blanc).

Sémillon (say-mee-YAW): A white grape found in the Graves and Sauternes regions of Bordeaux, France, and Australia.

Shiraz (SHEER-oz): A red grape grown primarily in Australia, aka Syrah.

Short-vatted: A term for a wine fermented with the grape skins for only a short time.

Solera system (so-LEHR-ah): A process used to blend various vintages of Sherry.

Sommelier (so-mel-YAY): The French term for cellarmaster, or wine steward.

Spätlese (SHPATE-lay-zuh): A white German wine made from grapes picked later than the normal harvest.

Stainless-steel tank: A container that (because of its ability to control temperature) is used to ferment and age some wines.

St-Émilion (sahnt ay-meel-YOHN): A district in the Bordeaux region of France.

St-Estèphe (sahnt ay-STEFF): A village and district in the Bordeaux region of France.

St-Julien (sahnt zhoo-lee-EHN): A village and district in the Bordeaux region of France.

St-Véran (sahn vay-RAHN): A white Mâconnais wine one step above Mâcon-Villages in quality.

Sulfur dioxide: A substance used in winemaking and grape growing as a preservative, an antioxidant, and also as a sterilizing agent.

Süssreserve: The unfermented grape juice added to German wine after fermentation to give the wine more sweetness.

Syrah (see-RAH): A red grape grown in the Rhône Valley region of France and Australia, aka Shiraz.

Tafelwein (taf'l VINE): A German table wine.

Tannin: A natural compound and preservative that comes from the skins, stems, and pips of the grapes and also from the wood in which wine is aged.

Tawny Port: A Port that is lighter, softer, and aged longer than Ruby Port.

TBA: Abbreviation for the German wine Trockenbeerenauslese.

Tempranillo (temp-rah-NEE-yoh): A red grape grown primarily in Spain.

Trebbiano (treb-bee-AH-no): A white grape grown in Italy.

Trockenbeerenauslese (troh-ken-bear-en-OUSE-lay-zuh): The richest and sweetest wine made in Germany from the most mature grapes.

Tuscany (TUSS-cah-nee): A region in Italy.

Varietal wine: A wine that is labeled with the predominant grape used to produce the wine, i.e., a wine made from Chardonnay grapes would be labeled "Chardonnay."

Veneto wines: A wine region in Italy producing Valpolicella, Bardolino, Soave, and Amarone.

Village wine: A wine that comes from a particular village in Burgundy.

Vino Nobile di Montepulciano (VEE-noh NOH-bee-leh dee mon-teh-pull-CHAH-noh): A DOCG red wine from the Tuscany region of Italy.

Vintage: The year the grapes are harvested.

Viognier (vee-own-YAY): A white grape from the Rhône Valley region of France and California.

Vitis labrusca (VEE-tiss la-BREW-skah): A native grape species in America.

Vitis vinifera (VEE-tiss vih-NIFF-er-ah): The European grape species used to make European and California wine.

Volnay (vohl-NAY): A village in the Côte de Beaune region of Burgundy, France.

Vosne Romanée (vohn roh-mah-NAY): A village in the Côte de Nuits region of Burgundy, France.

Vougeot (voo-ZHOH): A village in the Côte de Nuits region of Burgundy, France.

Vouvray (voo-VRAY): A white wine from the Loire Valley region of France; it can be dry, semi-sweet, or sweet.

Wood Port: Ruby or Tawny Port; they're ready to drink as soon as you buy them.

Zinfandel (zin-fan-DELL): A red grape grown in California.

Index

Note: Page references in **bold** indicate label(s) included on that page.

Gladys Horiuchi
Robin Kelley O'Connor
Alistair Robertson
LOUIS LATOUR
Marvin R. Shanken
LF Bouchard
Rodney D. Strong
Pio Boffa
James Trezise
David S. Stare
Louis P. Martini
Mike Stephens
Ed Sbragia

Alfredo Bartholomäus

Spencer McCarthy Claude Taittinger Jan Schlesin

Robert A. Caldwell Jean Hugel Jeffrey M. Pogash

John Philippini Walter Müller Pierre Emile Patrick Campbell Pierre-Louis Lopez

Darrell Corti Philip di Belardino Robert de goulaine

Jack Lakebreack Valerie Hugel Francisco Valle Zelma Long Danny Reiner

Pierre Villain

Edmund Sterland Georges Duboeuf

Harry Raymond Reynolds Michel Aubert

Edmund Jeremy C. Beck

Christia S. de Roger

Emil Müller Felipe Sepulveda Hubert Trimbach Jan Walty Rick Tw

Myron S. Nightingale Michael LeRoy